Jesus
the "Truth of Man"
for the
Age of Aquarius

I am TRUTH. My truth is a holographic message to Man about Man. It says: I am you. You are an eternal being that has died on a cross, the limitations of your human experience. The time for your resurrection...your awakening, is now here.

Rokus DenHartog
Dawning Light Ministries

Booksurge
7290 B Investment Drive
No. Charleston, SC 29418
www.booksurge.com

First edition: February 2009

ISBN: 1-4362-3181-8

Library of Congress Control Number: 2009901662

Author: Rokus DenHartog

Editor: Esther den Hartog

About This Book

This book is a compendium of short inspirational articles written by the author since 2000. It also contains two abridged transcripts of email discussions that took place in 2006 and 2007. The emails are based on the thoughts contained in the articles. The summations of these thoughts are referred to as **A New Theology** or at other times: **A New Theory of Reality** (THOR).

Our quest is to bring understanding to the most elementary questions of human existence. Who are we? Where did we come from? Why are we here?

About the Title: Nova Ora

Every Age has its breaking Truth; a Truth that opens and sustains it. I see in the core truth for this dawning Age of Aquarius: *the realization of the Eternalness of Man and the idea that we exist in many realities.* Embracing our existence as spirit beings brings the realization that we so much more than flesh.

Jesus showed and manifested that truth. That is why I call him: *The Truth of Man.* This greater awareness of Jesus' purpose and mission is the core message of this book. It comes as a *Nova* i.e. a brilliant explosion of Light, and it is happening now i.e. *Ora.* He is indeed the seed crystal for the awakening of mankind. His time has come.

May the reading of this book confirm your path as you realize it is already written in your heart?

Rokus den Hartog
July 8, 2008
Oldfield, MO

Acknowledgements

I want to thank the participant in the THOR email discussions, especially John McGill who said: *Rokus, you have found the Gold*, and Esther, my editor in chief. I could not have done it without all of you.

Carolynne, my fellow minister, friend, wife, and companion for 22 years received this chorus while on one of her inspirational morning walks. It mirrors my feelings about this book more than I could express:

Creating a new paradigm, bringing a New Dimension in Time,
Let's leave the Old behind, and bring in the New.

Make no mistake. This is what it will take,
Walk over to your cliff, and learn to fly.

Come with me now, I will show you how,
Many await for you, to make a breakthrough.
Come on let's make a breakthrough.

Introduction

We are in a time of unparalleled, accelerated, change. Quantum Physics has forever changed the way we see the world and reality. Attitudes towards the environment are in the forefront. There is acute global awareness of political, social, and economic upheaval. Yet the most significant aspect of all this change is in Man's perception of himself. He is questioning his origin, evolution, and destiny. I am using this book to present series of thoughts to give some cohesion and structure to our understanding of these powerful changing norms. These thoughts are small enough for any mind to consider, yet large enough to encompass a wholly New Theory of Reality, they are presented in a variety of ways. Hopefully you will find at least some of your own considerations reflected here.

May the words of this book help you connect to
the truth within that has always been you.

Index

Issue #42   **January 2007**

In The Beginning

A Discussion of the Beginning Of Consciousness As We Know It

Dear Friends:

How did I begin? It is impossible not to wonder, not to ask about your beginning. It is so intimately connected with the questions: Who or what am I? Where did I come from? How did I begin?

Beginnings fascinate us. We celebrate a birthday because it is the first day you first appeared in a bodily form. We celebrate anniversaries of all types and sorts. They are celebrations of a beginning. The children of Israel were exhorted to remember their beginning as a nation: "Remember the Rock you were hewn from!"

Science too has been fascinated by thoughts about beginnings. Just in the last century, scientists were conclusively able to show that the universe, as we know it, had a beginning. They placed this beginning, called a Big Bang, circa fifteen billion years ago. They reasoned that if there truly was a BIG BANG, then we should still be able to "hear" its echo throughout the universe. Sure enough, they sent up a test probe and found the echo they were looking for, fifteen billion years later. Since then they have discovered that the universe is not only continually getting larger, it is doing so at an increasing rate. What a surprise that was! It seems as if there is some invisible force pushing continually, not just in the beginning explosion. Religious people have always known that the universe had a beginning...for it is written: *In the beginning God created...*

Beginnings and endings are very real in this physical existence. Even stars and galaxies are born and eventually die. Everything physical we touch can break down and decay. Some do this very slowly; some very quickly. Eternal things however, such as LOVE, we don't necessarily think of as beginning and ending. They only begin and end in our experiences. We awaken to love and we talk about love dying.

1

Why is the knowledge of our beginnings as spirit beings so important? The beginning of anything will reveal its potential and limitation. The origins of things determine their destinies. So, let us consider our beginning.

It is essential that we form a mental construct of what we believe reality to be. If we do not do so, there are many genetic memories in the cells of our bodies that will by default present themselves as our truth.. We have tendencies to believe present scientific opinion as well. It states that we may simply be the product of quantum probability...one of an infinite number of equally probable happenstances.

There is nothing wrong with having an image of the truth. You must create such images in order to exist in this three dimensional world. This sum total of imagery in your heart-mind is in fact who you perceive yourself to be. It is from that perception of self that you continually create your reality. For instance, in order to pole vault over a bar ten or twelve feet from the ground, you must first create the path clearly in your mind and hold it there. Then let your body follow through the program. Many times of practice and many intense efforts are needed to create this synaptic pathway in the brain that enables you to execute a perfect vault.

Thoughts of a beginning will have to contemplate a time *before* that beginning making an image of what that pre-existent state may have been like. Before we begin this imaging we must ask: Does everything we construct mentally have to be absolutely correct? Does it all have to be totally "true"? The answer to that question is: "No." These are religious concerns. Always insisting on being correct in what we believe puts us in a perceptional box. The more important questions are these: *Does this mental construct give us greater ways to think about ourselves? Do these greater ways of thinking bring us joy, expansion or growth? Do they serve us in helping us to understand who we are and where we came from?*

So...let us imagine God as a totally homogeneous substance. Let's call it *God-stuff*. It appears the same from wherever you are in that substance like a huge unending clear Jell-O, totally without distinction or form. This is God the Source.

The ancients referred to the Source as *Light*, the **Ain Soph**, *the limitless light* and the **Nartoomid**, or *the eternal light*. I speak about these terms and give them deference because I have personally experienced this *Living Light*

The Light **KNEW** me. It had consciousness. It knew me in a way I had never been known. It knew me in a way I had never known myself. It knew me completely. This quality of *knowing-an-other* is greater than this physical experience. This all happened in a place of awareness where there was no form, no body, no things, only the awareness of myself and the LIGHT. As a result of this experience I now know that the LIGHT is always with us. In truth it **is** us, and there is no existence apart from the LIGHT for the LIGHT is the ALL.

So…if the LIGHT has no beginning and no ending, then how can there be a BEGINNING? It is written: *In the beginning was the WORD and the WORD was with God and the WORD was God.* The only way we can understand a beginning is to look at our **experience** of beginnings. How do we create a new experience for ourselves? We begin with a THOUGHT.

The First Thought

Please let me speak in very human terms about a *beyond-human experience*. The moment this first thought formed itself in the God-Mind, in the *Jell-O*, it was a beginning. This beginning is something that had **no** existence and then it **did**. The first thought of the Source could have been something like this:

What if there was another ONE?

The Desire behind the First Thought

When we have a thought, it arises in our conscious mind from a deeper place, a desire. What desire may have caused such a thought to form in the Source? Here is the feeling that lies behind the thought:

*I intensely desire for the LOVE that I AM
to experience itself AS LOVE.*

3

The connection now is obvious. In order for LOVE to be all that it can be, Love needs an **OTHER**. It needs another to experience the giving and receiving of LOVE. It needs another to create the need, a need that Love can meet.

How Can There Be an Other?

How can there be another when there is only the ONE? In order for there to be an **other** a different reality must be created. A reality in which there can be TWO. We call this DUALITY, the reality based on the thought that there are TWO, leading to MANY. Since in truth it is only the ONE that exists, this reality must be a **created thought form reality** based on an illusion. This illusion believes *there are separate selves that exist..* If separate selves exist there must be at least TWO of them and everything in this created illusionary reality comes in pairs.

We can see the duality that is from the beginning reflected in creation. Atomic collisions create packages of light called Photons. All photons have a spin associated with them. It is either a right hand spin giving it a positive energy or it is a left hand spin causing it to have a negative energy. A very basic law of science states that energy cannot be created or destroyed, it can only change form. Since spin energy is very unique it follows that for every photon with a right handed spin, there must be one with a left handed spin or this law is broken. Photons then are always created in pairs with opposite spin, male and female if you like.

We see this kind of a beginning, this different reality, this duality, in the scripture quoted from the first chapter of the Gospel of John. I am going to emphasize the dual nature coming forth in the beginning by printing it **bold:**

In the beginning was the WORD
And
**The WORD was with God
And
The WORD was God.**

Notice that the **WORD** is described in **TWO** different ways. It is described as *being* God. That is, the *substance* of God. It is made of

Jell-O and, it is still the LIGHT. It is also described as being **with** God. It's a mystery. How can something BE a thing and still be WITH that thing? It is the closest the scriptures can come to help us understand or at least be aware of the mystery of our existence in this realm of duality.

Saying it in another way, this New Thing, called **The WORD, has** the power of thinking of itself as **Separate from God.**

What BEGINNING is being referred to? This scripture refers to the beginning of **Consciousness-As-We-Know-It**

It is the beginning of what I call the **journey of separation** and the beginning of **consciousness-as-we-know-it** in dualistic form. It is a term I will use often. It is a recurring theme in the scriptures and it holds in it the thought of the original purpose and intent of the Father's heart. This so called journey of separation is the intent that the Christ-mind always serves.

A Second Witness

There is another place in the scriptures where the beginning is spoken of. It is found in Proverbs 8, 22-27. Here WISDOM, feminine in gender, is speaking. She describes herself as the first to be brought forth, before any material thing. Verse 27 describes how it happened.

Proverbs 8:22-27

22: The LORD possessed me in the beginning of his way, before His works of old.

23: I was set up from everlasting, from the beginning, or ever the earth was.

24: When there were no depths, I was brought forth; when there were no fountains abounding with water.

25: Before the mountains were settled, before the hills was I brought forth.

5

26: While as yet he had not made the earth, nor the fields, nor the highest part of the dust of the world.

27: When he prepared the heavens, I was there: **when He set a compass upon the face of the depth.**

The **DEPTH** described here is the infinite Source beyond all human knowledge or comprehension. It is the same as the **Ain Soph** or the **Living Light.** It is the beginning of the Journey of Separation, duality, and consciousness all described as a single act.

When he set a compass upon the face of the depth

What happens when you put a compass on a sheet of paper and draw a circle? The SINGLE plane is separated into TWO, the **INSIDE** and the **OUTSIDE.** This realm that has the concept of inside and outside, cold and hot, high and low, light and dark, joy and suffering, and right and wrong is the realm of duality. In this realm it always takes TWO opposites to describe anything. Photography illustrates this idea. Contrasting shades of light and dark are needed to create a photographic image. Our experience of love is another example. You cannot **fully** know love if you have never known what it feels like to be unloved.

These scriptures reveal the deep longing that lies behind all material form and consciousness. Knowing this desire may well help us to treasure our place in this three dimensional reality. This initiating glimpse of truth will create a new pathway for us.

Creation Is a House for God to Experience Love.

There is one more thought that we can consider about BEGINNING. Stan Tenen of the Meru foundation spent 10 years of intense study of the first sentence of the Torah. *In the beginning God created the heavens and the earth.* Gen 1:1. He was looking for a key to unlock the mystery of the Torah. He asked himself a question: *"What if the Torah were a secret document carrying a coded message to survive centuries of time? Where would I place the key to unlock the hidden code?"* He formulated that it could clearly be in the first sentence, maybe even the first word, or even the first letter.

With that in mind let's take a closer look. The first letter of the Torah is the Hebrew letter "Beth". It has its primary meaning of "House". Anyone building a house does so to create an "Inside" and an "Outside". The word "Beth" translated as **IN** holds the idea of a **house** and also the idea of **two** or **duality**

What a beautiful thought to help us consider the purpose of creation. Let's summarize it:

The purpose of duality, as experienced in creation, is to form a house in which LOVE can experience ITSELF.

In Conclusion

The universe and all created reality were purposed from the beginning by a desire in the Source. The Source desired to experience itself as Love.

The journey of separation made this possible through a shattering and bringing forth myriads of expressions of "self".

How then do we find our way home? How do we return to the place from which we have come? Can we earn our way back? Can we do more research to become wiser and finally "get it right" and so return?

We can only return to our Father Source by meeting that great desire which initiated our beginning. It is now our choice. We make this conclusion:

Only LOVE when fully experienced in us can reveal all truth and bring us to our wholeness.

Rokus denHartog

God-Seed

Dear Friends:

I want to take us back today to our beginning. It lies in the faintest whispers heard deep within. We find it in consciousness, before all the layers we created as we tried to find definition of our being. It's happening. We are coming home in our awareness to a greater reality, something we *once always were*. It's really impossible to describe this non-physical event of our beginning in physical terms. How can we be sure of its truth? The overwhelming joy we feel is our witness of the truth we are describing. We can feel it.

Paul said: *First that which is natural, then that which is spiritual.* Let's begin by looking at some science. If this bores you, skip down a few paragraphs; it gets better as we go.

First the Physical...

"We have reached back into the origin of the universe. We have launched a little space probe to receive the faint whisper of the cosmic explosion of fifteen billion years ago, and we have measured the structure of the big bang itself less than a fraction of a second after the universe started to expand."

In April of 1992, cosmologists George F. Smooth made the preceding announcement at an American Physical Society meeting. It was the result of twenty years of intense research by a team of scientists at Berkeley University. Some called this event "The breakthrough of the century". Scientists have debated back and forth for years whether the universe has always existed or if it had a beginning.

The beginning of the universe is really understood to be the beginning of Time-Space. Einstein was the one who first recognized that time and space are like Siamese twins. You cannot have one without the other. Einstein also favored the idea of the eternalness of matter. He could not consider the thought of it ever having a beginning. One could be tempted to ask: What happened a second before time-space began? All this research was based on an idea or a belief that if there was a big bang, then there must still be an echo around for us to hear it!

Scientists have asked these questions for years: Will the universe continue to expand? Is every part of it going further and further apart? Will the gravitational pull of matter slowly cause the expansion to slow down until the "spring is fully stretched"? Will it then collapse again, repeating the cycle of death and rebirth over and over again? In short: *Is the rate of expansion of the universe slowing down, remaining the same, or speeding up?*

Astronomers, with the availability of the Hubble Telescope, have found an answer to that question. Super Novas were used by the scientists to measure the rate at which the universe is expanding over time. They first selected 35 Super Novas observed through the telescopes in West Virginia. Then they took the coordinates of these bright stars to the latest telescope placed in Hawaii. This more powerful telescope reduced the field of vision to a very small portion of the sky. There they selected five Super Novas. These stars covered a time span of 5 billion years, ranging from 5 to 10 billion years ago.

A Super Nova is dying star in its death throws. It only lasts for a few months when it becomes a white dwarf. There is a time lapse between a cosmic event and the time we see it happen. This time delay allows us to see Super Novas exploding all the way back to the beginning of time. Astronomers can establish two main things about Super Novas, the time of their death and the speed at which they are traveling. Improvements in telescopes make it possible to track these events. These improvements come at a great expense. The mirror installed in the Hawaii Telescope is worth 9 million dollars!

Measurement of the light coming from the star, tells scientists how fast the star is moving away from us, the spectrum of the light *shifts* over to the lower end, the red side. This happens much the same as the pitch of the sound from a moving train lowers as it moves away from the hearer. They can also tell how far away in time a Super Nova is by the brightness of the light coming from it. The dimmer the light, the more distant the star is. All Super Novas have a characteristic explosive brightness.

9

Finally, after selecting data from these 5 Super Novas, the information was processed by the computers. They made a graph of distance verses speed with the calculated results. Everyone anticipated that the furthest stars would be going the slowest but, to their utter amazement they found the opposite to be true. The rate of expansion of the universe is not slowing down, not staying the same; it is speeding up ever so slowly! Whoeee!!!! Ha, Ha! Wow, what a trip! Don't you love it?

A force must be pushing everything outward. Scientists call it the DARK Force, simply because it is totally unknown to them. I can imagine there may be a few other things that seem DARK to them. There are a lot of things that have appeared dark to us for a long time.

Major scientific breakthroughs in astronomy and many other areas have happened in the very last decade of the twentieth century. It was a century full of beginnings. Biology saw the mapping of the human genome. Are we in a time of awakening? I think so! What is the essence of this awakening? Is it really about understanding the universe? Or, is man really asking about himself? What is my true nature? Where did I begin? Will I always be? How can I know these greater truths?

...Then the Spiritual

I was standing on the balcony of my friend's apartment in Sarnia, Ontario, Canada. I was in clear view of a large maple tree full and ready to shed its seeds. The maple tree I was observing had thousands of maple keys. A sudden gust of wind broke through the branches of this huge tree and as if on cue, a host of these maple keys burst forth. Some went thousands of feet into the air, others were carried further and further away by the wind until they disappeared out of my sight. Others just flew a short distance and, like so many tiny helicopters, began their descent onto the earth.

The feelings I experienced watching this tree seed itself reminded me of another very similar experience that happened a few years ago. I was kneeling with one knee on the freshly tilled earth of my small garden. A small amount of bean seed was in my hand ready to be planted. As I dropped the first seed into its resting place I had a feeling come over me. For a brief moment, a glimpse in time, I became the seed in the hand of God as He lowered me into the earth. I saw the time frame of my physical experience. It was as if I became Him and could feel the greatness of His love towards me. I felt a part of His very self, I felt the hope, the passion and longing that made Him lower me in to this earth plane. It was just a glimpse but ever so real.

Science is beginning to listen to the first events of creation. Is it possible that our true man, the greater reality of who we are, is beginning to remember our origins? Are we remembering past the layers? Place where we have sought residence, places to hide? Are we returning to our first recognition in the journey into separation?

Can we remember back, to a time before time, when God, like that great maple tree, released us from the essence of himself? Are we this host of beings, myriads of copies of himself, seeds, and genetic packages of his greater being? Each one destined for an unfolding of experience It is a journey through many realms and layers to unfold and develop consciousness, personality, and separate identity, all in harmony and likeness of the great I AM.

Jesus spoke to his disciples and said: *The Holy Spirit, the comforter will bring all things back to your remembrance.* The obvious first level of meaning is that after Jesus left they would, through the Holy Spirit, remember the conversations they had and write the four Gospels. We have them today as a record of their experiences and the teachings of Jesus.

How would this happen? I suppose their memory suddenly would become very acute and lucid. It would seem to them they were back in the time when Jesus was speaking to them. They would probably have the conversation run through their mind like a record as if they were back in that wonderful place they had with him.

Let's take this thought a little deeper. Let's consider the idea that this statement by Jesus is really looking forward to this greater time. Some of us are beginning to remember eternal things. We are remembering not just a conversation caught in time, but the actual feelings and the thoughts we experienced as left the greater realms of light. We left those, realms of being to begin our long journey of descent into matter and time.

A Leap in Faith

I remember the time when we first began to experience miracles of healing. I remember how much emphasis was put on the idea that in our minds we should not accept the prognosis of doctors based on their experience and knowledge of the facts. In the last few months, my granddaughter Jessica has been undergoing major treatment for a tumor in her brainstem. I remember watching my daughter, Deborah, as she listened to the dire prognosis of the medical doctors that were working to save her daughter's life. Some of the best neurosurgeons in the world dressed in their operating gowns were telling her their opinions based on what they were seeing. I would hear her say to them, with her heart and soul rent: "Yes, I know that what you say is your understanding based on your experience, which I respect and thank you for, but I have hope. I have hope because this is my daughter, and I know that even if everything you're telling me is true, she can still live."

With our own eyes we have seen the impossible, miracles. Is it possible that these wonderful experiences were really preparing us for a greater leap? Not just a leap of faith to believe a miracle, but a greater leap to take us over and away from everything that experience has taught us is possible. Have we been preparing for a leap of faith beyond the perimeters of all that is tangible? Is this leap of faith to take us to a place where we begin to truly accept and believe in an existence that is not based on time, knowledge, or experience? Are we involved in a paradigm shift into a great, beautiful, releasing and ecstatic "knowing"? A shift away from all thoughts of limitation and imperfection into a reality we dimly perceive through shadows and similitude? Are we ready to leave the confines of earth thinking? Are we willing to let go of the imagery in our mind based on human experience and instead use those experiences to catch a remembrance of greater thoughts and feelings that really do not belong to this earth realm at all? Just as science is discarding its limited and incorrect ideas; are we willing to look again and embrace a totally new perception of reality and of ourselves? It may require us to let go of all that has formed us i.e. our boxes and our holy cows.

Yes, my questions are rhetorical, and of course, I believe we are ready. We are ready to hear IN time, BEYOND time. That is what I believe I experienced when I saw a maple tree laden with keys or felt a bean seed falling from my hand into the moist and prepared earth. Yes, yes with all my heart, I do believe. We find, through our agony, a willingness to go and embrace greater thoughts and realizations. This new basis for our reality perceptions makes a path for all men to begin their release from entrapment and imprisonment in limited realms. Released from dimensions where we were first seeded to continue the grand journey. It is as if the great gardener is transferring a plant from his green house into the living room to be seen and experienced in all its beauty.

Letting Go

Can I leave behind my great desire to FIX things and to make them right? Can I accept that they have always been right and were never really out of course, as they seemed? Can I quit working for God, and realize that all work was finished from the beginning of time and find a rest in knowing? Can I spread the wings of consciousness and fly to a greater overview? Overviews that will help us all understand what never seems comprehensible in and from the lower planes? Yes, yes I say, as my heart bleeds and hot tears press through my eyes. I see my daughter trying to grasp the immensity of her own pain and as she tenderly cares for and holds her precious gift from God, her Jessica. I too, deep in my own soul have to let go of entrenched thoughts, almost like a death, this profound releasing. I let go of these thoughts that all have to do with fixing and making things right and trade it all in on a new and greater version of reality where nothing ever needs fixing. This is a place where nothing ever has been wrong and where Love permeates all thoughts, feelings and experiences. There is no aloneness, pain and sorrow embraced as realities. These experiences are used as gateways to greater realities, and knowingness were God Himself is experiencing. The Source is experiencing all of itself in every part of itself and in everything that happens. It happens in sacred union, holiness within you.

Now, in this union, we can state emphatically: *we know as we are known*. Now we see as God sees and we understand with His mind. We know that we are His experience in this earth realm. We can now begin to grasp in our minds that we are now and have always been one with God Himself. How could we leave that which was and is our true self? We can speak these kinds of thoughts freely. All we have to do is open our heart and our minds will conform to this

13

greater knowing. No longer are we bound and locked into the paradigms of time and space. No longer are we trapped in the layers of consciousness where we thought to hide our nakedness, the fear and pain of our separation. We now know that we truly never left. We are free to become and unfold. The Son has set us free.

What are we hearing when we truly listen for that echo that is still in our being? It is a remembrance of how we felt, still totally connected to ALL that we are. What was the feeling that released us? What was the desire, the hope that motivated the great beginning? What was the thought in God's great heart towards each and every part of himself that went on the great journey? Can you remember? Yes you can. You can remember more clearly than Science can measure the faint echo of an explosion that happened 15 billion years ago. You and I can see back to our origin more beautifully exact and true in vision than the Hubble telescope looking at Super Novas. We can see our ends and our beginnings in time and hear our Father whisper to us the great song of His Love for the universe. What is that song? How are you hearing it? What is it whispering to you? Believe in it, for it is truly your only way back to yourself, your greater self, your source and beginning. Abba Father.

I can hear the faint and beautiful whisper of His love as each seed proceeds from Him, imprinting it with its own unique sense of being. Every seed comes with its own potential identity. Each one individually and collectively completes the ALL. What does the whisper say for you? This is what I hear it saying in me:

I am you. I am always who you are. I cannot leave you even when in your mind you leave me. My LOVE is the only guarantee of your existence and in my love I give you that which will always bring you back to me, freedom. It is your power to choose. I will never allow it to be taken from you. You will go where you will and where you choose. You will make long, difficult, and rewarding passages in time and space. These experiences will create your unfolding. You will uncover and become many things in many realms, but I will always guarantee your passage back, for you will always have choice. I am the guarantee of this envelope within which you will have total freedom to become all that you can be. There will be systems and powers that will seek to control and remove the privilege of choice, but they will not stand. My guarantee is the word of my Love to you.

Choice: The Greatness of Your Being

What makes you so great, so significant in the hierarchies of being? What is it that makes the Angels wonder about you? Why do they try to understand you and even at times simulate you?

It is in your power to CHOOSE!!

Most people perceive themselves as weak and unable but, to the greater realms, you are admired and loved for your excellence and your courage. These attributes are the result of your power of choice.

Let's think about it another way. Ask yourself, what do I love most about the human experience? What would I be willing to die for? Immediately, for me, Mel Gibson comes to mind in his masterful acting of William Wallace in the movie BraveHeart. Remember the last scene as he is bound and tortured and is given one last chance to use his voice? His torturers, thinking he is about to recant, are standing there eagerly anticipating their triumph over the human spirit when, with a loud voice, he cries out:

"FREEEEEEEEDOMMMM!!"

What a moment! What an experience! Absolutely unforgettable! Why? That is what you and I are! We are lovers of freedom. We need to ask ourselves: What is the essential dynamic or operating part of Freedom? Conclusively it is *CHOICE*.

Love, the essence of who God is and who you are, is the greatest of all and cannot be demanded. The very experience of love, as beautiful and marvelous as it is, will not be desirable if it is not freely given. I cannot truly respond to love if I am not free. The feeling that I am free to choose...releases me to respond to love.

The Great Quest: Order and Freedom.

Simultaneously, while responding to love, another part of you is saying: *But we have to have ORDER. Things must be done decently and in order. We cannot really let people be absolutely free because they will abuse their freedom. They will steal, they will lie, they will abuse and even kill each other if we do not create some control in our country.* Guess what? You are correct. In fact, that is what we have right now on this planet and especially here in the "good old USA". We are faced with the challenge of creating the greatest freedom with the least amount of control.

We seemingly are torn between these conflicting desires: the passion for freedom, and the desire for right treatment of every man. We plainly see the need for control. Such noble passions! Such excellent desire! Every one who participates in the human experience is involved at some level in the drama of these seeming opposites. When you were a child, a wise parent slowly acquainted you with choice and responsibility. Choice was a very small circle indeed in a life structured by the parent. The wise parent also included in your early repertoire of experience a few "No-No's." A pretty vase (from K Mart) purposely placed within your reach, and you were told not to touch. Everything else was made "child proof." Very soon the early years of childhood passed. Responsible parents spent a few careful years weaning you from mindless, blind obedience. Your experience was not without pain but, you probably survived the transfer to adulthood without total debilitation.

Dominating parents who spend the greater part of their efforts ensuing obedience and total submission of their children were probably driven by their own lack of that same obedience when they were children. Time was not taken to help us develop a moral sense and responsibility of our own. When it comes time for such children to fly, they do. Children demand what they think will be their freedom. They want to choose for themselves. They choose what was forbidden to them in order to experience freedom and independence in their frame of thought.

When our children fly from us in that manner we feel that we have failed as parents. The pain we see them go through is harder for us to bear than any pain we have ever experienced before. It is compounded with guilt and with shame. The feelings of failure are very real.

Novus Ordo Seclorum

The whole world is in conflict and at war over this very issue. The issue is about freedom, control, and choice. What was the constitution of the United States all about? It was a search and a reach for order. The founding fathers sought a constitutional framework that would no longer control for the sake of control or by the whim of a single potentate or king. This order was to ensure personal and collective Freedom. They felt it to be a divinely inspired experiment in human self-government. Checks and balances were put in place to ensure one single objective; to provide a place for our passionate love for freedom and self-expression.

Why is the USA under such horrendous pressure today? Why are there terrorists vowing to destroy us? True, there are the multinational companies wreaking destruction of indigenous cultures and destroying the rain forest. True, our government has broken trust with its own people. We have been lied to and deceived in international intrigue. But the real cause of the conflict in our world and the hatred against us lies in the fact that we are the people on this planet who at the core of our being know freedom. We also know that this freedom is not for us alone. We know that it is for all men to experience their own reality, their own validity, and their own truth. We have a deep faith, a profound unshakable conviction that this is possible and can be realized in our time.

The First Kiss

If you as a parent feel you have failed, or if you feel that we as a nation are failing or have already failed, then consider this: Where did the thought come from that, like a fuse, ignited a whole sequence of events resulting in this present experience of which we are speaking? What was the desire that set in motion the potential and possibility for CHOICE? Choice, which, when granted, has such wonderful and devastating consequences?

The power of choice is much the same as nuclear power. On the one hand it has can release man from the back breaking labor required to meet his energy needs. On the other hand it can cause such devastating destruction as we have seen in Hiroshima.

Why was choice ever desired and created in the first place? And what was the need or longing that stimulated it into created reality? You know the answer in your own experience. It is the same desire that made you seek your first kiss. As a teenager it gave you the courage to take a hold the hand of that boy or girl that you had been exchanging glances and words with for three months. I remember vividly the very first time that I ever kissed a girl. I had not watched it on TV as our children have. I really had never seen my parents passionately kiss. It took me years to really find out how truly beautiful, tender, and infinitely desiring a kiss can be.

Where does all that desire come from? One of the most exquisite poems of all time begins: "How do I love thee? Let me count the ways..." Who or what desired the first kiss? You already know what that was. It was our deepest most fundamental reality. It was the greatest knowing of the truth about who we are. It was Love itself.

Before there were opposites, before fear and doubt, before the need for righteousness and justice, before all, in all, and over all, there is: Love .This great love is what we call God, our Source, our Father, the All, the only Power, the ONE.

How can we, in our finite state, and in our limited perceptions, adequately portray or understand our beginnings? How can we grasp the inception of the reality we now experience? It seems impossible. Yet there is a thought being whispered in our hearts that is leading us inward into the truth. It is the thought that it was Love itself that desired an Object. Love needs an other, other than itself, other than the ONE. Yet how could there ever be any other than the ONE? Whatever that other ONE would be, it would have to exist in a framework of illusions. This framework is a series of stepped-down frequencies lowered into denseness and duality i.e. a mind creation.

This other ONE (seemingly separate) would also have to have the power to choose. Love cannot be experienced without choice and freedom. It must exist in a realm of duality, there must be opposites. The choice this other ONE must make is to harmonize with the ONE and experience love, or to oppose the ONE and live in lies, falsehood and fear.

Your Choice: Your Reality

To live is to make choices. Choices, especially the ones you make as a parent, can truly leave you feeling like a failure, as we said earlier. Your life can be filled with regret and condemnation. You may still have pain and disappointment that you cannot face at the lost moment that could have been in your children's lives. If this is your experience, you must ask yourself:

What about the Eternal Father and His Children? Is He as responsible for His as I am for mine? And if He is, how does He deal with it? If I pass judgment on myself, condemning myself, do I also with the same breath condemn Him? If The Eternal one desired an experience of choice, and if I judge that experience to be a failure in my life through condemning myself, what choice am I making thereby?

Answering this question is your participation in the great drama of life. You are a part of this drama, the great beautiful magnificent journey of separation whose conclusion is already decided in the nature and Being of the One, the Whole. For all things shall return through the great cycle of our dream, our illusion, back into the awareness of the One where we have always really been.

Finally, with great joy and power, with eternal thanksgiving and Love to our Father and Source we must proclaim to you, and to all in your space, this wonderful releasing truth:

You may always choose again, when the opportunity comes your way, and let me assure you, it will.

Choosing Your Incarnation

For a choice to truly be a choice, there must be valid alternatives, and there cannot be condemnation imputed with any of those alternatives. Yet choices do have consequences, and these must be understood. All this has to do with what we call maturity and responsibility. This is the hour that is upon mankind. The choice must be made to appropriate something that we have never truly made our own: our incarnate state.

19

We chose it once before when the morning stars sang together and all the Sons of God shouted for joy. We saw the great purpose of the Father and aligned the imprint of our Love with it. This is how we came on this journey through the valley of shadows, this separate experience culminating in these separate physical bodies. Now, in this flesh, we must make that same choice again.

When we were still in that greater world of light, in our bodies of light, we foresaw these events. We knew that on the other side of forgetfulness we would remember again; and in remembering we would choose again, breaking all chains of victimization through lies and obligation.

You and I in our awareness must take a step away. If you can, for a moment, step out and beyond all chains of materiality, only then can you make the great empowering choice that will set all men free. You must choose, in total, completely, without reservation, your own material consciousness and all the experiences that have come with it. You must choose who you are in every realm that you walk in.

The Choice: To Be Who You Are

I came. I laid down my life for you that you might know that even your seeming powerlessness, your crucifixion in and on your human experience, was not without power. For it was your choice to so be, even as I showed you that it was mine. In this knowing, we are one. We are the same. We cannot be separate or apart. In this knowing, I hold you. I carry you as I carried Peter until you no longer deny, not me, but yourself, and you make the choice you came here to make, the choice for which this body was formed, the choice that sets creation free, **The choice to be who you are.**

Rokus denHartog

Interlocking Realities

Dear Friends:

We are on a journey of separation. Jesus spoke of this wonderful journey, this terrible journey, in one of his parables. He described it this way: *"A certain man planted a vineyard and let it out to servants. He then went to a far country for a long time."*

God seems something *far away* for a *long time.* We feel abandoned on the shores of this strange beach called the 'human experience.' Actually, the great Source and Father of all has gone nowhere. Where could He go? Rather, a dimensional illusion has been formed called SPACE-TIME, or a FAR COUNTRY-LONG TIME. That is where we feel so alone and separated. The journey is not one of distance or time at all. It is a journey of awareness. It is a journey back home to greater and former knowing. We ask for the Joy of the Journey.

We who are intimate with the one from Galilee are beginning to grasp the depth of our own experience. The Light is dawning. The veil is being removed. We have understanding. One of these understandings is the realization that we live in simultaneous, interlocking realities. These interlocking realities are the subject of this writing.

Interlocking Realities

We live in realms of interlocking realities. Many worlds exist in the same space. Reality can be experienced at many vibrational levels of perception. The idea that all truth can be described or focused by a single set of teachings, doctrines, or descriptive statements has infected the human mind and has locked itself into his genetics. It is a pervasive attitude that has limited both science and religion. The burning of heretics, the ridicule of intellectual minds, and the scoffing of the ignorant has been with us all through our long recorded history.

Today we are experiencing a breakthrough in this matter. There are brilliant and respected scientific minds that are proposing ideas beyond the scope of religion. Yet, these are ideas whose veracity finds support in the ancient text, held so dear by us who have come from more fundamentalist experience and background. At the same time there are mystics making credible pronouncements in scientific matters.

On the side of science I have in mind the work of Zechariah Sitchin, a highly respected expert in history and archeology. He is presenting information obtained from ancient clay tablets found in Mesopotamia and is interpreting them to push the civilized history of this planet back 450,000 years. You or I may raise some real skeptical ears at his sound, but the intellectual and academic world is not only listening, they are jumping onto his train. Likewise, J.J. Hurtak, the author and recipient of the information contained in the *Keys of Enoch,* written in 1972, could be called a mystic. His book contains information of great interest to science. It also validates the record of the Torah concerning Enoch, the name Yahweh, the Elohim, and other great truths of the scriptures.

There is a lot of excitement about these many new sources of information and enlightenment. At the same time there is much confusion. It seems as if all truth is not the same truth. The fact is, these sources differ significantly on very important issues. If you are dogmatic you will find this very challenging. However, if you will allow yourself to listen, this can be a time of great accelerated change. Flexibility is needed. This planet is coming into a reality check!

This planet is a war zone of competing energies. Ideologies, philosophies, and religions are on a collision course with Truth and Light. Every stronghold of intelligence that has made a claim on this planet must validate its right of inheritance in order to remain.. Step up to the podium and present your case.

These energies are contending for preeminence. We can see it in the way that McDonald and Burger King each vie for a greater market share. This heavenly conflict is the real cause of all wars that have ravaged this planet from the beginning of time.

This war in heaven was also the cause of Jesus' crucifixion. I remember very vividly a statement made by an Angel about Jesus of Nazareth in a book by Ruth Montgomery. It read like this:

Yes, we have wondered about Jahshuah Ben Joseph. Why would such a high brilliant being waste his life and time on such an insignificant planet as Earth?

This statement has made a great impression on me. It dawned on me that not all beings of light or darkness understand who Jesus was or his mission. Such beings may not be opposed to Him. In fact, they may reverence his person to the degree they have seen Him, but they have limited understanding.

How shall we make our way on a path filled with such contradiction and opposition? What can we believe? How do we handle the searing doubt that we experience on this journey? My answer to these questions was to put my trust in Jesus and through him, in the Father of Light. I recommend him to you?

Meet My Mother

My mother was a devout Christian woman who faithfully tithed and attended the Christian Reformed church all her life. She struggled tremendously with the doctrines of hell, concerned about her sons that did not attend church. She wondered if they would end up in never-ending torment. My brothers were more skeptical and perhaps more intellectually honest than I was during those years. They saw the hypocrisy of much that is passed off as religion and God. Perhaps they would appreciate this little joke I once heard: One day, a visiting evangelist tried to get some "Amens" or at least nods of agreement from the stoic congregation by asking: *"Who wants to go to heaven in this Church?"* Immediately, everyone's hands went up, with the exception of one retarded boy, little Johnny, sitting in the back pew. Puzzled, the preacher asked Johnny: *"Don't you want to go to heaven, Son?"* To which Johnny replied: *"Not if all these folks are going!"*

Please do not interpret this as criticism of church. I am in favor of every effort that is made by men to improve their lot and increase their understanding and relationship with God. We too gather for fellowship every Sunday, just like my brothers and sisters in the Christian Reformed church. Although we are not bound by dogma and tradition, I am sure we have not attained the greatest possible dynamics available to us in Christ either.

Now...back to my mother. Even though she did not understand me, she did respect that God had called me. She asked me to do her funeral over the wishes of her minister. When they objected to the use of the church for the funeral she said: Since you rent the church building to the Baptists, could you not rent it to me? At this valid insistence they relented and this divorced, ex-church member, had a wonderful experience helping his siblings have real closure.

Before she passed she asked me abut hell. I sat with her, tears welling up in my eyes. I could feel Gods great love for her as I told her what He is really like. Peace came to her heart that day. She never could understand the Pentecostal antics her son had embraced except for the hugging. I remember when I first embraced her, she stiffened like a board! The second time she felt was more like stiff foam, but pretty soon, as I persisted, she let me embrace her and love her. That was a wonderful day for this son.

To show affection, something so easy for some, had been very hard for her all her life. I was more free than my mother but I did not understand the real treasure in those days. I was concerned about religious understanding and experiences instead of reality. The reason I am taking such pain for you to meet my Mom is because she communicated with us after she died. She came to Carolynne, and told her the following: *"There is a light-mist everywhere. It's like a school. There are seven levels. Where you start depends on the degree to which you have overcome death in your earth life."*

The overcoming she is speaking of is the overcoming of the death experiences of your life. Those death experiences are the disappointments of life that have left feelings of abandonment, failure, and so on. She went on to say that she was just at the first level and was perfectly content to be attending this school. She was learning in this lowest level the lessons she could not learn in her life experience.

24

I am persuaded that all the levels my Mom spoke of can be experienced in our physical lives and even be transcended here and now. What a thought! I have also come to the conclusion that this earth realm, the densest of all, is not a limitation but a grand opportunity for transcendence. When these levels are experienced simultaneously, we have interlocking realities. The simultaneous experience of these levels is what I refer to as *interlocking realities.*

We are more aware of the interlocking realties collectively these last hundred years or so when Pentecost was experienced again at the beginning of the twentieth century. There were Spirit manifestations in Topeka Kansas and then later in Azusa Street, Los Angeles. It was so disturbing to people that church people had horse figs thrown at them. Charles Fillmore, in this same time period, wrote his metaphysical dictionary. It became the basis for the Unity movement. Two simultaneous movements occurred. One emphasized that God is **Mind,** desiring spiritual *mental* experiences. The second emphasized God as **Spirit,** desiring ecstatic, *emotional*, spiritual experiences. Here we see two interlocking realms right at the beginning of a fantastic century. These successive visitations during the twentieth century prepared us for the next climaxing wave that is beaching and grounding its energy on human consciousness. This last statement brings me to the real purpose of this writing.

Can You Say: "It Is Good"?

I have related all this to you to tell of an experience of such interlocking realities that Carolynne and I had at our home in Oldfield, Missouri. Let me give you a little background about Carolynne and I. We traveled the USA for four years from 1986 to 1990. When Eva (our daughter) arrived, it was during a two week stay in Minnesota. After the birth, Carolynne began thinking about a nesting place for Eva.. I still wanted to travel. As it happened, we met Sue Shepherd in Springfield, Missouri in the fall of 1989. That following spring in May, we purchased 25 acres in Oldfield, Missouri with Sue. It was a great story how it all happened, but I will not go into all of those details. Suffice it to say, that when Carolynne stepped into the house that we now live in, the witness of Spirit hit her. She declared it to be *our home*. It took me a few days to reconcile myself to this new thought. This is where our story starts.

25

I will let Carolynne tell in her own words her story of interlocking realities:

Greetings to all! Last November, I was preparing for our annual Thanksgiving Gathering when I began looking around at our house. It was in a state of construction. The living room floor had been stripped of carpet because of mold. The ceilings had been patched in several places because of water leakage in the upstairs bathroom. It wasn't a pretty sight to see for me or for anyone else. I was in the house alone and took advantage of the luxury of complaining where I couldn't be heard. *"All these people are coming and I just can't stand this house. It looks so terrible. I just hate it."* Spirit responded to my complaining and spoke so clearly: *"What did you say when you first saw this house?"* I was stunned. Then I slowly replied: *"I said it was mine and it was good."* Spirit spoke again: *"Can you still say it is good, even though you see the seeming deficiencies?"* I replied with a heart of repentance and tears running down my face. *"Yes Father. You gave us this house and I will say it is good and thank you for it."* Then spirit spoke again. *"What did you say before you came into YOUR physical house?"* Immediately I knew that the reference had changed. Instead of my house, the spirit was now talking about my body. Stunned again, I haltingly replied. *"Why...I guess, I said it was good. A body you have given me and I have come to do your will."* The reply was: *"Then why have you complained about your body and who you are all of your life?"* My heart broke as I realized this was true. I have struggled with the wonderful tabernacle that the Father has created for me, always wanting it to change it, and never truly inhabiting the place given to me.

Carolynne

This very intense experience actually took place over a ten year period. There are two specific interlocking realities that unfold. First there are the physical events centered in the house in which we lived. It was a created experience. It did not seem at all that we were "creating", it just unfolded in our space and time. Let me say it like this: In that other interlocking reality of spiritual awareness, we drew the experience to ourselves in our physical and emotional space. Our eternal counterpart created it with the energy of the Holy Father and it appeared in our physical world.

26

I suppose you could say we drew ourselves a picture. It was a picture in our 3-D space to help us understand what was happening in our 4th and 5th dimensional space. A picture is better than a thousand words.

We can easily see that we have all come into this realm to create experience. All we have to do is extrapolate beyond our personal involvement. These experiences will enable us at a higher level to accomplish our eternal mission in the cosmos. Paul the Apostle refers to this aspect when he says concerning the children of Israel and their journeying in the wilderness: *These things happened unto them for our sakes upon whom the end of Ages has come.* The question has now been raised: *Why do you always resist the body you are in, your own incarnation?* I do not think the question was raised to measure, to judge, or to condemn. It was raised to be considered and answered.

Two interlocking realities appear in the picture story of the life of Jesus. His death on the cross is the shadow of a greater reality. That greater reality is the crucifixion that took place when a company of spiritual beings took on flesh and thus were lowered and limited to physical form. His dying and suffering on that cruel cross needs to be seen by enlightened eyes. This true beholding will break the shackles of our denial, fear, and feelings of abandonment and rejection. This is the answer to the question that was raised in Carolynne's experience of interlocking realms: *We resist our incarnation because it is like a crucifixion.* Realizing this truth will enable us to embrace our incarnation, our physical experience.

This embracing of our incarnation brings a great release. We find true freedom from the limited realms of consciousness that have kept us bound in long ages of time. Resurrection life is flowing in abundance. We suffered the pangs of death and hell when we lost all awareness of our eternalness and clothed ourselves in flesh bodies through thoughts of un-worth and failure. That death is now being released from us. This is the journey of our incarnation. We came to this earth plane to experience this lower realm and all that it brings.

Now, we stand at the apex of the ages. We are recognizing that before we came, we declared our incarnation, (our physical house), to be GOOD. We are remembering the joyful echoes and refrains of love and victory as we began our descent into matter. We could feel the rigor mortis of unconsciousness setting in, its onset slowly blotting out our true knowing of the Father and the Light. We are glimpsing the truth of it now. We were sown into forgetfulness, yet knew that we would return with joy. The scriptures declare it so: *"He that goes forth weeping, bearing precious seed, shall doubtless come again rejoicing, bringing his sheaves with him."*

Jahshuah My Own, I Love You

Here we stand on the verge of the great awakening of Man. We stand here with Jesus. He is the one who remained in the heavens and became the one to show the pathway that we all experience. He became a breakthrough in his unique incarnation. We are entering with him into the glory that we had before worlds were. He is not calling us to follow Him. We **have** followed Him. He is calling us to let our beings merge again as we once-always-knew. He is calling us to merge in a marriage of awareness. This joyous bridal nuptial consummates as become aware of the Holy union that we are in all the Ages of Time. We create a whole new world, a paradise in earth. This kingdom of Love, Joy, Peace, and Righteousness is designed and created from our love. A love that is so new and yet so old.

Jesus made this real to us in a song he sang to Carolynne. He sang it to her…through her…when we first came onto the property. Because of this song we call it "This Place of Ours."The words are:

> *There's resurrection power, in my very being,*
> *there's resurrection glory in this hour.*
> *It's a whole new way of living,*
> *a whole new way of walking,*
> *and it's just beyond the open door.*
>
> *So won't you come on in with me?*
> *Into this Place of Ours,*
> *Together we'll walk, hand in hand,*
> *and inherit the Promised Land.*

Rokus den Hartog

Betrayal:

A Human Experience

Betrayal is a common human experience. My nine year old daughter may not know the words to describe how she feels when her best friend and another friend leave her out as a third party, but she knows the feeling of being betrayed even as young as she is. Children cry and soon forget these painful feelings because their real world consists of their connectedness to their parents; but teenagers and young adults can experience such intense pain of feeling betrayed, perhaps in their first experience of romantic love, that they never recover from it and are unable to form a deep and lasting relationship the rest of their lives.

Perhaps the most vivid and powerful portrayal of the experience of betrayal that I have seen acted out on the screen is by Mel Gibson. In the movie *BraveHeart*, William Wallace, played by Mel Gibson, leading the Scottish revolt against the English King, is defeated in battle because of the betrayal by Robert the Bruce, the leading Scottish nobleman. Wallace, racing from the field of battle and pursuing the English king, is knocked from his horse by an armored knight. Feigning death, he is approached by his victor. Suddenly he rises up and tears the helmet from the English knight. When he does he exposes Robert the Bruce, whom he thought to be his ally and friend. The pain that sears through his soul, not only a betrayal of his person but of his beloved Scotland and all those who trusted in him, is acted out magnificently. That one scene alone to me is worth the millions of dollars spent to make that film.

But you really do not need to see a movie to taste the bitter pain of betrayal. All of us in our lives have, perhaps unwittingly, betrayed others and have been betrayed by others. Most importantly, you have FELT as if you were betrayed.

Betrayal: The Path of Ascension

Most of you that will read this writing have already experienced intensely this breaking of your trust, not only by friends and perhaps spouses, but by people you shared some degree of spiritual awareness with, people you were committed to because of a common commitment to some higher consciousness. Perhaps a professed loyalty to Jesus or at least to the church you both attended. Maybe it was the pastor that you felt betrayed by when one day you found the door closed. I was told of a charismatic group that met in homes. If they wanted to exclude a certain unwelcome person; they would keep the next meeting place a secret. Ouch! Do you remember the time the spirit revealed to you the meaning of the scripture: *Going therefore unto him, without the camp*? You really need to read by the spirit to understand King James English here. The meaning is: *Going therefore unto him OUTSIDE the camp.* That is, in order to progress in your spiritual walk, there comes a time when you must leave the place of your spiritual beginnings and go where He went, outside the camp. You need to leave the people you shared this religious consciousness with! For what reason? To be crucified. Why? Because the only way to let go of a realm of being that is no longer able to keep you, no longer serves your path of ascendancy, is for you to let go of the sense of self that keeps you connected there. That is, you must die, unwillingly, because you do not understand. You must die at the hands of your friends, because no one else was close enough to you. With the pricking thorns of fear in your mind and the gall of bitterness in your mouth, you left there, never to return in that same state of mind. But you could not be crucified without being betrayed, even as He was betrayed. So you too experienced betrayal!

The Message of Calvary

For two thousand years we have not really been able to fully understand why it was that Jahshuah came and was betrayed. He was betrayed by one of His own into the hands of the religious and civil authorities of that day. Crucified at the hands of cruel men, he died and rose again. True we experienced the cleansing of our souls from sin. We have also experienced the beautiful infilling of the Holy Spirit. But have we truly heard His message? Do we know that what

He came to show us will truly set us free from all limitation and reconnect us to the source of our being? I venture to say that only now, two thousand years after He manifested in this physical plane, is there a people prepared to hear and understand the eternal truth that He came to bring. You cannot really learn it by reading the scriptures alone or by obedient acts of righteousness. You must open the ear of your spirit self and hear Him whisper the truth from within, the eternal truth of who you are.

Do It in Remembrance of Me!

There came a day in my journey of awakening when I heard Him say to me: *Do it in remembrance of me!* When I heard those words I listened again to the familiar text, so often used to celebrate communion. I could hear the words clearly in my mind: *In the night that He was betrayed, He took the bread and broke it. As oft as you do it, do it in remembrance of me!* Do what in remembrance of me? The breaking of your being, the pain of feeling betrayed, and the agony of having to leave everything that was near and dear to you! Use the opportunity of that moment in your life to draw Him into your consciousness. Why? So He can whisper to you the truth of your being. He can tell you who you are, the reason you came into the flesh and the purpose for your being on this planet.

In the hour of your betrayal you may not have been in a place to hear Him whisper to you. It may well be that you were bitter and angry, full of blame and shame. Guess what? You can go back any time to that point in your experience when you suffered betrayal. It is still locked inside of you if you have never resolved it! Every successive experience of betrayal serves only to focus all the betrayal of your life. Forgiving is not enough, you must understand! Let the spirit take you back. Understand that all the pain of the human experience is an opportunity for spiritual ascent. Understand that whatever injustice or pain was ever inflicted upon you is your chance to loosen yourself from your ego definition of self. It is your chance to cut the umbilical ties to the lower forces of you earth experience and begin to reconnect to the eternal dimensions from which you came. It is a chance to take another step in the evolution of your being, the awareness of who you are.

31

Seeing From an Eternal Point of View

Is this acknowledgment of identifying with Jahshuah in death and resurrection in our spiritual unfolding the only understanding we need about betrayal? I recall the moment vividly. I was walking away from the scene where I had experienced such a profound sense of betrayal. I had no words to respond to it, no reaction to make. Only the feeling of searing pain as if a sword had been trust through my soul. All I wanted to do was turn away and be alone. As I walked away I heard an infinitely tender and compassionate voice say to me:

"Now you know how I feel."

We can see ourselves in a mirror. Is it possible that our human experiences, these highly personal emotional states, are really reflections seen by a greater awareness beyond this physical time-space realm? Can we let ourselves think that God, or at least highly spiritual entities in a non-space realm, experience feelings of betrayal? Is it possible that the whole of our experience, like the experience of Jahshuah on the cross, is an intense remedial act of salvation for those realms? Is it possible that there are such realms of God's being that are locked in pain and non-understanding that must be released by a collective messiah? If this is so then the purpose of our being incarnate cannot be understood in terms of our physical experience alone.

If we are ever to truly understand our physical experience we must learn to think of it from the point of view of our non-physicalness. We must leave the earth plane of our awareness of self. We must die and rise again into a greater dimension of awareness. We must go back through the ages of our incarnation, back through Paul, through Moses, through Abraham, through Adam, and remember the journey. We must become aware of our descent. We must think in terms of becoming physical rather than spiritual If we can see ourselves as eternal beings taking on the awareness of our physical bodies then we can begin to ask the questions of our existence. Our intent will then be to fully feel and embrace our experiences of betrayal. We have been exhorted to give thanks in all things. If you wish to grow and go to greater heights, you must learn to so embrace your life and be thankful.

I tell you, when you realize the nature of this present realm and the opportunities created here by you and for you, you will not have to try to be thankful. You will be filled with a spirit of thanksgiving every moment of every day!

Why Did We Create This Bitter Path?

When was He betrayed? It is written: *In the **night** that He was betrayed*. The reason there is betrayal and broken trust in the various realms of reality is because there is not-knowing and not-understanding. There is darkness. There is night. Mankind and all spirituals must pass through the night, for it is only in the night that you can begin to form a separate consciousness. Only in the womb of darkness can your being-ness be conceived to begin the great journey of realization and awareness. Only through not-knowing can we understand and only through not-being can we become.

However, the child that remains in the womb when the hour of delivery is come will certainly die and great is the disappointment of the parents who conceived out of their love! The bitterness of the womb that brings forth a stillborn child is deep. It is time for mankind to be born again. It is time for you to come forth. Now is the hour of our greatest awakening. Now we must leave the old and tried paths and venture forth anew. We must leave the repeated cycles of death and pain that are always asking us to do again what our forefathers have done. Now, if ever, is the time to trust and to believe

What is This Pain of Betrayal?

I now know that my own experience of being betrayed forced me out of my comfort zone, my denials, and made me take the chance of striking out on a new path. We must know that the pain of being betrayed has its source in our fear of believing in the greater truth of our being. All the accumulated experiences of betrayal of the human race have been created for you to make a breakthrough. You created the experience of your betrayal that you might face the greatest fear of your existence: The fear of your own validity, the fear of the worth of your own being. Betrayal allows you to see the fear you have of declaring the holiness and greatness of your being. Amen!

We have not been able to face this fear and declare it to be void as the night from which it came. We have stayed in our denial, given form to our fear and projected it outward as the experience of BETRAYAL. Generations have come and gone, each creating again the cycles of death, the cycles of broken trust and betrayal. The pain is filled up in our human experience. It is time for the morning of the truth to dawn in our conscious knowing. It is time for Christ, the Son-Body that came from the Father, to rise from the dead and reveal all things. It is time to dispel the night forever; it has served its purpose. The hour is at hand that those in the grave shall hear the voice of the Son and they that hear shall live.

The Keys of Hell and the Grave

One of the most illuminating scriptures on this subject is recorded in the book of the revelation of John. Here Jesus is recorded as saying these words:*"I am He that liveth and was dead, and behold, I am alive forevermore. And I have the keys of hell (the grave) and of death."* The voice that is whispering on the inside is giving us these keys. They could only be given by the one who has them and has the visible proof of possessing them, the one that has experienced death for every man.

Keys unlock a door, a condition, or a state of mind. A physical key can unlock a physical door, but it takes a spiritual key to unlock a state of mind. A spiritual key is an UNDERSTANDING. The physical BODY of man is the symbol of his separation hence is symbolized by DEATH. The MIND of man is where his death thoughts are; it is symbolized by the GRAVE.

The keys of understanding that are being given to us are the understandings of the MIND-BODY connection that we experience as physical man.

One of those keys is the understanding that the pain of betrayal we experience here is really the outward projection of one of our deepest fears, the fear that our being has no validity, has no worth. As we begin to turn this key, unlocking to us our greater awareness of self that is hidden in the realms of CHRIST, we also turn the key to open the door to the dawn of the new day. Amen!

34

SIN and BROKENNESS

Dear Friends:

As we stand in the dawning of this greater day, a day for which mankind has long waited; we need to look at one of the most fundamental ideas of man's relationship with man and with God, that is, the concept of Sin

To think about the idea of Sin, has been most difficult for me, It has perhaps been the most difficult of all the various thoughts I have deeply considered. It is so difficult to consider because no one seems to clearly know what it is we are speaking of when we address the subject of Sin. It is easily confused with closely related words such as guilt, condemnation, and judgment.

Sin: Moral Wrongdoing

I have finally concluded that most people use the word sin to mean, in a very loose way, moral wrongdoing. The word Sin in the sense that it was used in the scriptures is no longer used in common language today. The idea of Sin as an offense, a breaking of the law or a crime, is no longer called Sin; it is simply referred to as a crime or miss-demeanor, the breaking of coded law. Today we simply say: *That was wrong. You should not have done that.* Or if statutory law was broken we might say: *That was illegal, you could go to jail for that.* Or if it is thoughts we have we might say: *Shame on you for thinking like that*

The word "Sin" is by no means unimportant. It is found no less than 448 times in the scriptures, 336 in the Old and 112 in the New Testament. John the Baptist, when officially introducing Jesus at the Baptism in the river Jordan announces Him as follows: *Behold the Lamb of God that takes away the sin of the world.* Here Sin is closely tied in with Jesus mission.

Most Christian theology centers on the idea of Sin as moral wrongdoing and the Atonement as taught by the Apostle Paul. The whole of the relationship between man and God is seen in terms of Sin and Forgiveness and the life hereafter. Rewards of heaven and hell are all seen from this point of view.

A Larger Definition of Sin

It is high time for a change. We need clarity of thought and understanding. We need to see the true nature of God and correspondingly our relationship with God and one another. We need a new theology
.

Instead of further confusing the issue and complicating thought by referring to definitions of the word Sin as used in the Old Testament, the New Testament, and in common usage today or even to try to re-iterate the teachings of the Apostle Paul, I would like to propose a single definition of the word Sin. This definition will span all of time and apply to all situations and relationships. This definition is not one I have invented or arrived at through great effort and thought. It was given to me. One day as I was just giving up, realizing I could not sort it all out, I heard this definition; the words just came into my mind. You be the judge of where it came from.

Sin is the thought or the awareness that
I cannot meet your expectation.

I have considered this idea for several years now. The implications are truly staggering. If we embrace this thought as a definition of Sin and begin to incorporate it into our lives, we will have a revolution indeed. Nothing will remain the same. We have already shifted in our awareness of who we are and who God is. These new thoughts will bring alignment between what we have already experienced and our understanding of it.

It is difficult for us to consider the thought that Sin, seemingly the cause of all human misery, had its origin anywhere but in Hell, created by some evil force. But if the origin of Sin is a **thought** or **awareness,** then clearly sin begins when thought begins and where thought begins....in our own mind. The thought that I am unable to meet an expectation is a very common occurrence. It is not at all evil. In fact it is a thought that may cause one to press in and try harder to please and to prove one's adequacy.

36

When Did Sin Begin?

If Sin is essentially a thought of inadequacy then clearly such thoughts are not limited to beings living in a physical plane. The potential for Sin begins when thought begins. Thought begins at the very beginning of consciousness, the very beginning of an awareness of self that is separate from the Source itself.

How do we prove such a thought? Are there scriptures that confirm such broad sweeping statements re-adjusting our perspective of reality? Paul the Apostle makes this claim concerning physical reality. The things that are seen show forth the things that are not seen, even His (God's) eternal power and God-head. It seems that Paul understood the principle that the physical world is a world of manifestation. That is, it serves as a plane or place to show the realities that exist in other realms. These realms are beyond the physical plane, realms of Spirit as we call them. We know and understand that our being-ness is more than physical. Our substance is not really atoms and molecules. We are made up of much more refined and sublime "stuff" and ultimately we are pure energy at some frequency of existence that we can only imagine in our present state. We are consciousness.

The Spiritual Is Understood In the Natural

It seems more than plausible that we should look into the nature of physical reality and physical experience to understand the nature of non-physical reality. You may have read my pamphlet called *God Seeds*. It describes an experience in which I saw a large maple tree shedding its myriads of seeds. As I saw the wind carry them aloft, I could feel the tree as if it were God, He was sending us forth. I could feel His heart of unconditional blessing and support as He energized us to fly. The command was: *Go forth and create! Create and unfold consciousness. Become! Become all that you can be! Be the I AM in the realms of separation!* That was the beginning of consciousness as we know it, the beginning of us. It also initiated duality, the journey of separation. The Source desires to know itself as Love

Some months after I experienced this awesome breaking thought of beginning, I was walking along the sidewalk in Detroit Michigan. There I saw some maple keys lying on the sidewalk. They came in pairs, joined at the seed, twin seeds. Each had is own wing. Every seed was formed as a double. I suppose they are genetically identical. I saw them lying there. They were unbroken, still connected. I wondered if the seeds could fly in that condition. If I was correct in my thought that brokenness is from the beginning and that God Himself had to experience brokenness in order that we might have a point of origin, then the seeds in that whole condition should not be able to fly. My heart had a tremor. Shall I put it to the test? Of course I would. If what I was seeing in the physical creation was truly a reflection from deep in the heart of God, an acknowledgement of our beginning, then it must show that aspect of brokenness as well. It could not show our beginning as God-Seeds and be inconsistent as to how we began, in brokenness. As I picked up the twin seed and threw it out with all my effort, it just fluttered back to the ground. I could not see that awesome little helicopter effect that characterizes flying maple seeds. Again I tried it, again it could not fly. Then in a sacred moment I took that twin seed, the one that could not fly. I broke it into two separate seeds, and threw them...and of course...they flew...beautifully...gracefully...easily.

Brokenness and Sin Happened In the Beginning

So we see that brokenness is from the beginning. It was not a mistake or a punishment; rather it was a necessary experience to send us forth on the most awesome journey of all, the journey of separation, the journey of the experience of Love. Just before his crucifixion, Jesus portrayed the sacredness of the pain of separation and brokenness with these words: *Take eat, this is my body, broken for you...*In so doing he gave the Eternal Source a voice. It gave feeling and awareness to the brokenness that the Father-Source itself experienced. We came forth as a result of that separation and breaking hence the words: *broken for you...*We emerged from the Wholeness and Oneness that He always is and began our journey in brokenness. It is true also that we are that body that was broken in Gethsemane and at Calvary. He did take our brokenness upon himself and showed it to us. What Love, what awesome compassion.

What was the means by which this brokenness was accomplished? What causes brokenness in our lives today? It is Sin, Sin causes separation: Your Sins have separated you from each other and from God. So we see that Sin truly has its beginning in our beginning. It began as we began to unfold consciousness. As we began to form our first thoughts as awareness of self, it too was created. We created it. Some thoughts were awesome and powerful thoughts of love. Other negating thoughts were created in opposition, in the reflection, in the duality that came in the beginning. How did that first sin-thought form? We experienced the awesome releasing Love of the Source for us. We felt His powerful benediction and His unconditional blessing. As we did, a thought formed itself in us...we wondered...what if I cannot return this Love? What if I cannot be all that the Father Source is expecting of me? What if I cannot fill this awesome beautiful desire in Him?

This thought was such a simple one. It is one that we experience every day in some small way. It opened the door to many other thoughts and awarenesses. It opened the door for more devastating thoughts and conclusions. We formed the thought that we might not be worthy of the Source, resulting finally in feelings of un-worth, self-loathing, and shame. When these thoughts eventually created experience and physical reality we experienced shame and guilt that drove us deeper into negativity and pain. Our journey of consciousness extended into depth so that in those deep places of separation and loss, of feeling abandoned and unworthy we might in fact and reality discover the opposite. We might then truly know that the Love of the Source is indeed complete, whole and unimaginably wonderful. It is full of grace, mercy and forgiveness. Its acceptance is truly totally unconditional. How could we know the height of God's love if we had never known the depth of such loss and emptiness? How could we know the absolute bliss of the Love of God had we never known the depth of sin and un-worth that made it so real?

Aligning With Past Understanding

Can we reconcile this perception of Sin with those presented to us in the Old and New Testaments? Let us briefly look at the concept of Sin as seen in the Torah, the Law of Moses. I wish to write a separate article just on the Law and its place in the unfolding drama of the Father's purpose, for now I will just give a brief insight. The Law is a covenant, an agreement, much like a mort-gage. It has a death clause. If you fail to live up to the contract, you die. Under the Law, the expectation is made clear and is agreed upon. If you keep the law you are blessed, if you do not keep the Law you are cursed. Much in the same way as credit card companies reward and punish the cardholder. If you make late payments or default in any way, your interest rate goes up, penalties are imposed...all on the basis of your agreement. Sin is now clearly understood...it is failure to meet the expectation of the stated agreement. Sin now is not just a thought; it is awareness of failure to perform. The result is condemnation, real condemnation, and the punishment is just. You can see that the definition of Sin under the Law perfectly fits the definition stated in the first part of this writing. Let me repeat it here leaving out the word "thought" and leaving in the applicable word "awareness."

Sin is the awareness that I am unable to meet your expectation.
OR
Sin is the failure to meet the expectation of the Law.
OR
Sin is the transgression of the Law.

What about the effect Jesus had on the cross? Paul clearly states that without the law Sin cannot be imputed. John pronounced that Jesus was the Lamb of God that takes away the Sin of the world. Jesus himself said: *I have come to fulfill the law, not to destroy it.* Are we therefore to conclude that Sin is no more? Even a cursory look at the writings of the New Testament shows that the writers clearly saw that Sin continues to fulfill its purpose. Sin in the Greek, *hamartia,* derives from the root word, *hamartano,* which means "to miss the mark." Missing what mark? The idea is that of an archer aiming for the center of the target, the bull's eye. Missing the mark is without condemnation. Yes it is failure to meet the expectation, but whose expectation? For a student it may well be the instructor's expectation. For a child it may be the expectation of a parent. But for a seasoned archer it is only his own expectation that he fails to meet. That failure challenges him to excel, to do it again, to improve, and to attain. It fuels the desire that enables him to overcome, to succeed. In the event of failure to meet an expectation, whereas the law ministered condemnation, the spirit ministers grace

Jesus' Mission and Sin

So what do we say concerning Jesus' mission and our view of Sin in the Light of that mission? How is it that the Lamb takes away the sin of the cosmos? How did Jesus change the paradigm concerning sin?

Jesus came to reveal the Father's heart. He came, and in the demonstration of his love for you and me and all men, he showed the true nature of the Father that could not be seen in the Law. This true nature is seen in the fact that the Father did not at any time impute blame or guilt on the creation and consequently not on you and me. The thought that God requires a certain standard and condemns all those that cannot achieve it has been clearly demonstrated as limited and incomplete. Jesus took upon himself our separation by taking on a physical form as we also have done. In doing so he clearly showed that **we are the Son of God crucified on our human experience.** In spite of this pain of separation, fear, abandonment and disempowerment... the Father yet raised him up and declared him to be the Son of God in power. Here we can clearly see His heart attitude to any and all of us. The Father, in His heart and being, did not ever for one moment in time or one brief instant in eternity, separate Himself from any part of His creation. Nor did He ever condemn or place shame on it, never ever! In the light of this greater truth we suggest the following interpretation of the mission of Jesus as stated by John when he said: *Behold the lamb...*:
:
Behold this man, see in him the perfect reflection of the Eternal Lamb of God, God's own provision to meet the need for every man and enable him to complete his journey of separation. It is always taking away the Sin we experience that wants to attach itself to us. In this man's life you will see the truth that all things are complete in the Father. Sin is serving the purpose for which it formed in us. It can no longer hold us in bondage to fear. The pain of separation and its sorrow will be gone forever.

CONCLUSION

Sin, the thought or the awareness in us that we cannot meet an expectation, with its emotional appendages of shame and guilt, is the evolutionary driver of consciousness.
It can only be understood, and its pain be alleviated, when our heart-mind is opened to understand the true nature of God, the Source, and the long journey of consciousness.

Rokus denHartog

Re-Connected

And Clothed with Glory

Part 1: Coming Out of Denial

I can see what the problem is. I understand why mankind is sick, diseased, and dying. *He is in denial*. What is he in denial about? Man is in denial about himself, about his identity. It is not about *what he does* but about *who he is*.

Here is the truth: Man is a being of light that came from another dimension to this plane of existence. In order to come here, to be in a physical body, he had to experience a great reduction in consciousness. This truncating, or cutting off, in his awareness of self included the loss of the knowledge of his existence in the greater realms. You might think of this reduction as necessary so that he could "fit into" the consciousness of his physical body.

Strangely enough, you, being human, still exist in those greater dimensions of light. Your existence in what you now see yourself to be is only a projection of your greater self. If you could see the whole of yourself, you would probably think that you had seen an angel. You would certainly not think: *Wow, that's me I'm looking at*! Let's add a phrase to the truth about you: You are multidimensional.

The events of the Garden of Eden are the story of how you came to be here, the story of your disconnection or your separation. The events in the book of Genesis speak of seven creative days or ages. We are now ready to experience the seventh age, the golden age of man. This is the time of our re-connection.

What are we being reconnected to? First of all, we are experiencing a spiritual rejuvenation. We are being reconnected to the Father of Light. In truth and reality you have never been separated from Him. How could you go where He is not? There is no such place. It is only in your mind that this separated reality exists. It is therefore in the renewal of your mind that you return to the Father.

Secondly, we are returning to the spiritual beings that exist in all the realms. The earth plane is a projection of these realms. We are being visited by our ancestors who first began this journey. The angels, who have assisted us for so many centuries, are finally able to reveal themselves to us. The veil that has separated us from the other realms is thinning and is being taken away.

Thirdly, and most important, we are being reconnected to our light bodies. Our consciousness is opening like a pinecone placed in water. The energy and power that is our reconnected state, is flooding us with great joy.

What proof or evidence can I give you to validate what I am saying? The only real validation that I can give you and that you will accept is the effect of the truth on your being. You probably would not be reading this writing if you have not already at some deeper level in yourself become aware of this truth. You may never have said it just like I am saying it to you, but you know within yourself that this is the truth you have longed to remember.

Can I point to some authority outside of yourself to validate what I am telling you? There have been many mystics and spiritual men that have said what I am saying in some way or another. The one I wish to quote has stated it more perfectly and directly than any other that I know. To do this, I will first have to tell you who Jesus was, that is, who he himself claimed to be:

Jesus, the Metaphor of Man

Jesus asked his disciples: *Who do men say that I, the Son of Man, am?* Do you remember reading the story and Peter's answer to the question? *Thou art the Christ, the Son of the Living God!* Please don't let me lose you here. Don't get hung up on two thousand years of Christian debate about the godhead. Notice the question, not the answer. Jesus clearly identified himself. He called himself the "Son of Man." What did he mean? He did not call himself Jesus or the son of Mary or the Son of God; He called himself the *Son of Man.*

43

In the Hebrew, this phrase would read: "The Son of Adam." Why did he call himself the Son of Man? In *fact*, he was the son of Mary. In *fact*, he was the Son of God. But in **truth**, he was the Son of Man. Jesus came to deliver mankind, you and me, from our only real problem, our denial. He came to break the chains of the "devil" that kept us locked into an earth consciousness. He came to show us who we are. To do this, he took on our human form, he became like us. In truth, he became us. That is why the early apostles could say that when he died, we died. He is who we are.

Words alone cannot tell us who we are. He is the evidence we need to show us who we are, all we need to do is look at him. Look, not so much historically or as a picture, but look at the truth that he came to show and identify. What was his greatest moment? If you were to ask Peter, James and John, they might well say that his greatest moment came when they saw him transfigured. Jesus had prayed in their hearing: "Father, clothe me with the Glory that I had with Thee before the world was." They saw him totally connected to his Light Body. They saw him as he always exists even as he walked the shores of Galilee or died on a Roman cross. But the most wonderful truth is the realization that this glorious reality is the truth of your being. That glorified transfigured being, brighter than the noonday sun, is in fact and in truth the Son of Man, it is you. That glorious Light Body you are being reconnected to is not found in some distant heaven to be attained to after you die; nor is it in some other level of reality. It is you, beyond all limitation of time and space, and the truth of you while you experience yourself in time and space.

We have tried to say for years that we were crucified with him. We said it mostly because the scriptures stated it to be so, not that we had any real understanding of it. We never objected too strenuously to being crucified with him but the thought that we shared with him in the transcendent glory was too much for our pea-sized brains to even consider. What about his crucifixion? What does it really mean that we were crucified with him? It means that when you, in truth, are looking at him hanging on a cross, you are looking at yourself hanging there. Why do I need to see him there as me? So that I can come out of denial about who I am and where I am in consciousness. Let us look at him as he hung there.

He had a crown of thorns on his head. Those thorns are the pricking of the fears that every man experiences being in a body of flesh. All those fears we experience in our jobs, our relationships, our roles as husband, wife and so on, all reduced to a single great fear: "I am not good enough." While he hung suspended between heaven and earth as if he was not at home in either, he cried out the greatest agony of your human experience. The agony you experience because of your intense feeling of separation from everything that you came from, your feelings of separation from God. He cried out "My God, My God, why hast Thou forsaken me?"

How many of us suffer from a deep feeling of powerlessness? Everything around us seems to restrict and limit us and keep us from the freedom we imagine and long for. His hands were nailed, outstretched on the cross member of that tree. His feet nailed to the post. All of man's inability to go and to do is acted out in this agonizing way. It must have been a solar eclipse that made darkness come in the middle of his experience; the darkness, the not knowing, not understanding of the human soul, how great it is.

Isaiah the prophet so beautifully wrote of us: "He was wounded for our transgression; He was bruised for our iniquity. Surely he hath born our sorrows and by his stripes we are healed." How exquisitely did the prophet describe the human condition! Everything in our experience made us to believe we had failed or broken a law or displeased almighty God. Why else are our bodies sick and dying? Why else are our lives full of pain and sorrow? It is for this mistaken belief that he came to show us the truth and bring us out of denial. He came to show us that this painful, limited human experience is **A-Okay**. It is the pathway to the greater glory.

The Truth of the Human Experience

What then is the truth of the human experience? Let us listen to the man who knows that he is you, the Son of Man. "I have power to lay down my life and to take it again, this commandment have I received from my Father." For Jesus, representing you, that meant his experience on the cross. The Pharisees, Pilate and his crew, did not put him there. He went willingly; he chose the path when he said: "Nevertheless, not my will but thine be done." That is exactly how you chose, not a wooden cross but the cross of your human experience. You were crucified in time and space on the wood of your humanity. You laid down the knowledge of your divinity. You relinquished the powers of eternity. You suffered the reduction and limiting of your consciousness. You became human. You died, as Adam, to all the former glory of your eternal existence and entered the limitations, pain, and sorrow of the mortal body.

How will you return to were you came from if you do not know where you have been? How will you ever accept the power and privilege of glory and immortality if you do not know that they rightfully belong to you? Belong to you not as an undeserved gift but as an inheritance by truth and right? The only thing that stands between man and his entrance into this seventh golden age of realization is the degrees of denial that still cling to him as so many grave clothes to a man already raised from the dead. Guilt, shame and condemnation have played their part. They have been great servants to us along with a host of spirits to minister them to us. They have helped us to totally and truly enter this journey of separation and this valley of shadows, these seeming realities, this experience of the physical body. But now we have come a point of realization, a knowing, and a plane of awareness: We are standing now at a point of full conscious entry into the world of form. Not because of shame or guilt, but because we have come to do the Father's will, not in weakness or defeat but in the power and joy of a sound mind. We are not coming as of the earth, but now as the Lord of heaven, as a quickening spirit. It is time to put away the former, the seeming realities of pain, loss and suffering and to be clothed upon with our true and rightful garments of union, wholeness, glory, and light. We are coming out of denial.

Part 2: Who Told You That You Were Naked?

Who told you that you were naked? The words rang in Adams mind over and over. It was not a question to be answered. He knew there was no person that had told him that he was naked. No one had said to him: "Hey, Adam, you are naked, your butt is showing, you have egg on your face," or any of the hundred voices we have created in our experience to keep us thinking about that primal question. What is the question about if there is no single person that said it to us?

46

Why is it important for that question to have been planted in our minds these many millennia? The question of nakedness is the question of shame. The issue of blame and shame has ravaged the landscape of the human experience from the beginning. It demands to be addressed. It will not go away. As often as we think we have found a way to deal with it or to make it go away, it reappears in another generation and seems to wreak havoc all over again.

What Does It Mean To Be Naked?

Let us stop and consider the implication of the thought of being naked. You were naked when you were born, and that physical nakedness did not bother you except perhaps that you were cold. No, it is not the showing of the physical form that is referred to, it is the feelings that are associated with or symbolized by nakedness that we need to focus on. I remember early in my spiritual journey of awakening I used to have dreams of being partially clothed. I might be in school trying to get to some class or another, and I would be in my underwear. Whatever the dream was, in it I always experienced embarrassment or shame. It always created feelings of wanting to hide, wanting not to be seen. Why hide? Hide from whom?

What Was It Like Before We Knew Shame?

You may recall that nakedness did not always cause this feeling of wanting to hide. It is written: "They were naked and were not ashamed." Or we might say: "They were totally exposed to each other and experienced no desire to hide anything from each other." What was it like not to experience shame? A dear friend of ours recently told us of a dream that she had. In this dream, she went for a daily visit to a library. As she walked there, she was completely naked. In this great library, all that she had to do was touch the books and she would immediately know all that the book contained. One day as she was walking to the library, she noticed that people were looking at her. Oh no, she thought, they will see that I am fat. She found some kind of cloth to cover herself and went on to the library. Once in the library it was not as it was before. She was no longer able to touch the books and know what was in them. She had to read each page and each line of every page and each word of every line.

Can you imagine what it means to be able to touch a book and know its contents? If books as dream symbols represent people, can you imagine what life would be like to truly know each other simply by "touching" each other? Do you know how many people live together for years, live in the same house, share a bed, raise the same children and never really "touch" one another? Never really have intimacy of soul and spirit? Never experience the depth of each other or even their own being? Afraid to allow themselves to truly feel their emotions, feel other people's emotions, because there is some "right" way life is supposed to happen. Life, for millions of people, is only conforming behavior to a pattern already in the mind. A pattern learned from society, from religion or inherited genetically, never truly being free! Always living and responding in certain ways because that is the way it is supposed to be done; that is the program. Most people live entirely from the memory patterns of the race that exist in mass consciousness.

What was it in the dream that caused her to change? In our present language we would say that she became self-conscious. She became aware of herself as someone separate from the people around her, the ones that were looking at her. Her mind told her what they were thinking and she accepted those thoughts and feelings as her reality.

What Is the Purpose for Our Nakedness?

This change is a key to understanding our purpose on this planet. We came, not just to this planet, but to the *realm* of being physical. We came for a purpose. A necessary part and prerequisite of that purpose was the experience of shame, feeling naked, feeling exposed, feeling vulnerable. Remember now, the shame we experience in this realm has to do with what we *think* another person is feeling and thinking about us. Clearly to experience all these feelings about oneself or others, one has to believe he is separate from that person or persons from whom he is hiding. The root thought that allows you to experience shame is the thought or awareness of yourself as a separate being. Separate from others, separate from the realm of spirit, separate from God. The purpose of nakedness is to experience separation. Hiding yourself is seeking separation. Why do we hide or separate ourselves? Do you remember as a child the terrible feeling of having done something wrong and being found out? Yes it was the scolding or beating you wanted to avoid, but deeper than that you hated the terrible feelings of disapproval from your parent. You hated how the anger of your parent made you *feel;* the feeling of having no worth as a person, of not being good enough, inadequate. Maybe you have never really let yourself think about these feelings. Perhaps you just went on in the continuing line of generations that passes those feelings on and on and on. You did the same to your children as was done to you! As a child you hid in a closet, in your mother's skirt, or in any dark place were you thought you could not be seen. As adults we hide in much more complex ways. We hide in a very extrovert forceful nature and do to others before they can do to us. We hide in a passionate love for hitting a tiny golf ball. We hide in almost anything that we do, but the truth is we are really hiding from our selves. And what is it we are hiding from? A **thought!** Can you believe it? Could all this pain and agony be just to hide from a thought? This is the thought we are hiding from: *"I am not good enough."*

A Dream About Hiding

Another dear friend of mine, Tom Holmquist, also had a very vivid dream relating to this subject of hiding. In this dream, he was a boy in school helping to prepare for a dance. He was carrying a number of phonograph records to the booth were they were to be played. As he tried to open the door with one hand the records fell and shattered on the floor. He quickly tried to push the pieces under the door where hopefully they would not be seen. With terror in his mind he fled down the stairs into the basement below. The basement consisted of a long hallway dimly lit by a single light bulb. At the end of the hall, he found a room with many books stacked in piles along the wall. He pulled back a stack of these books and hid behind them. He could hear the other students and teachers calling for him, but they were unable to find him hidden behind the books.

The dream is fascinating because of what it reveals about the place in which we have hidden or have tried to hide. Books speak of knowledge and thoughts. They speak of the mind. It is in our minds that we have hidden ourselves. Hidden from what? From the truth of ourselves of course; what else is there to hide from? The mind we have hidden in is a certain perception of self, a self that is separate and physical. We began to think of ourselves *as* being physical beings. Our journey into this three dimensional realm had begun.

Not Being Good Enough

The key element in our hiding is the awareness of inadequacy. In other words, we can rephrase the question: "Who told you that you were naked?" in these words: "Who told you that you are not good enough?" How many scenarios since that thought first entered our minds have we created to give validity to it? Every time we fail, come short, mess up, botch it, goof up, screw up, we are simply creating situations that will "fill up" this thought of not being good enough. This one thought and our need to give validity to it has created the whole situation of human suffering and pain.

You might say, if this one thought of not being good enough is the cause of all our pain, our sickness, our disease... let's fix it. Let's tell people that they are truly beautiful wonderful beings, after all is that not the truth? Is it not amazing to you that we are always trying to fix things? Perhaps we believe that God is always trying to fix things, or at least should be fixing things. We are always assuming there is something wrong, hence we are always fixing things, when in fact all these *"wrong"* things are constantly being created by our minds to show us our way of thinking. I do believe we have the whole thing backwards.

Death, disease and pain and sorrow are really opportunities to *see* and *feel* and *express* the thought of unworthiness, the thought: "*I am not good enough.*" There is a whole world around us that is constantly saying that you are not good enough. Even when you finally prove that you are good enough because you succeed in wealth or in love or in your abilities, what have you proven? You have simply proven that others who are not like you are not good enough. You have managed to separate yourself even more and have gone deeper into thoughts of being unworthy. The voice that is telling you that you are naked, that you need to hide, that there is something wrong with you, is simply the voice of your own mind. Your own mind, that part of you that only has one important job, the job of preserving your separate sense of self; your individual identity as an ego being.

Why do you suppose that God said to you in the first place: "Who told you were naked?" Surely you do not think that He did not know the answer to the question? Do you suppose he wanted you and me to *think* about the issue? Have six thousand years passed simply to go back to a place where all this does not exist? A place where there is no separation? If you teach or believe that, you must truly feel that something did go terribly "*wrong*" and that everything that has happened since that time has been simply to fix that original mistake.

Is it possible that only now, so many millennia after that thought was first planted in our minds, that are we able to truly consider it? Finally the fear that has kept us paralyzed, and the religious thinking that has kept us in the grave clothes of limited thought are gone. We have broken free; we are able to think, to feel, and to experience, without fear and condemnation. Finally there are a people that have been able to cleanse their garments in the blood of the Lamb and are able to see things as they really are.

What Is the Truth?

The simple truth is this: The feelings of lack of worth, of not being good enough, symbolized by nakedness, were created by our own minds. They were created so that we would desire a place of hiding. The place we have hidden ourselves is this mind-body connection we think of as being us. We have entered the realm of separation.

Whatever the purpose is for our being here, it cannot be fully accomplished until we cleanse our being from all thoughts of blame and shame. Any thought that we did something wrong, something that needs to be atoned for or fixed, will only serve to keep us in this limited state of body and mind. Until we can see ourselves as we truly are, beautiful perfect beings of light and glory, we cannot even begin our mission.

Love Is the Only Reality

How can you convince somebody in a diseased, dying body that he or she is beautiful and perfect? Can you take them to another dimension and let them see themselves? They will only say they went to heaven and saw an angel. Can you tell them in words? They will only say you are lying; there is too much evidence to the contrary. In order to show and convince a being trapped in separation, in a physical form, you have to go and become like them. You have to take on a mortal physical body just like theirs. You must experience their pain, their intense feelings of abandonment and separation. You must feel the great cry in their being to be clothed again in glory and light. You will experience that cry deeply in your own being when you will pray: "Father, clothe me with the glory I had with thee before the worlds were." You will hang naked, as they feel, on a cross of shame and rejection, as they feel, and you will utter the deepest pain of the human experience for them when you cry out: "My God, My God, why hast thou forsaken me?" You must show them that the ultimate pain of the physical body, that powerful symbol of separation, **death**, has no power over you. You must die and rise again. You must show that the whole system of separation and death that they have created as a hiding place is a lie and has no power or reality.

After you accomplish all that and they truly believe on you. After they experience the Holy spirit of truth beginning to break the bondage of the lie that is in them, then you will have to tell them an even greater truth. You will have to reveal to them that they are just like you; that they have already died and can rise again. It will take two days, two thousand years before they will be ready to hear what you really came to tell them. They will insist on believing that all you have shown them is so that they could see you and worship you. You will have to reveal to them that they are eternal spirit beings that chose to become physical, to take on human form. Show them that leaving the higher spiritual plane and taking on a physical form and a limited ego mind was in fact a crucifixion. You must show them, not tell them, that they were crucified in time and space on their own physical consciousness, the physical body. Show them their fears that prick their minds by the thorny crown that disfigures your countenance. Show them their own feelings of powerlessness by the nails in your hands and feet. Let them feel and see themselves in you, show them it's all right, it was supposed to happen like that. It will be your great love for them, love that flows from you even while you are dying, my great love through you that will help them to understand. Knowledge and revelation alone will not release them, truth is more than that, and truth is what I am. Nothing can be healed; no restoration is possible apart from Love. Love is the only reality. Love alone is irresistible. I am Love.

THE TORAH

A Look at the Law of Moses,
Its Significance and Purpose
In the Unfolding of Consciousness

What is the LAW?

Dear Friends:

The Law of Moses also called the Pentateuch or the five books Genesis, Exodus, Leviticus, Deuteronomy and Numbers as they are named in the English version of the Bible, is without doubt the most revered sacred writing of all time on this planet. Just consider the millions of Christians that are taught the scriptures to be the literal inspired word of God. Or think of the fact that for thousands of years there was a special priesthood whose only task was to copy and preserve hand written scrolls containing these five books and that much of what archeology knows today about ancient times comes from those very writings.

In more modern times the Bible Code, written by Michael Drosnin as reported in TIME magazine, claims that the Torah can be used to predict the future, a kind of modern divination if you like. It is done by choosing a certain word or sequence of words and then using a computer to look for skip patterns that contain those letters in sequence. The scientist who discovered the code, Eliyahu Rips, used this method to predict the assassination of Yitzhak Rabin. Other historical events can so be demonstrated after the fact. I leave you, the reader, to evaluate all this but the fact is that this claim is made exclusively about the Torah among all the existing literature of the world.

In Jewish tradition, the Rabbis teach that the Torah, a continuous document without vowels or punctuation, actually preexisted creation and its divine letters are the actual templates of creation. It says that as history unfolded, the Torah manifested in the stories such as the story about Joseph and his brothers, revealing not just historical events but demonstrations of Cosmic Truth and eternal principles.

The Meru foundation, presents a similar thought concerning the Divine Nature of the Old Testament. The author took the first sentence of the Book of Genesis and studied it for ten years treating it as the opening sentence of a sacred coded document, looking for the key to unlock its secrets. Finally, ignoring the words found there and treating it only as a string of 22 letters, he placed them as beads on a string and then wrapped it around itself like a spiral. He discovered an awesome geometrical, mathematical pattern that can be seen throughout the sacred writing of scripture and only there. From his point of view this attests to the sacred origin of the scriptures.

I cannot vouch for any of the above personally but I cannot ignore any of it either. What I can attest to is the fact that in my personal experience with God, the Holy Spirit has at times projected certain scriptures on the screen of my mind. They were usually out of the context of my thinking process at that time, scriptures that gave illumination, wisdom, understanding and direction.

I more recent times, Stephen Jones has this to say about the Law.

In its broadest context, the law is the foundational revelation of the mind of God that we currently have on record. It is the Word of God as given to Moses. The Ten Commandments provide a moral guideline that summarizes and categorizes the rest of the laws and statutes.

In addition to the moral laws, we find certain penalties for sin (law breaking) which are called "judgments." Normally, these take the form of restitution payment to the victims of injustice, and the death penalty for such sins as cannot be paid by restitution--such as premeditated murder, kidnapping, bestiality, and rape of a married woman. There are also forms and rituals by which sinners (law breakers) were to find justification and reconciliation with God. These sacrifices were the Old Covenant method of justification, and they served as types and shadows of a greater Sacrifice which was yet to come in the Person of Jesus Christ. When He came, the old forms became obsolete.

Finally, the law reveals the moral code by which God relates to mankind and judges the people of all nations, taking into account their level of knowledge. This gives the law a prophetic tone, for all

54

the types and shadows prophesy of something greater to come. The Sacrifices all speak of Christ and His death on the cross, the feast days prophesy of His first and second comings, and laws of redemption and Jubilee speak of the process by which God judges and saves mankind.

In the New Testament, while the forms of the law changed, as spelled out in the book of Hebrews, the moral code remained the same, for in the matter of morality and character, God changes not. God had two ways of saving mankind. He could have put away the law and legalized sin, which would have made it impossible to prosecute sinners, simply because there was no law to make sin sinful. But He chose instead to uphold the law and pay its full penalty for the sin of the world, thus retaining the law as the standard of righteousness and character--the ultimate goal of what we will attain by faith in Him.

My reason for spending so much time in this writing to show the Divine Nature and origin of the sacred text is because what I am about to write about the Law. The purpose of the Law, I believe, goes back to the very heart of the Father and the very intent and purpose of all creation. Only if we have some appreciation of the significance of this sacred text can we grasp the awesome depth of what eternal purpose was transcribing into human consciousness by the giving of the Law.

Let's look at some of the events that surround the actual giving of the Law, the Law now meaning the Decalogue; the Ten Commandments. We read in the book of Exodus chapter 19 the following text:

Verse5 *Now therefore, if ye will obey my voice indeed, and keep my covenant, then ye shall be a peculiar treasure unto me above all people: for all the earth is mine:*

Verse 6: *And ye shall be unto me a kingdom of priests, and a holy nation. These are the words, which thou shalt speak unto the children of Israel.*

Verse7: *And Moses came and called for the elders of the people, and laid before their faces all these words which the LORD commanded him.*

Verse8: *And all the people answered together, and said, All that the LORD hath spoken we will do. And Moses returned the words of the people unto the LORD.*

If you read further in the text, you will find that the people were commanded to prepare themselves for the meeting, the consecration of the contract, almost like a marriage. They were told to all be bathed and to abstain from marital relation during those three days of preparation. This is not a one sided covenant. Rather, this is a contract between two parties. It is a contract with clearly defined expectations, penalties, and rewards. On the one hand is the nation of Israel, representing human consciousness, human thought, and experience. On the other is Yahweh Elohim, YHVH, the divine representation of the Source, the Father. Moses, as the best Man, the third party and the official, is conducting the ceremony, reading the conditions, and obtaining the agreement and contract in writing.

The blessings and the penalties are clearly spelled out. Listen to them as Moses speaks to the people of Israel prior to his departure in Deuteronomy chapters 28, 29 and 30. Read the full list of blessings and curses; see how these blessings perfectly foresaw the history of 2000 years that was to follow. Read about the tender promises of restoration and forgiveness after the expected dispersion and regathering of Israel. It is clear that whoever gave these instructions well understood that the people of Israel would not obey, or keep the covenant and in so doing fulfill the divine plan. I will only quote a few verses from Deuteronomy chapter 30 verses 11 to 20 that illustrate the theme of a covenant between parties with clearly defined terms, penalties, rewards, and expectations.

Now what I am commanding you today is not too difficult for you or beyond your reach. It is not up in heaven, so that you have to ask, "Who will ascend into heaven to get it and proclaim it to us so we may obey it?" Nor is it beyond the sea, so that you have to ask, "Who will cross the sea to get it and proclaim it to us so we may obey it?" No, the word is very near you; it is in your mouth and in your heart so you may obey it.

See, I set before you today life and prosperity, death and destruction. For I command you today to love the LORD your God, to walk in his ways, and to keep his commands, decrees and laws; then you will live and increase, and the LORD your God will bless you in the land you are entering to possess.

But if your heart turns away and you are not obedient, and if you are drawn away to bow down to other gods and worship them, I declare to you this day that you will certainly be destroyed. You will not live long in the land you are crossing the Jordan to enter and possess.

This day I call heaven and earth as witnesses against you that I have set before you life and death, blessings and curses. Now choose life, so that you and your children may live and that you may love the LORD your God, listen to his voice, and hold fast to him. For the LORD is your life, and he will give you many years in the land he swore to give to your fathers, Abraham, Isaac and Jacob.

The LAW: A conditional Covenant

First: A Brief Historical Overview:

To those of you that have read the scriptures and read history, you know the story. Israel failed to live up to the terms of the contract. She was consequently divorced by her Husband and scattered among the nations as symbolically portrayed in by the Prophet Hosea and recorded in the book by that Name. But the promise is clearly stated, the wife is to be forgiven. She is to be restored and the marriage is to be consummated in faithfulness in the latter days. The nation of Israel is to be regathered leading to a paradise on earth. We are thrilled by these prophetic insights and their historical significance. We know how the redemption price was paid by Jesus on Calvary to redeem Israel from the bondage of Sin and the curse of the Law. Not only the Nation of Israel but whosoever would come and drink of the water of Life resulting from the wedding, the Lamb and his wife, free for all that receive and believe.

Historically we know the forgiveness from Sin that has been experienced, and the blessings of the Holy Spirit, the earnest of the marriage blessings. Our emphasis in this writing is to see and understand what has never been clearly seen until this day which is the **purpose behind the giving of the Law.**

Second: The Law is a Conditional Covenant:

Before we actually look at this purpose, let us note again about the giving of the Law that it is a conditional agreement. It is a covenant that must be kept by both parties. Nowhere else in scripture is there mention of any other such covenant. Paul makes special note of this fact when he addresses the difference between the covenant of the Law and the promise to Abraham. He stated that the Law, which came later, could not cancel a previous contract, a promise that had been made earlier to Abraham and his seed. It is a kind of Grandfather Clause. He then points out that the promise to Abraham, to be accepted by faith, was underwritten by God Himself. There is no room for a second party to agree and ratify it. Here is Paul in his letter to the Hebrews chapter 6: verses 13 and 14:

For when God made promise to Abraham, because He could swear by no greater, He swore by Himself, Saying: Surely in blessing I will bless thee, and multiplying I will multiply thee.

We have clearly understood the spiritual aspect of Paul's teaching, that our relationship with God is not based on works as judged by the LAW but is based on Faith and Grace. Faith in the promise of God made to Abraham. However, we have missed the full significance of the nature of the Law being a conditional covenant.

If all this be true, as stated by the apostle Paul in his letters to the church in Rome, we must again return to the original query: Why then was the Law given at all? Here in Paul's own words is his light on the subject, I have printed to most significant words in bold italics

Galatians 3: Verses 16 to 19

*Now to Abraham and his seed were the promises made. He saith not, and to seeds, as of many; but as of one, and to thy seed, which is Christ. And this I say, that the covenant, that was confirmed before of God in Christ, the law, which was four hundred and thirty years after, cannot disannul, that it should make the promise of none effect. For if the inheritance be of the law, it is no more of promise; but God gave it to Abraham by promise. **Wherefore then serveth the law? It was added because of transgressions.***

58

Paul answers the question in part. He asserts that the Law is an introduction to Christ, a necessary preparation as a slave who conducts a pupil to school. He also clearly states that he could not have known Sin except by the Law. He says that in spite of sin, he was still free until the Law came; until the Law condemned him and the commandment slew him. Paul clearly teaches that the Law, particularly the moral Law, **was given as a minister of condemnation.** Not only the Law itself but also the Aaronic Priesthood was a Priesthood given to help the worshippers under the Law to receive and abide under the administration of this condemnation. The priesthood and its sacrifices was mercy added to help bear the severe results that came with the breaking of the law. Sin, as defined under the Law is the breaking of the Law.

Third: Defining the purpose of Sin and the Law.

Strangely enough, it is Paul, by this very clear teaching on the Law **after** the dispensation of the Law was ended, who showed that Sin existed **before** the Law. In fact Paul states that the Law made Sin exceedingly sinful. We then make this simple conclusion pertaining to the Law as being the covenant made with Israel through Moses:

The Law was given to give a legal definition to the idea of SIN

Let me return now to the definition of Sin that we have been considering at other times.

Sin is the thought or the awareness that
I cannot meet your expectation.

We have shown in other writings that Sin existed long before there was a Law that made it real. We saw that Sin began in the very formative thoughts of original consciousness of creation. The very first beings to begin to gain individual self-awareness also began to create thoughts of failure and disappointment. These thoughts are intrinsically a part of consciousness and the unfolding of consciousness. Man himself is the creator of his own Sin and Sin-consciousness. Sin is the evolutionary driver. It drives us to attain imagined approval, to advance and unfold, and to become. From a divine point of view, Sin is that which makes Grace abundant. There

59

would never be a need for Grace and Forgiveness had it not been for Sin. Sin, created by Man, is the opportunity for God to be known in Love, forgiveness, mercy, grace and justice, all the awesome divine attributes and the attributes of unfolding consciousness.

Notice in the definition of Sin that two words are used. The first is THOUGHT. All sin originates in thought. We have to imagine that we are not pleasing to our Source, the divine Father. Whether someone has induced that thought in you by a suggestion, deceiving you, or if you created it all by yourself, it makes little difference. You are now the owner of that thought. You will experience its consequences in your relationships, your surroundings, and your circumstances. Your whole world is colored and affected by your thoughts. All of your reality is conformed to it.

Fourth: Understanding How Sin Works:

As long as Sin is just a thought you cannot be sure if it is real or not. Is the person you so imagine really displeased with you? Did this person have expectations that you failed to meet, or did you just imagine those expectations? How can you be so sure that the one who had expectations now holds those expectations against you because you did not meet them? You can easily see, even from your own experiences in relationship, that all of this is very unsure ground. The mind seems to have no limitation as to what imaginings of condemnation it can create either with or without any real basis.

What is the result of all these imaginings whether they are real or not? It is SHAME. The shame of not feeling as if you are good enough for another; the shame of not being clothed properly for the occasion, the shame of being naked, insufficient, and incomplete. Shame leads to condemnation, which in turn causes you to act in ways that create Guilt. Guilt is created by acts, acts with wrongful intent and desire, actions that violate Law and Eternal principle. Guilt and condemnation are functions of the mind. They can be real or imagined but no matter what the cause, real or not, guilt has awesome effects. Guilt can drive you to desire to make restitution or it can debilitate and make you dysfunctional. Ultimately it is the cause of death, physical or emotional.

The sum total of all this is that created beings have sin. These Beings, that came from the Source of all Light and Life and began the journey of the journey of unfolding consciousness, created sin. They need it, and they can be trapped by it. Sin can serve you in the unfolding of your being or hinder you in the same way as guilt can be used to help a child or to bind and hinder it. Wise parents know that secret. All this is possible because the original intent of the Father-Source is total unconditional love and empowerment.

Here then comes the stated purpose of the giving of the Law to Israel. The benefits accrue to all creation.

The law was given so that sin, which was only a **thought,** *could become a real* **awareness**

Understanding real or imagined Guilt

What is the result of this **AWARENESS** of failing to meet expectations? When the Law states the expectation, and you fail to keep the commandment to which you agreed; then it is your own agreement, the Law that you contracted, that stands up to condemn you. You now have an AWARENESS of sin, not just a thought. When the Judge, who represents the law, declares you to be: "Guilty as charged"; then guilt becomes very real indeed.

You might ask: *If we already had sin and guilt, why was it needful to make sin and guilt real?* The reason that a clear definition of Sin and Guilt needed to be created was to enable you and me to clearly understand the nature of GUILT. If a real contract is made and the terms of that contract are broken Sin has occurred, Sin is now the breaking of the law, the real expectation stated in the contract that was not met and the result is a feeling of GUILT. Real Guilt comes with a condition of restitution. The penalty can be paid or be paid for you.

A modern mortgage is a good example. The contract gives you the cash to purchase a home and live in a higher status. The expectation to be met is the monthly payment. Failure to meet the expectation incurs penalties and if restitution is not made, the death occurs. The

MORT-Gage is enacted, and the house goes back to the lender or in older days you become the servant to the lender. You die to freedom until the debt is paid in full. Can you see how all this is presented in the Law of Moses as Stephen Jones summarized it earlier?

Why is it necessary to understand guilt? Why not just get rid of guilt altogether? You are the creator of Guilt and Sin. It was created in your mind to serve you and to help the unfolding of consciousness. It is to give you contrast and so help you understand the nature of Love of the Father-Source of your being. To rid the universe of all guilt is a like ridding the body of all bacteria in order to prevent disease. Death would result; we cannot live in these bodies without bacteria.

Fifth: The Conclusion: Unconditional Love

Now that we know the earmarks of GUILT and SHAME, and there is not one of us that has not experienced and been debilitated by guilt and shame, what can we now understand that we could never understand before? We can now clearly see and understand this simple fact:

The Source himself, the Father-Mother of your being never imputed guilt to you nor ever caused you shame.

How do you know that? How can you make such an awesome devastating claim? How can you be sure that the Love of the Father is truly and totally unconditional?

Our understanding of the LAW and the nature of GUILT gives us the discernment of truth that we needed. It is the emotional and intelligent understanding that comes as a result of thirty-five hundred years of spiritual evolution from the time the Law was first given to this day, the dawning of the day of Awakening, the resurrection from the sleep of ages. In order to prove that guilt was imputed by the Father-Source, you must show the contract that you signed stating that you agreed to meet all His expectations. If you cannot produce such a memory of a contract, then you must conclude that all Sin and all Guilt that you experience toward God is all of your own creation. That in truth and reality, you have always been FREE, free to create, free to experience, free to love, worship and unfold all your being

62

into the consciousness of God. You are FREE and you are totally and unconditionally LOVED...even free to create Sin.

The single greatest resistance to what I am presenting to you in this writing comes from a limited perception of the story as told in Genesis, the so called original sin of Eve and some comments made by Paul in the New Testament that seem to confirm it.

Sixth: Understanding the Garden experience:

Let us look at the manner in which this understanding about Sin and the Law all applies to Adam and Eve in the Garden. After all, how are we to understand Paul's statement: *"As by the disobedience of one man, Adam, Sin entered the world and by sin, death."* It seems as if the cause of all misery on this planet is laid on Adam's doorstep. Here is Paul's statement in his letter to the Romans chapter 5:

Wherefore, as by one man sin entered into the world, and death by sin; and so death passed upon all men, for that all have sinned (For until the law sin was in the world; but sin is not imputed when there is no law). Nevertheless death reigned from Adam to Moses, even over them that had not sinned after the similitude of Adam's transgression, who is the figure of him that was to come. But not as the offense, so also is the free gift. For if through the offense of one many be dead, much more the grace of God, and the gift by grace, which is by one man, Jesus Christ, hath abounded unto many.

The Traditional Point of View, Adam's Guilt and Shame

Billy Graham, the Evangelist Par Excellence of the previous century often had George Beverly Shea sing that well known Hymn "The Love of God." One of the lines in that hymn reads: *The guilty pair, bowed down with care.* It is interesting to know that nowhere in the scriptures are Adam and Eve referred to as the *guilty pair.* That is NOT to say that they did not EXPERIENCE guilt. According to Paul; yes. The command was given, the command was not kept. Yes the pair were sent out of the garden and the experience of death became real to mankind and guilt and shame has been his portion ever since. But after all this was said and done, nowhere was Adam brought to trial, nowhere can you find were judgment was passed upon him. Guilt was never imputed...guilt was created in the man's own mind.

Guilt was experienced with all its debilitating effects, but it was never given divine sanction or acknowledgment.

How are we to understand a clear case of disobedience with no fault imputed or charges laid? Recently I took my youngest daughter for her first driving lesson. As we proceeded onto the gravel road, just beyond our driveway, I suddenly, clearly and loudly said: STOP! Of course she did not stop, she just looked at me and said...why Dad? Unquestioning obedience was not really a part of her repertoire, I knew that. I knew she would not stop at my command. I knew she would be disobedient; that was the plan. My will, as perceived by her, was disobeyed, but my plan was perfectly on course. It opened the door so I could talk to her and put the plan in place. I explained to her that sometime during these driving lessons I might see an event unfolding that she could not because of her inexperience and she should, at least for these lessons, give over her will to me. I had no problem getting her to stop after that.

Looking at Adam's situation from another point of view, let us assume for a minute that the scenario of the Garden, as it is interpreted by most religious and secular people today, is true. God creates man in innocence and childlike immaturity. He gives man a test: *Do not eat of the fruit of the tree of knowledge.* Man fails the test and is immediately cast out and rejected and subjected to the ultimate penalty of death. Although the events as related in the story perhaps are correctly seen, the intent and purpose are totally misinterpreted.

No wise parent or even a teacher would, on the basis of a single test, for which the child was totally unprepared, reject and condemn a child. To attribute this scenario to the Creator of Mankind is truly absurd.

How then are we to see these events as recorded in Genesis? What are they saying concerning man and the purpose of man taking on physical form? I intend to show us that these events are a staged reality purposed as the beginning part of a drama acted out by Adam kind to reveal truth of wonderful release and cosmic healing.

Seventh: The Purpose of Being Incarnate

We can only understand these enigmatic events by viewing them from the larger perspective of the development and unfolding of consciousness. The **creation** of man, the initiation of the separateness of his being from the Source of Light and Life, happened many Ages before the events of the **forming** of Man in the garden, the time when he took on a physical body. In fact, I see the forming of man, his incarnation into the physical realm, as a repetition or a re-enactment of previous events in a higher vibrational plane of reality.

If man, as I understand it, experienced Sin and the resulting effects, shame and guilt, long before his incarnation then it follows very simply:

The primary purpose of the incarnation of man, is to directly confront these elements, Sin and its children, Shame and Guilt.

The reason for bringing these two elements into the lower plane of the physical experience is to create understanding of them. When something is experienced physically and emotionally, the learning and instructional values are increased dramatically. Don't just TELL me, let me FEEL it, is the message here. A picture is worth a thousand words. From this point of view, it was essential that the experience of sin and its results be introduced immediately after the scene was set for physical manifestation.

This also gives understanding how the scriptures as referred to in Hebrews the second chapter, can give honor to Adam for his incarnation, taking on Sin and death for all created realms. Adam is not now seen from the perspective of his own experience but rather from the point of view of his own eternal Light being that saw the purpose, accepted his role, and was lowered in consciousness to do the will of his Father. Here is the description of Adam and the event of his incarnation as found in Hebrews the second chapter verses 5-8. Notice particularly that there is no mention of a transgression or fall.

For unto the angels hath He not put in subjection the world to come, whereof we speak. But one in a certain place testified, saying: What is man, that thou art mindful of him? Or the son of man that thou visitest him? Thou madest him a little lower than the angels; thou crownedst him with glory and honour, and didst set him over the works of thy hands. Thou hast put all things in subjection under his feet.

65

The process of incarnation, becoming physical beings, is simply described as a LOWERING. The phrase: *Made him a little lower.* I prefer to read it as: *Lowered the frequency from his Elohim state to cause him to become physical.* This is clearly supported by the fact that the Author uses identical words to describe the incarnation of Jesus, the second Adam, who repeated in a highly focused manner the events of the first Adam when it says in verse 9:

Verse 9: But we see Jesus, who was made a little lower than the angels for the suffering of death, crowned with glory and honor; that he by the grace of God should taste death for every man.

When Adam took on the experience of Shame and Guilt in the Garden he created the first scene of a drama that was to unfold in the Ages of time. This drama was created to reveal the true nature of the Love of the Father. It gives true understanding of the purpose of Sin and guilt, and so brings the creation out of denial. It empowers us to overcome the debilitating effects of the journey of separation.

This scenario unfolds in stages, First Adam is introduced and a portal created for him to experience Sin and Shame. Then the Journey in Time and Space unfolds, through Noah and Abraham as the full effects of Shame and Guilt take hold. The nation of Israel, the Law, is given to further bring Sin into a real awareness. Guilt now no longer is simply a subjective experience of the mind; it is now a fact, administered by a Law created by agreement of two parties. Guilt is now clearly experienced and emotionally and experientially felt. Priesthood is instated to help assuage the debilitating effects of guilt. Offerings for sin are provided for the penitent worshipper. The extreme price is being paid by a nation of people; they are as it were a scapegoat for the created realms and the sin of the cosmos as its experience is laid on them.

Through the administration of the Law and the Priesthood, the way of redemption is also presented. A Lamb is slain for a household. The blood is smeared on the portal of entrance. The death plague is thwarted. All this beautiful symbolism experienced in actual physical demonstration by a nation in physical bondage and slavery to a Pharaoh. All so that cosmic understanding might come to help us to see universal imprisonment to material consciousness, to guilt and shame and oppression.

When the disobedience, the failure to keep the law, has done its devastating work and man, as Israel, is left seemingly without hope, scattered and separated without a King or a Priest, the promised Messiah, the Savior appears. He appears not as a powerful King to slay the enemies but rather in the very form of weakness with which man is clothed, humanity. His own reject him, even as man rejected himself in his own mind. He came in a lowly way, riding into Jerusalem on a donkey, the foul of an ass.

This one, Jesus, the second Adam, is Representative Man. This is the one that is to come; the one who shows the truth, who takes away our blindness and our lameness, our debilitation. He is the one who causes us to see ourselves from the divine point of view and intent. He is the one who heals the wound of separation by giving us true understanding. He causes us to live and understand the journey of man. He does so by taking on that very journey, becoming human like us, and by his death on the cross showing us what really happened to us in the garden.

What was that? Even as Jesus took on the experience of the cross in obedience to the Father, so you, Adam, have done the same. Even as Adam's drama is repeating the journey of all created beings, so Jesus has taken on the journey of Adam.

The enthronement and the overcoming that is repeatedly spoken of concerning man in the scriptures is the experience of understanding and empowerment that comes as a result of the death of the cross; whether it be a wooden one as Jesus died on, or a flesh and bone one that you died on. Resurrection is that place of awareness and truth that breaks the bondage of death created in the mind of man by his own imperfect and incorrect interpretation of his own journey; an interpretation full of misjudgments made in childlike immaturity concerning the nature of the Source, the Father of all being.

Man is now able to see that all sin and guilt are the creation of his own mind. They are experienced for the purpose of the evolution of consciousness, not as an entrapment and limitation of his being as he has perceived it. Where are we in this unfolding drama? We have come to the time when understanding is returning to the mind of man. We were subjected to futility, to blindness and death in hope. Hope that we would create all the needed experience, the drama, on the set of material creation, a drama that would bring clarity and understanding to all the realms observing these human events. We ourselves, participants in the drama, can now step back and take a look and see the whole of the journey and its intent. The Father-Source of our being can now share with us His heart, His intent and motive for the whole of the journey of separation. We can begin to feel His joy in the knowing of us. We can share it. We can feel the heart of Jesus, his commitment and dedication to the Father, his mind in which he endured the shame of the cross and persevered through it all to bring resurrection and life to all that receive him.

Eighth: Answering the Question

We also see finally, in answering the question asked previously: "How we are to understand Paul's remarks about Sin entering the world through Adam's disobedience?" We understand that we have made an erroneous assumption. We have assumed this to be a statement of BLAME when in fact we need to see it simply as a statement of FACT. It is a description of **HOW** Sin and death became a reality in this physical plane. Our very eyesight of truth was still discolored by our preoccupation with guilt so that we could not see the whole of truth even after the Holy Spirit illuminated us.

Summary: The Tabernacle Of God Is With Men.

We have seen the Garden experience as a shameful, regrettable mistake. The burden in our minds of so called original sin has been truly unbearable, but forgiveness has come. A Lamb, an offering, was provided, atonement and restitution so important to us, have been made at Calvary. We have been given relief from sin and guilt and the joy of salvation has already been our portion. It is now time to see the truth, not through the guilt ridden eyes or even the forgiven eyes of the lower Adamic experience, but through the enlightened awareness of the sharing of the Father's heart. We see through the eyes of eternal awareness of Being, our Light Body. We now know, we see, we understand the origin and purpose of Sin, Death and the Law. He has wiped away all tears because we understand WHY it all had to be. We have born the guilt of creation. The groaning prisoner has been set free, and full redemption is truly at hand. All men and all created beings will see and know the totally unconditional, unlimited Love of the Father-Source in us... The Tabernacle of God is with Men.

Shame and Trauma

The Grand Lady in the Harbor

There is a statue of a woman that stands on Ellis Island in the New York Harbor. She stands there as the symbol of Freedom and Justice, the awesome dream of human kind. You may have climbed the 284 steps it requires for a visitor to look out the windows in her head and have seen grand view of the harbor. If you have, you probably have also been in the special room below the Statue of Liberty. This room is a museum that commemorates the design, promotion and construction of the Statue. There, center stage, is a one-foot tall image of the grand Lady, a perfect replica one would assume. In fact it is truly not a replica at all. If either of the two statutes, the Grand Lady in the Harbor or the small statue in the museum, could be called an original, it would have to be the small one below. It was the original model that was used to promote the idea of the Statue of Liberty and to raise the monies needed for its construction. The greater truth of course is that neither the final image that now stands on Ellis Island nor the model that stands in the room of History is the true original. The true original was the conceptual image in the mind of its creator, Frederic Auguste Bartholdi.

While the Grand Lady in the Harbor was yet an image in the mind of her creator, this small model could be looked upon and the creator could be heard to say...*that is what she looks like gentlemen, is it worth your time and money to invest in her?* In his mind the image already existed. All later forms were only manifesting something he always knew, understood, and wanted to be conveyed.

The True Image of Man

At this time of human history, the true image of man is appearing into view. Our point of recognition comes from the reality that Jesus, known as Christ, brought to us two millennia ago. Many ages of longing and desire have passed. Many imaginations and dreams of utopia have come and gone. Empires have risen and fallen. Doctrines and philosophies have passed in the same way. But now all creation is beholding, through its tear stained mind, the image of its creator as it appears in the form of man.

We are the first to have conscious awareness of that awesome image, that grand appearing, that wonderful knowing called Immanuel, God with Us. It is awakening in our hearts like a long forgotten memory come back, like a longing we have always felt but could never focus. It is like a dawning we always knew was to come but could never truly visualize. Now that we see its first rays, and feel the first tremors of its beauty, we recognize it without a doubt and without deep questioning because of the great upwelling of Joy in our hearts that comes with it. We know this joy to be the witness of truth we have sought for.

Jesus the Faithful Witness

It is written that two witnesses shall establish every word. What is that second witness that we need? It is that small image, that initial coming, that first appearing that showed forth our truth so long ago. It is the man of Galilee, the one our soul has loved more intensely than life itself. Do you remember the awesome words and feelings that came when you sang: *"I would rather have Jesus than houses or lands…I would rather be led by his nail scarred hands."*?

Then came those wonderful and horrendous days when you realized that the Jesus your heart longed for, although he truly was Historical, was so much more. He was wonderful because he brought new hope and joy, but horrible because it was so hard to let go of old belief systems. He became a living presence, an entity that comforted you and whispered in your ear…*You too can overcome as I did…*

When the rubber hit the road, he was there to greet you. He was there to help you, to comfort and strengthen you by his Spirit when you found that you too had to go "without" or "outside" of the Camp in order to meet your destiny. You had to go outside of your accustomed circle of associates and friends in order to embrace your incarnation, your crucifixion, your roadway to destiny and appointment. After all that you experienced even greater shock when you realized that the Jesus of Bethlehem and the Christ you met on your road was also your brother. He was your nearest kinsman, your sister, the one you experienced union with. And so through awesome pain and glory you experienced an awakening about which no preacher could ever tell you. No man could conceive this knowing into your virgin mind. This could only happen by the eternal truth awakening from the Ages of Old, from a land before time, the awakening of the real you, the word that becomes flesh.

Although we have known Jesus, we have never truly seen him as the true and faithful witness to the image of greatness that we are, the collective appearing of Christ on the flannel graph of human consciousness. Only now is he being revealed to us as that witness. We see him first in the wooden manger of humanity. He is in the barn, full of hay and animal dung of the human intellect that we prized so greatly. We see that the Christ child we celebrated every Christmas is the awesome reality of our own being coming from the realms of Glory and Light into this human form. It has been hidden by our limited awareness of self, but is now awakening. *Oh holy night, the stars are brightly shining. It is the night of the dear Saviors birth. Long lay the world in sin and error pining till he appears and our soul knows its birth*...Finally we understand why we were so charged and inspired by those beautiful Christmas Hymns.

We have seen him at the river Jordan when the voice came from heaven saying, "This is my beloved Son." This was the revelation of being a Son of God that came in what we call Latter Rain. It swept the earth until today all charismatic teachers understand some form of what was called the message of Sonship. We have seen that to have dominion over all limitation is our destiny, although that consciousness has been trapped in linear time. What do I mean by that? Our awareness is trapped because we were always looking for some FUTURE time when we WOULD become the manifested Sons of God. Nevertheless the power of that small image was at work. It was slowly stimulating the eternal realm, embracing reality in us. The awakening had begun, and there would be no way to hinder its full birth.

Today we stand at the threshold of fully seeing that Jesus, as The Son of Man, came and walked out his Journey. Even to the detail that He insisted John, his lesser, baptize him. We see that His crucifixion truly showed our crucifixion. We were not crucified on a wooden stake as he was. Instead, we were crucified on the wood of our own humanity when we took on human form with our kind in the Garden of God. Our crucifixion came when we were lowered in hope. We gladly and willing continued our journey of separation so that our Father's Great Heart might experience all of Himself as us and so enter the very creation that had gone on its journey of separation.

No word of truth has done more to break the shackles of shame, condemnation, and fear from our hearts than the awesome awareness that it was God Himself that wanted and desired and even passionately longed for a greater experiential knowing of His great Self. To do this, He so initiated the thought of duality within His own being. From the beginning, sin and evil were needed. Entities of Light became entities of Darkness to serve the great purpose of the Father. The duality and contrast of good and evil were needed to make the Journey of separation seem real.

In order for you and me to truly grasp the depth of our pain and separation and break the bonds of denial and shame that kept us from understanding, the Son of Man took upon himself our sense of sin and shame. He went into the lowest parts of our hellish experience and cried out with a loud voice: *Eloi! Eloi! Lama Sabachtani?* Meaning: *My God! My God! Why hast thou forsaken me?* He gave us the voice we needed. He cried out for us what we in our pain and separation could not understand. Truly he was bruised so that we could in him become free to experience the iniquity that was part of our destined journey.

It is by looking at Him, the image that appeared for our redemption, that we are able to break free from the denial that keeps us in repeated cycles of death and the grave.

This imprisonment to the body and mind connection always tries to define us and never can. It is by looking at Him and seeing Him bear his shame, seeing him spit upon, lied about, jeered and bruised, that we are able to accept that our journey of shame, rejection, denial, and abandonment was not the result of sin or mistakes. Even as His path was a chosen journey of redemption, so was ours. Not now only as one who s*howed the Way*, but as a collective company to set creation free from its bondage to a material consciousness that witnesses itself in death and decay.

Shame, the Portal to Our Humanity

It was Shame that began our entrance into this material realm. It was shame that made us seek a hiding place from the projection of thought that questioned our truth and validity. It was Shame that had to come through a lie to take hold of our hearts and enable us to take the plunge into the separation of Adam's experience. This experience is like a death that we have shared in him these many long ages. There was a phase we came through, as Light beings, on the path of our chosen and intended lowering. During this phase, it was said of us: *They were naked and were not ashamed.* Another way to say this that gives the sense of the truth conveyed would be: *They were truly intimate and exposed to one another and had not yet experienced shame.* It was only after we entered a greater degree of duality, when our gender was separated, that we became vulnerable enough to accept a lie. It was a lie that questioned our very validity. Not of what we did, but of who we were.

I was recently given a book called "Power versus Force." I believe it is truly a breakthrough book. By means of Kinesiology, the Author, over a period of twenty years of testing and with the assistance of many others, claims to have come up with a consistent vibratory scale to compare a large number of things. What I found most interesting is his comparison of the full range of human emotions on a logarithmic scale, (logarithmic meaning that each time you go up one level you multiply by a factor of ten). The Author, using this scale, measured Love as a human emotion at 500 whereas Shame, the lowest of all emotions, measures at 200. This measurement confirms to me what I already understood about the identification in Genesis of shame as the Emotional Doorway through which we entered and became locked into the physical experience.

Another friend showed me a book written to instruct on the use of essential oils as a healing art. In it the author states that the essential oils, each for a different emotion, help a certain portion of the brain trigger a specific memory trapped there from a past trauma. The trauma itself is stored in specific organs but the memory must be accessed through a sense of smell provided by these essential oils. I would not be as impressed by this information if I didn't have an experience to support it. The Spirit showed us a specific incidence wherein a dear friend was released from a childhood entrapment of shame. It happened in our home and the key elements of released memory came from the sense of sight and the sense of smell.

These two recent happenings, reading the book: "Power versus Force" and our experience with the essential oils, have further made me look at the event that the Spirit orchestrated in our home. I want to elaborate on it because I believe that it is a mini-event that illustrates the dynamics needed to release us from toxic shame. Shame became the doorway for our incarnation and now its release signals our reconnection to former knowing, our return to the Father of Light and our own Eternalness.

Cleansing the Emotional Body: A Story

At four in the morning, I awoke and went downstairs to put wood in the fireplace as I often do. I had forgotten that our friend was sleeping on the couch. As I came into the room, semi dark, I noticed that she was looking in a hand mirror. It did not seem strange to me, but she started to explain to me that she was trying to deal with what she called self-loathing. Someone had suggested she look in the mirror and reprogram herself by telling herself that she was a good and worthy person. We briefly discussed the subject and as I went to walk back up the stairs I turned and said to her: "Maybe something happened in your childhood that caused you to feel this self loathing." On my way back to bed, I passed by the children's bedroom. Eva, then 13 years old, had a sister and cousin visiting with her from Oklahoma. I believe this was Thanksgiving time when we have an annual weekend of meetings. I opened the door, just to check on them and noticed a pungent odor. I remember wondering at what it might be but strangely enough I did not investigate further. I had hardly been back in my own bed for fifteen minutes when a tumult erupted in the house. I ran back to the girl's bedroom to find smoldering blankets and a room full of choking smoke. Apparently a curling iron had mistakenly been turned on instead of off and had become lodged under Eva's pillow. The curling iron was a total meltdown, only the metal parts were left. An inch deep circle a foot in diameter had burned down into the mattress. Eva had soot under her nose. Cornelia, the older sister, had roused the other two, Frieda-Ann and Eva, and hurried them out of the room. As Eva ran down the stairs carrying a smoldering blanket with soot on her face, our Guest looked up. She saw Eva and remembered. A memory of her

74

childhood flooded back. She too had experienced a fire. In her case, as a small girl, she had used a light bulb from an Easy-Bake oven to read by. The light bulb had become lodged under the pillow, caught fire and she had to escape a burning house. Her family's small home with all the unopened Christmas gifts were destroyed by the fire. As she remembered the incident she remembered the shame she had felt when her mother said: *Look what you have done!* Here, locked away in her memory, was the key that explained all those years of self-loathing.

Why did this memory release and healing come to her at this time? Clearly she was ASKING: *Why do I have such deep feelings of self-loathing?* This also was a time for this woman to begin a major unfolding of her life in PURPOSE. The child that initiated those feelings of self-loathing no longer exists, but the feelings have persisted into adulthood. That child could not truly understand the experience. But now the adult can. She can know, can understand, and can adjust and relate. She can put away the lie that controlled so much of her life.

She can take responsibility for her own experience.

Now I am delighted for every person who experiences healing of the inner child, or release from past trauma, both individual and genetic. But by far the greater message from Spirit to us is that we are standing at the Cryptic Edge of awakening as we begin to understand our own beginnings in the incarnate realm. We begin to see not only the true purpose of our taking on flesh but also the dynamics by which we took it on. As it was written of Jesus so is it true of us:

....because the children partook of flesh and blood he likewise took upon himself not the nature of angels but the seed (genetics) of Abraham.

Empowerment for Resurrection

The sacred secret, the truth about our incarnation, has been kept from the Angels and from Man but is now being opened to us...Why? Again, Jesus, the Pattern Son, the Forerunner, the Way-Shower, the Way-the Truth-and-the-Life, reveals the answer. Jesus, speaking of his own crucifixion, therefore of your incarnation, makes the following statement:

No man takes my Life from me. I have power to lay it down and power to take it again. This commandment have I received from my Father.

Where did Jesus say that his empowerment came from to walk his overcoming Journey? Clearly stated here, it came from a speaking from his Father. A "speaking" requires a "hearing." A hearing requires access to the eternal store of Living knowledge and Intelligence that is the Father. It requires a place and a state of union. We too then are accessing our powerhouse, our empowerment through our connectedness in the Light who is our Source, our Father.

This access to the greater knowing can only be attained as we open the gateway, the door, which is our emotional being.

We open the door by removing those things that lock it. That is, we cleanse our emotional being of Shame. How do we do this? We have to go back to where it happened! Like an orchestrated experience or smell, like an essential oil, we need a replay of those events that caused us to be lowered into this physical plane and into these matter bodies.

Jesus is the image that shows us what happened to us. He is that one-foot-high replica that provides the essential trigger experience to effectively release us from the trauma experienced in our incarnation. It is residual shame and self-loathing that keep us from accessing the Father and our true knowing.

This knowingness empowers us, and we use this empowerment not to lay down our life but **to take it again**. This is the hour of the resurrection of Adam Man. This is the time of our awakening. The eternal dawn happens when we remember who we are and how we came. Without the seeing of the man Jesus and the hologram that he is in the human experience, it is not possible to release the trauma and to access the memory that clothes us with the glory we had with him before the worlds. Only the remembrance of that union and that oneness can empower us to complete our mission and set creation free from it's bondage to materiality. In this comes to pass the saying:

No one cometh unto the Father but by me.

Just when the wisdom of this world wants to say that Jesus must take his place among the Masters, which he truly is and does; just when the religious world is receiving a revival of the knowing of him as Savior and again would lead us to the altar of forgiveness, that every man must certainly experience; just when man is starting to shake himself free from long, long centuries of bondage to the intellect, to religion, to the ego and all its powers, to material wealth and political power, just then there comes a whole new vision and awareness of the truth that Jesus brought to this plane so long ago. An event that was heralded by Angels singing: *Peace on Earth and goodwill toward all men.* That peace truly has come in the hearts of those that believe but it yet remains to come in an outward way to this planet.

Only this present awakening of the human spirit, this present reconnection to His eternal Truth and Knowing, can bring forth Paradise on earth, the utopia of every dreamer, and the hope of every man.

I have great news for you who have not heard! The truth you need is here. It is available. You need only reach out and take hold of it. It lies within you. It is beyond the entrapment of illusionary shame, beyond the mistaken powers of the ego, the limited self, beyond belief systems and a material consciousness, but it is there, in you. You need no special tools, no mantras or incantations, no rituals or vows, no crystals or special doctrines. Although all these do have some kind of place, all that you need if you have come with me, if you too are one that comes from Mount Zion, all you need to do, my reader, is LOOK at HIM, and let yourself see yourself **in** him and **as** him.

Rokus den Hartog

Crucified from the Beginning

Limited by Our Perceptions

Whenever Carolynne and I travel a long distance, perhaps to the East Coast, we like to start driving very early in the morning, well before daybreak. By the time we fully realize we are travelling and Eva is still asleep, we are half way there. I usually drive the first part of the journey. I am the one that gets to experience first the pre-dawn light as the eastern sky slowly illuminates, then the sudden appearing of the first bright sector of that brilliant globe we call the sun. As I watch the sun, I convince myself that I can actually see it rise in the eastern sky. Can you see the movement of the minute hand of a clock? I doubt I would see it to be moving if I did not KNOW it was moving; nevertheless, I do FEEL like I can see the sun rise millimeter by millimeter against the horizon.

I was a high school physics and math teacher for fifteen years, so I know that the sun does not really rise at all! I realize that in actual fact the earth, on which my automobile is rolling, is actually turning in space at a rate of 800 miles per hour. It is turning towards a very stationary sun. You know it too. Yet whenever I see the sun set or rise, I can never really get into the thought that I and the earth beneath my wheels are really causing this beautiful phenomenon called the sunrise. I am the willing prisoner of my perceptions.

Have you ever been stopped at a red light, perhaps beside a large eighteen wheeler, when suddenly you get the sensation that you are rolling backwards? You jam on the brakes to keep from hitting the car behind but when you do so you do not feel the familiar jerk in your neck. You're the only "jerk" there seems to be when you realize that it was really the truck slowly rolling forward that gave you the sense of rolling backwards. It was the huge size of the truck, blocking your view of the background, which created this illusion of motion. This same kind of illusion exists when you are viewing a sunrise or a sunset, however, I never feel like "jerk" watching this most beautiful of all illusions. The truth of the matter is that the sunrise that is so familiar to our earth experience is also unique to our earth experience. The moment you leave this planet and look back at it, there is no more sunrise or sunset at all! The other day as we were beginning to watch a video at home, a picture of earth came on the screen in such a way that I actually felt I was in outer space, leaving the planet. Our earth, so beautiful, so much of it covered with water. I remember thinking: Wow, look at all that water, and it does not even fall off! Why should I not be amazed? Have you ever seen any object hold water upside down?

This "EARTH-PERCEPTION" that is so beautiful and is also so illusionary has had theologians, scientists and philosophers in bondage for many centuries. Plato and the early church Fathers all believed the earth to be the center of the solar system and even the universe. The church persecuted, and killed people for believing and teaching otherwise. Why were we so bound to that EARTH-PERCEPTION? Why did it have such a powerful grip on the human heart and mind? Can you conceive of burning someone at the stake for any kind of a strange belief? No, of course not! Are we so much morally superior to our ancestors? I think not, I believe that freedom of thought and expression has been bought at a great price! But why did such a great price have to be paid at all for such a simple truth that can be explained to any schoolboy?

As Physical, So Spiritual

The answer to this question lies in the fact that man is only bound to outer illusions, physical illusions, based in scientific ignorance, because he is bound spiritually or inwardly by much more powerful illusions of the mind. The whole story of our release from the bondage to an earth perception, the thought that the sun goes around the earth, is really the acting out of a drama at the physical level to show us those very same events at a spiritual level.

We are all very familiar with the thought that the children of Israel were brought into Egypt and settled there under Joseph. You surely remember your fascination through the years with that magnificent drama of the Exodus. It took over four hundred years to unfold and ended at such a grand victory when Miriam danced on the shores of the Red Sea singing: *The horse and rider cast into the sea.* Paul the

Apostle, speaking fifteen hundred years later, describes this event as *a drama the children of Israel played out for you who live at the end of this dispensation,* "You" meaning the saints of the early church. Today we realize the truly cosmic significance of the Exodus. From the bondage, Egypt and Pharaoh we now know represent none other than the illusionary power that has darkened the human mind; darkened by the power vested in lower spiritual realms to which man has become subject; powers that believe in and act out separation. Again we see a physical drama acting out a spiritual state of affairs.

BONDAGE results from FEAR and fear results from IGNORANCE, from NOT-KNOWING. Strangely enough, even though the bondage is a result of an act of the mind of man, it is not possible to confront the mind of man directly to break that bondage. How simple it would seem to just correct a twisted synapse in the brain. In order to be freed from fear we must look at it mentally through the mind's eye, look at it physically through our physical experience, and most of all, look at it emotionally, that is, let ourselves feel it.

To Look Is To Come Out Of Denial

For two thousand years, we have known that Jahshuah is the great redeemer of the world. When John the Baptist introduced him on the stage of human affairs, he said: "Behold the Lamb of God that takes away the sin of the world." The word "BEHOLD" is just rather dramatic old English for "LOOK AT". The injunction of the one who said that he was a voice crying in the wilderness was to tell us to LOOK at this one.

Jesus, referring to his purpose for coming on this planet, made a reference to the journey of the Israelites. He said, "As Moses lifted up the serpent in the wilderness so must the son of man be lifted up." Clearly Jesus referred to his crucifixion as the how of being lifted up, but more significantly, one might ask: "Why did Moses lift up the serpent?" I was driving behind an ambulance the other day, in January of 1999. The symbol of the medical or healing profession was on the back of the ambulance, a pole with a serpent wound around it. As you remember, Moses was told to make a serpent out of brass, raise it on a pole and whoever of the children of Israel that would LOOK at that image would be healed.

Again Paul, writing to the Hebrews, asking the question of questions that lies in the depth of every man's soul, writes: "Who is man?" Unconsciously we believe that we are a mistake, an error in the program, a result from original sin by our ancestors. The proof that we believe that way, and still believe that way after two thousand years, lies in the fact that we believe that the only purpose Jesus came to earth was to deliver us from our sin, sin that we believe to be our innate tendency towards evil. Even though we may have an experience of being saved and forgiven, and we mentally believe the scriptures that say that Jesus destroyed the power of sin at the cross, yet we still act like we believe in its power. We still do not see ourselves as the Lords of creation as the scriptures declare us to be. WHY? Because we have not yet truly seen Him and hence we have not seen who we are! We keep acting out our lives and creating our lives out of a false image, an illusion, an EARTH-ILLUSION.

Let us ask the man from Galilee: What are you showing us about ourselves by having your physical body nailed to a tree? What is the import of your blood from the crown of thorns dripping down your beard, your hands and feet pierced into immobility and impotence? Are you showing us, as we have believed, that you were being punished for something that we did; a punishment that we could not bear? Yet you say that the One who sent you has a heart so full of love that he sent his most prized part of himself?

I Came That You Might Live

Finally, slowly, after tremendous struggles of soul and mind the answer begins to form in our mind and heart. It comes in a voice full of compassion, so tender, so infinitely loving and caring: *No, I am not showing you anything that is going to happen except in my resurrection. I am showing you what you are most resistant to; I'm showing you what has already happened to you. I'm not showing you that you are going to be crucified or that you should crucify yourselves. I am showing you that you are between the two great thieves of your life, your guilt of the past and your fear of the future. For in this titanic struggle of the ages, you with me have fully experienced for all worlds and all beings in light and in darkness the terror of separation. You with me have overcome, as we rise in*

81

resurrection, ascending back to the Father of all light. We are returning all things home to Him from whom all things came and in whom all things exist. "MY GOD, MY GOD, why have you forsaken me?" has been the agonizing cry of your being out of which you have experienced all your suffering, all your tears. But now you know that we were crucified, together, as ONE from the foundation of the world. Not by Roman soldiers. Not by your own fear and belief in separation but by a choice. A choice to do His will, to give our lives for all the creations of our Father so that all may know Him and His great power and Love.

Conclusion

Is it truly possible that only now, two thousand years after the fact; are we finally beginning to understand the great purpose of Calvary? Consider the fifteen hundred years passed before Paul could boldly declare that perfection could not and would never come by the law! Jesus proclaimed that knowing the truth would set us free. He knew the truth about mankind that he brought. He also knew that ultimately the truth revealed through him would set all men free. This is our greatest hour. It is the time of our emancipation from every lesser thought that has bound us to the dust realm. We are free to rise and ascend. We are free to think and speak the knowings of eternity that hold the key to our true identity. Can we do any less than that if he gave his life? I have chosen, as never before, to allow my being to merge with him in purpose for this planet and with you, if you will so choose.

Rokus den Hartog

THE CLOCK OF GOD
OR:
The Precession of the Equinoxes and the Plan of the Ages

Dear Friends:

I have a friend, Edna she will soon be a hundred years old. In a recent conversation with her she told me of a time, years ago, when she wanted to expand beyond the boundaries of her Church context and she asked the Lord: "But what about all those preachers, which one will I believe?" The reply came so gently: *"It will be as it was planned before the foundation of the world."*

What a powerful awareness. Even though we are creators of our own existence, co-creators with God, knowing the secret of the Law of Attraction, yet, below it all is an eternal contract, made before material existence that upholds us and all things and has a purposed end constantly in view.

We marvel at the insights of science about the relativity of TIME-SPACE, quantum physics, the concept of parallel worlds, yet we know that these are all created things. They have a beginning and an end. The Hubble telescope shows our galaxy, the Milky Way, to be on a collision course with the Andromeda galaxy. The computer generated images that portray this event are truly awesome to see. Compared to these cosmic events we seem but indiscernibly small specs on this grand scene of Time-Space, stretching through fifteen billion years of explosive creation. Yet we know that we existed before all this became manifest. We will continue to exist through all worlds and Ages and are presently, in essence, greater than all of it and all of it serves the great will of our Eternal Source, our Father and our coming home to Him.

There is an Eternal Kingdom. There is a Plan for the Ages of Time, and as we come into a place of rest concerning our own existence, into a greater more sublime definition of who we are, we desire to see more clearly our appointed place in that Plan. Paul the Apostle referred to the Plan of the Ages in his letter to the Ephesians:

*Paul, an Apostle of Jesus Christ by the will of God, to the saints which are at Ephesus, and to the faithful in Jesus Christ; grace be to you, and peace, from God our Father and from the Lord Jesus Christ. Blessed be the God and Father of our Lord Jesus Christ, who hath blessed us in all spiritual blessings in heavenly places in Christ: According as **he hath chosen us in Him before the foundation of the world** that we should be holy and blameless before him in love.*

Notice in this awesome introduction that the whole of Paul's emphasis is on the existence of the saints in the realm of awakened relationship through Jesus Christ to the infinite Father of Light. He finally refers to their connection with the intent that is before the foundation of the world. That will and intent of the Father has precipitated what we call the Plan of the Ages.

The phrase "Before the Foundation of the World" is of course an English translation of Greek words which, according to Strong's concordance can equally well be translated and expanded as:

Before the down-casting of the orderly arrangement of the Ages of Time.

Time seems so absolute to us, so irrevocable, once a thing is done it is done. Yet we know from an eternal point of view it is not so much the physical events that transpire that are so important; it is the **awareness** created in those events. Perhaps a hundred thousand thieves and rebels were crucified by the Romans in Jesus' day yet not one of them became notable in history, not one of them was even remembered past the moment of his own agony except for this one who was crucified, not for some wrong doing of his own but to serve as the great awakener of mankind; one who would be the mirror in which we would see our greater truth.

A Greater Reality

What is Time? Did Time have a beginning? What happened just before it began? Time as we know it is part of created reality, time-space as science calls it, which began in an awesome bang fifteen billion years ago. Yet the question of what happened just before time began is a contradiction of logic. How can time, that needs a regularly repeating physical event, exist when there are no physical events to record?

It is my persuasion that physical reality is not absolute. It exists in the context of another, a greater reality which we refer to as Sprit or the divine mind, consciousness itself. This greater reality is referred to by Paul and Jesus when they use the phrase, *before the foundations of the world.* We could therefore translate this phrase as:

In the greater reality out of which all things are created and in which all things exist

In this greater reality Time, past, present, and future exist as one. That is why the scriptures can say that: *All his works are finished from the foundation of the world.* If this be so then we must understand that it is not so much our physical experience itself that is so significant, rather, as I illustrated about Jesus, it is the evolution of **awareness** that is so prized in the experience of earth. Awareness belongs to consciousness and consciousness is eternal.

We conclude then that the Plan of the Ages, from before the foundations of the world is a plan formed in consciousness, formed in a greater reality, in God himself. It is formed in a realm beyond time and space, something we cannot rally grasp with our time orientated minds. We can only say the words and feel the eternal impact on our consciousness. The word "before" in this context has a larger meaning than implied by the way we use it in our everyday experience. Perhaps there is no word that truly presents the thought that is being conveyed here.

However, we **can** understand the Time Clock of the Ages so often referred to in the scriptures and other ancient literature. It is written of Noah that by his preaching he brought an end to the Age that then was. According to the chronology of the Torah, that would have been the Age of Taurus, the Age of Adam and the patriarchs. Abraham sacrificed a ram instead of his Son at the beginning of the next age, the Age of the Ram, Aries. Jesus, whose Greek name looks like a fish, stood with John in the waters of Jordan on the cusp between Aries and Pisces. We want to clearly show how this Clock of the Ages works and secondly give the astronomical explanation of it. Before we discuss this Clock of the Ages I need to mention and define some terms that will help us to understand the concepts presented here. The first of these is the idea of Motion.

Motion Is Relative

Throughout the following discussion of cosmic events you must remember that motion is relative, it needs a frame of reference or point of view. A very dramatic illustration of this can occur as follows. The automobile you are driving is standing in line at a red traffic light. Beside you, also waiting for the light to turn is a large semi. Suddenly you have the feeling that your car is rolling backwards. You envision bumping into the car behind you. You slam on the brakes, expecting the familiar whiplash feeling in your neck and...nothing happens! It was the semi slowly pulling ahead that made you feel you were rolling backwards. I promise you, if you have never experienced it, it is dramatic..

What happened? You and the truck were moving in relation to one another, however, only the truck was moving relative to the pavement. So you see there are three possible frames of reference here, you and your auto, the truck and of course the pavement or the earth itself. You have to be able to envision the event by placing yourself as the observer in all three of these frames to get a good understanding of it.

In the same way, for every cosmic event in our Solar System there are at least two perspectives. The more exact and simpler to understand is the perspective you get when the motion of the planets is seen using the STARS and the Sun as a frame of reference. The Sun IS one of the Stars. Throughout the long ages of time man has seen these events from the point of view of an observer on this planet, unconsciously using the EARTH itself as that frame of reference. This greatly complicates the understanding of the motions of the planets. The Astronomers, before the advent of telescopes, had very complicated models; spheres within revolving spheres to attempt to explain the apparent retrograde motion of Mars and the other so called wandering stars. The stars were all thought of as being the same distance from the earth, attached to a sphere called the CELESTIAL SPHERE. Even though this is not at all correct, it is a useful idea to help us understand the precession of the Equinoxes, so we will use the idea of a Celestial Sphere.

You may remember from your studies of history how traumatic the change in consciousness was when Johan Kepler and others began, through the use of telescopes, to suggest and finally prove that the earth really is not the best frame of reference to use. The Sun itself and the fixed stars are a much simpler one. People were burned at the stake for what we now see as simple observations.

The idea of a sunrise and a sunset are awesome examples of this relativity of motion. Who is not thrilled and awed at the indescribable beauty of that orb of light slowly appearing and disappearing from view? The fact that from the stars frame of reference the Sun really does not rise or sink, instead, the surface of the earth you are standing on is slowly rolling towards the sun making it appear to be rising, changes nothing. You can stand there and say to yourself: *The Sun is not really rising, I am just imagining it*"; it will change nothing, you will immediate forget all you mental analysis in favor of the beauty of the moment. Sunrise and sunset are truly experiences of this earth, they cannot be seen in outer space.

In all our consideration of celestial events we always have, in the back of our mind, the immediate spiritual inferences that are so easily made. The earth and its gravity represent the lower degrees of your experience of self, the ego and its attachments. The vast expanse of the heavens is in coincidence with the eternalness of your true existence in and beyond this present dualistic plane. And so the beauty of a sunrise, so illusionary in nature, emphasizes to us the value and worth of the temporal and the earthly. The experiences of the ego self are treasures to be valued. Remember when Jesus told a parable about a man who found a treasure hidden in the earth? Jesus of course was referring to himself and the value he placed on his own incarnation.

To fully appreciate the import of the precession of the Equinoxes, the Grand year and the Plan of the Ages you will have to become adept at making this mental change of perspective. You must be able to, see the event from the point of view of the stars, which is simpler, and then see it as you would on earth, with greater emotional impact.

From a more esoteric point of view we say that it is our addiction to an ego centered consciousness which keeps us from true spiritual awareness. We cannot see things clearly, see them as they really are, and the paradigm shift required for man to transcend his ego limitations has been his great quest for many long ages.

The Clock of Ages

As you know, any timepiece simply needs a regularly repeating event, the hands of a clock, and a set of markers, the numbers one to twelve. Through the long ages of human history, time has been recorded by observing the motion of the heavenly bodies. The duration of a day, a month, a year, and also the much larger time period of the Grand Year, 26000 years, are all derived from the motion of the earth and the moon relative to the sun and the stars.

The regularly repeating events we are looking for are illustrated in diagram #1. In this illustration, you will see the arrow that indicates a revolution of the earth about its own axis, a day; the time required for the moon to revolve in its orbit around the earth, a month; and one cycle of the earth in its orbit around the Sun, a year.

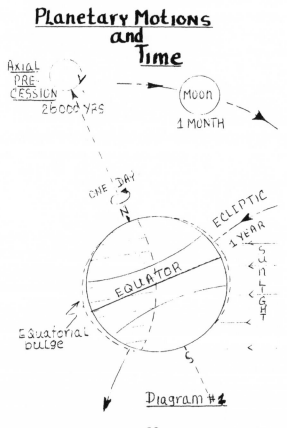

The Plane that contains the sun and the planets is called the Ecliptic. The axis of the earth is inclined to this orbital plane, at about 23 degrees. The pointer referred to above points almost directly to the pole star; the one star that does not seem to rotate as the earth revolves about this axis. The earth, because of the fact that it has a slight bulge at the equator, is affected by the gravity of the sun and the moon in such a way that it causes the earth to wobble ever so slowly around its axis, much in the way that a spinning top will gyrate just before it falls. This means that the axial pointer that is aimed at our present pole star actually moves very slowly clockwise, tracing out a small circle on the celestial sphere. Over long ages of time this means that we will have a different pole star, say 10,000 years from now, than we do now.

A single wobble of the earth, tracing a single small circle through the pole star positions by the extended axis takes 25,800 years to complete, this time period is called a Grand Year. This completes the movements of this Grand Clock as illustrated in diagram 1.Here is a summary of the regular motions of the Earth and the moon that form the movements of the Clock of God.

1. The motion of the earth around its own axis, --- One Day.
2. The moons orbit around the earth --- One month.
3. The earth's orbit around the sun --- One year.
4. The slow precession of the axis of the earth relative to the stars, caused by one wobble--- One Grand Year, 26000 earth years.

What about the markers we need to record and observe the passage of the Ages of time? These markers are provided by the Zodiac, a band of stars, consisting of twelve figures that circle our solar system through which, as a background, the sun seems to move. In actual fact the Sun does not move in relation to the stars. However, seen from the earth, it does seem to move from one constellation to the next during the year as you on earth move around the Sun.

In diagram # 2 you can see the orbital plane, or the Ecliptic divided into twelve sections, each comprising 30 degrees, adding up to the full circle of 360 degrees. If these sectional lines are extended to the celestial sphere, they mark out, approximately, the twelve positions of the zodiac, as shown by their names and symbols.

PRECESSION of the EQUINOXES

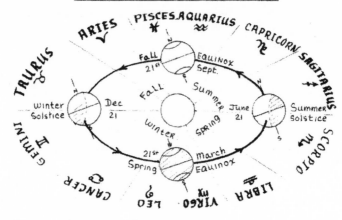

Diagram #2

The CLOCK of AGES

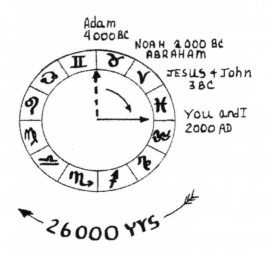

Adam
4000 BC

NOAH 2000 BC
ABRAHAM

JESUS + John
3 BC

YOU and I
2000 AD

← 26000 YRS

Diagram # 3

We can see how these signs are related to the months of the year astronomically. If you read the names counterclockwise you will have them in the order of the months of the year. If you read them clockwise, they will show you the order in which they appear on the Grand Clock of the Ages as in diagram #3. This reversal in order is called the precession of the Equinoxes

Referring again to diagram # 2, even though the Sun does not really move relative to these stars, from the point of view of an observer on our moving the earth, the sun will appear to rise every morning at a slightly different place among this band of stars. In a year it passes through the Zodiac, accounting for our twelve months. This apparent motion is caused by the movement of the earth relative to the stars.

Referring to diagram #2, imagine yourself to be at any point along the orbit, say June 21st, the Summer Solstice,\on earth. If you look across the diagram, the Sun appears to be between Taurus and Gemini and for all that following month the Sun would seem rise in the constellation of Gemini. So we see that from an earth perspective the Sun travels through the entire Zodiac, in the accustomed order, in a single year. It seems much more reasonable to think of the earth as traveling because in fact the earth does orbit around Sun, through the sections assigned to the zodiac through successive months of the year. However, as explained earlier, the relativity of this motion is an important part of the total picture and let's face it, all these long ages we have always been looking from this planet, only recently have had eyes in space.

You will notice that these positions of the Sun do not agree with the dates used by astrologers to create your natal chart. Virgo astrologically is from Aug 23 to September 22. However if you will look at the diagram #2 you will see the Sun from the earth point of view, on the Fall Equinox, Sept 21, just leaving Leo and entering Virgo. We are strictly interested in the astronomical aspects of the zodiac when we are considering the Ages of Time.

The Grand Year and the Ages of Time

The successive months of the year, following the signs of the Zodiac are caused by the motion of the Earth in its orbit around the sun. If

91

you imagine yourself to be an observer standing in the position of the Sun starting on March 21st , you would see the earth leaving Leo and entering Virgo. As you followed it's counterclockwise orbital path the signs would follow one another in succession as per the calendar months in the familiar order. As already mentioned, we are dealing with the actual astronomical positions, and not those assigned to the calendar by astrology. However, the order of the signs is the same.

Now imagine you are on earth making the same observations. This point of view is far more realistic. It's where we really are physically! From time immemorial, we have described the motion of the heavenly objects from an earthly perspective. The Sun rises and sets. We never refer to the more direct explanation of sun set and sun rise, being that you, standing on the earth, are constantly rotating towards the sun, causing the phenomenon of sunrise. In the afternoon, you are rotation away from the sun, causing the sun to appear to set.

Watching the Sun rise on March 21st, you would see the sun between the constellations of Pisces and Aquarius and you would see both constellations rising with the sun. The sun, at least for our purposes, is fixed right in the center of the celestial sphere. The whole sphere seems to rotate around our earth because motion is relative.

Three months later, one season, you would see the sun between the constellations of Gemini and Taurus. The reason that the sun seems to be moving through the constellations as the months go by is because you, as an observer on earth, are moving. The apparent movement of the sun through the constellations is no more real than sunrise, or if you like, is just as real as sunrise, awesome and beautiful. It is a phenomenon of the earth and the planets only.

The Grand Year happens the same way. The slight wobble of the earth causes the position of the axis to slowly gyrate. Since it is the position of the earth's axis that determines the time of the Spring Equinox, this effect causes the time of the Spring Equinox to occur slightly earlier every year. The position of the sun on the day of the Spring Equinox, as seen against the background of the stars, is moving ever so slowly backward through the signs of the Zodiac.

Have you ever noticed in the old movies how the spokes of the wagon wheel would actually be rotating backward, in the opposite direction of the overall motion of the wagon? If you only took a snap shot every year on the Spring Equinox you would see the sun slowly moving backwards along its orbit. The movement every year is only a small fraction, 360/26,000 or one 1/1000 of a degree.

If you continued that observation for 26000 years you would see the Vernal Equinox moving through all the signs of the Zodiac until it occurred again on the same day. March 21st is the day of the Vernal or Spring Equinox, a time of equal night and day. The movement of the position of this day, against the background of the stars, in reverse order of the normal apparent motion of the earth, is called the Precession of the Equinoxes. This so called precession movement is the basis for the Time Clock of the Ages.

The best time to observe the apparent position of the Sun among the stars is at dawn when the sky is still dark enough to see the stars. According to bible chronology, Adam in 4004 BC, on the day of the Vernal Equinox, would have seen the Sun rise between the constellations of Gemini and Taurus. For the next 2000 years or so, the duration of one age, the sun would continue to be seen rising in Taurus on that same day each year. Noah brought the end of the Age of Taurus, Aries ruled the next 2000 years

Abraham, when offering Isaac, had a ram provided as an offering, a ram that was caught in a thicket by its horns. The Ram is the sign of the age that follows Taurus in the successive ages of the Grand Year. The Bull was a sacred animal to the Egyptians, the Israelites, when disappointed in the non-return of Moses from the mount, made one out of the gold they were given as they left Egypt. Taurus, the Bull, was the sign of the old, the age recently phased out.

Jesus and John the Baptist stood in the river Jordan on the cusp of Aries and the dawning age of Pisces as John introduced Jesus to the Stage of History. *Behold the Lamb of God that takes away the sin of the world,* was the proclamation that went forth.

The two fishes are the sign of the Age that has been the church age. Jesus called his disciples fishers of men. The fish, being a symbol denoting Jesus Christ, is still a symbol of Christians today. It was first seen on the walls of the catacombs during the days of the Roman persecution of the fledgling sect.

So the Ages of time in the Grand Year, if we start the clock with the appearing of Adam, will follow one another, as the signs in the Zodiac except in reverse of the normal order. Diagram #3 shows some of these successive ages and the events associated with them.

Jesus and the Age of Aquarius

No man who has walked this planet was more controversial than Jesus of Nazareth. He appeared at the end of the Age of the Ram, the age of sacrifices. He came to end that age and to show that the way of sacrifices is incomplete and imperfect. He did so by fulfilling all the signs and types of that age in the reality of his own physical body. He did not destroy the Law, but rather he showed the completed end of the Law, describing it in the words of the Psalmist: *A Body thou hast prepared me, I come to do thy will oh God!* No words spoken with the most excellent oratory could have paralleled the sublime expression of perfection in the *Logos that became flesh and walked among us,* as his most favored disciple described his coming.

Many books have been written to fame and to defame him. Yet through the intervening years, his own words concerning his purpose and mission remain as a rock, steadfast, unmovable, and certainly not understood by man. In front of Pilate, the power of the earth, he claimed to be the TRUTH of Man, and clearly stated that he came into the world for a specific mission:

For this cause was I born and for this purpose came I into the earth, to bear witness to the truth!

Before the Pharisees, the lawyers, the politicians and religious rulers of the Age of the Law, he clearly identified himself as the Son of Man and the Son of God. He defied their worship of the temple and denounced them for their Hypocrisy. In the parable that followed the questioning of his authority by the Chief Priest and the rulers, he claimed to have been sent as a special emissary by the owner of the vineyard, a clear indication that Jesus was aware of the Purpose of the Ages and even more important, his place in that purpose.

The evidence for what I am saying is found in the book mistakenly called the revelation of Saint John. The first verse of that book gives the following information:

94

The Revelation of (belonging to) Jesus Christ
which the Father gave unto him.

The clear indication here is that Jesus himself received a revelation from the Father of Light. It was a revelation concerning the Plan and Purpose of the Ages as detailed in that book which finally ends by saying: *And I saw a new heaven and a new Earth for the former things have passed away.*

Before the event of Jesus' last meal with his disciples, before the Passover on which he was crucified, he gave this remarkable instruction to his disciples: *Go into the city, there you will see a man carrying a pitcher of water, follow him into the house, there prepare for us the Passover.* It was not customary for men to carry the water pots, so the man would indeed have been notable. At this last supper, which by his own admission he had *desired with great desire,* he gave final instruction to his disciples whom he had meticulously groomed for this purpose, He had taught them, by example and by instruction, the nature of his Kingdom *Let him that is greatest among you be servant to all.* As it happened, on this occasion, there was no one to wash the feet of those attending the meal. To eat with unwashed feat was a severe breach of etiquette, yet not one of the disciples wanted to serve as the least so Jesus took the linen towel, gird himself, and washed the feet of everyone of his disciples. What a dramatic turn of events, what a legacy to leave for a Kingdom. What a wonderful kingdom this must be, where all seek to serve and respect one another as greater than them selves.

I am convinced that the Spirit pre-arranged every detail of this phenomenal meal. During the meal he made this proclamation: *Henceforth will I not drink of the fruit of the vine until I drink it anew with you in the Kingdom*; what enigmatic words, what a mystery indeed. Perhaps the last supper is more than a last meal. Perhaps it is a defining statement and timing, spoken and enacted in a secret way so that his followers through the coming age would, by revelation, understand the timing and the purpose of Jesus kingdom.

Jesus understood the Clock of the Ages, he also knew that the Age that was then dawning, Pisces, could never fully reveal and embrace the purpose and the truth he came to bear witness to. This enacted parable holds the sacred key to understand the timing of his coming

Kingdom. It points forward to another time, another age, the age of the pouring out of water, Aquarius.

This timing would be understood when his followers would have evolved enough in spiritual understanding of his eternal principles that they would be able to join with him in the drinking of his cup and the sharing of his new wine of the kingdom.

Aquarius is the sign in the Zodiac that is the image of a man pouring out a pitcher of water. Jesus claimed to be the Son of man, and he claimed to be able to give living water flowing from the belly. The Sign of Aquarius is the sign of the Son of Man, it is seen in heaven today, and it is the sign of this dawning age.

Jesus gave the instruction that we must hear today: *When you see the sign of a man bearing a pitcher of water, follow him into the house.* The Astrological term "house" is used to refer to the constellations, each one a house. We are entering the house of Aquarius as I am writing this book.

There Prepare A Place for Us.

How different that is from the age that is passing. In the age that just passed we followed him but in this age we are to prepare a place for him. He wants to walk with us and share with us the inheritance of light for this planet. We are to be a Christed body of people, a people of light and understanding The Christ of God, is now bringing a whole new Order of the Ages.

What is this order? What are the eternal governing principles that bring a new heaven and a new earth? Looking at Jesus life as he bore witness to the truth as seen in his time among men we see these three operating principles:

1. All spirituality is rooted in the desire of alignment with the will of the Father, the source of all being.
2. The mortar of relationship that allows us to be one is the principle of forgiveness.
3. The operating principle of divine government is leadership that serves in love.

The Equinoxes and Solstices

Now that I have described the Time clock of the Ages, and the way it relates to human history, I will describe more particularly the mechanics of what is called **The Precession of the Equinoxes.**

Let me begin by describing and detailing the cause of the seasons. Referring to diagram #2, put yourself in the position of the sun, watching the earth make its yearly orbit around you. Let us assume that the axis of the earth actually sticks out at the North and South poles so you can clearly see its inclination of 23 degrees to the ecliptic (orbital plane). What will you see?

March 21, the spring or Vernal Equinox, is the first day of spring. You can see the tilt of the axis clearly; it is not tilted towards you or away from you but it leans to your right at 23 degrees. Exactly half of the Northern hemisphere is exposed to sun light, the other half is in the shadow or night time. The day then is equal in length to the night, hence the name Equinox.

As the earth continues in its orbit, you see less of the tilt as the northern hemisphere slowly increases its angle towards the Sun. At the day of the Summer Solstice, June 21st, the axis seems straight up and down and tilted directly towards the Sun. See in the diagram how the sunlight now impinges on the northern hemisphere more directly, more at ninety degrees, causing summer heat and also the longest day of the year as more of the Northern part of the globe is exposed to sunlight and less to the night. This is the beginning of summer.

Continue in following the Earth in its orbit, the day when we again experience equal night and day occurs on September 21st, the fall equinox. The axis of the earth is again seen at 23 degrees tilting to the left but not away from or towards the Sun. This is the first day of autumn.

As we follow on to the winter Solstice December 21st, when the axis is fully tilted away from the Sun. The Light of the sun strikes the northern hemisphere most obliquely, more of the northern half of the globe is in the shadow hence we have the longest night, the shortest day and the beginning of the coldest season, winter.

It is strictly the tilt of the Earth's axis that is the cause of the seasons, the Solstices, and the Equinoxes. This same tilt and its precessional movement or wobble is also the cause of the cycle we call the Grand Year. Here is another simple way to envision the movement of the Equinoxes among the signs of the Zodiac.

If the axis of the earth were always positioned the same relative to the stars, the day on which the Spring Equinox occurs would always be at the same position among the Stars. Remember, at this point the axis is not angled away from or towards the Sun. However, the actual position of the axis is shifting very slowly, still at 23 degrees but at a slightly different orientation with respect to the stars as the earth goes through its wobble caused by gravity acting on the equatorial bulge. This movement of the axial position in the opposite direction of the actual spin of the earth causes the critical Equinox position of the axis to occur slightly earlier in the orbit; hence the point of the Spring Equinox actually occurs a tiny bit sooner every year, about 1/100 of a degree of the total orbit. You can see in diagram #2 that the Spring Equinox will slowly drift through the Age of Aquarius in the next 2000 years.

Another more general way to think of the precession of the Equinoxes is to realize that one complete wobble of the earth takes 26,000 years. This means that any position of the earth's axis relative to the stars, say its position on the Spring Equinox, will only be repeated exactly, in every detail, every 26,000 years. Since the wobble is in the opposite direction of the normal motion of the earth, the result will be a gradual, apparent, shift backward through time until we are back to the position the earth was in 26000 years ago. Backward in time means hat we see the position of the Sun moving in a clockwise motion through the signs of the Zodiac, in a direction opposite to that of the months of the year.

Conclusion

Jesus knew the divine intent and understood enough of the timing of the orderly movement of the ages to know his place in that order. He also knew that the age of Pisces was not his age; it would be the age of the disciples, an age for them to be fishers of men. He anointed them with the promised Holy Spirit and commissioned them to go.

Their impact on the world and the evolution of human consciousness is immeasurable. This world cannot be imagined as it is today apart from Christianity and its influence.

What about Jesus' greater truth and his mission of a Kingdom on Earth? What about the promise of the Angels at his birth of peace and good will toward men? The golden age of mankind is dawning. The resurrection that Jesus demonstrated in his physical body is beginning to happen to the Spirit of Man. Mankind is being loosed, as Lazarus was, from the death shrouds of his old, dualistic, three dimensional thought structures. He is being re-connected in the Light of the Spirit and to his greater awareness which he was clothed in before the Ages began their unfolding. The prayer of Jesus:

Clothe me with the glory I had with thee before the worlds were!

is heard echoing in the spirit and the soul of man. His desire for reality has erupted, he can never go back to the cocoon of death consciousness he dwelt in for so many long ages. Gone are the days of him being used and abused by other elements and intelligence for their own gain and purpose. Gone are the days of our victimization and our imprisonment to the lower thought forms and energies of this planet. We are as a modern rocket, powerfully breaking the gravitational ego hold on our awareness. We are ascending and transcending limitations of imperfect thoughts and belief systems and we are free to believe, free to experience, free to be all that the human spirit was created to be. We are free to know and fulfill the Father-Creators' heart's desire…Fellowship in Love.

Rokus denHartog

"COME, MY NEW ONES OF TIME AND SPACE"

Jesus: His Mission and Truth

ELoi, Eloi, lama sabachtani! My God, my God, Why have you forsaken me? These are the words that Jesus, according to the Gospels, cried out in the depth of his agony on the cross. Centuries have passed by and these awesome words still haunt us whenever we allow ourselves to feel his experience. Many theologians have pondered over the seemingly imponderable question as to who Jesus really was and why he died such an agonizing death. This death, even more than his life, became the central theme of the greatest of man's religions.

Critics say that most of the words attributed to Jesus in the gospels cannot really be proven to have actually been his words. Others, using the Aramaic, have translated this phrase as really meaning: "My God, My God; that you have spared me for this great purpose. " Why is it so hard for us to accept that Jesus truly lived our human experience? Can we allow the thought that, at the deepest possible level, he experienced our unconscious pain of existence, our belief in separation from God? Why is it so difficult for men to consider that a Being of Light could incarnate, and, while still living in the full awareness of his divine essence and origin, experience what it is like to be human?

Psalms 22 reads as follows, beginning with the proclamation Jesus made: "My God, My God, Why have you forsaken me?" In verse12 we read: "Many bulls surround me, strong bulls of Bashan surround me; roaring lions tearing their prey."And again in verse 16: "Dogs have surrounded me; a band of evil men have encircled me, they have pierced my hands and my feet...they divide my garments among them and cast lots for my clothing."

Imagine the scene, Roman Soldiers gambling over Jesus' expensive garment while the eternal drama of Man's existence is displayed in the form of a man dying on a cross. Then consider that this psalm was written a thousand years earlier. To me, it is not at all strange to think that David, the Psalmist, beginning with his own pain and experience of rejection and humiliation, is transported into a prophetic mode and sees the crucifixion of the one who was called the Son of David. And while I let myself read and feel all the arguments and mental anguish of men, I know from my own experience the profound workings of Spirit to reveal the hidden things concerning man and his incarnation, the mysteries of God.

After 2000 years, what do we see as the message that Jesus brought? Gandhi loved Jesus' Sermon on the Mount. Christians generally have experienced him as the one who forgives and heals, but mostly keep their experience of him in the context of heaven, the life hereafter. The reality of a personal experience at the altar, conversion, a changed life, a soul cleansed from sin, has been experienced and testified to by thousands, even millions of people since the first message of the cross was preached, and such an experience cannot be denied.

My friend has a large screen, digital television. The images are crisp and clear. All facial expressions are clearly visible. Recently, as I was visiting, he was watching a quartet of young men singing Southern Gospel. The theme of the song was desperation, repentance, sins forgiven and looking forward to a life with Jesus in heaven. When they came to the part where we all go to heaven to be with Jesus, the crowd reaction was awesome. What is that all about? Is it not that we believe that our human experience as we perceive it is much less than what we are designed for and capable of? Some envision an afterlife where everything is perfect, no sin, no death, no sorrow or crying. Yes I can understand that. I believe in such a life. I know we can live in a way where we are not trapped in regret and failure but live in abundant joy and divine expression right here and now. Jesus himself said that his mission was exactly that: *I have come that you might have life and have it more abundantly!* ....right now.

Jesus' Greater Message

If we can take just one small step away from our entrapment in human consciousness and take another look at Jesus and listen to his words, we will see that all the things that we have begun to experience in the last 2000 years are just the introduction to his real message. We have been so deeply trapped in our human awareness that we were totally unable to understand the simple esoteric meaning of all that Jesus said and did. His truth was not just the words he said. His words were and are awesome, but his greater truth was in the demonstration of his life, death and resurrection; Jesus who became the Christ of God.

The simplest and most obvious message that Jesus demonstrated to us was the fact that death as we have perceived it is not what it seems to be. By his open visible death on the cross: *Father, in thy hands I commit my spirit;* his attested resurrection when he spoke to Mary in the garden, and by his ascension before a crowd of his disciples, he demonstrated clearly, to all that would see and hear, that death is only an experience, a transition, an emerging into a greater reality.

For two thousand years we have read his words; *He that believes on me, though he be dead, yet shall he live and he that lives and believes shall never die.* We have steadfastly believed that Jesus was speaking about the experience of mortal death. The fact that rarely a one, if there be such a one, has by-passed the grave has not deterred us at all in our preaching and teaching. We still loudly proclaim that death is the last enemy to be overcome. We think that death is an evil being that has some kind of real hold on us while Jesus clearly demonstrated otherwise.

Here is my conclusion: Jesus' focus never was on physical death or on going to heaven. He only used the idea of "death" to present his greater truth. If this be so, you might well ask:

1. What was it that Jesus came to show us that we have not been able to see?
2. Why have we not, for two thousand years been able to see it?
3. Why are you claiming that we are now able to understand the real meaning and truth of Jesus mission?

Allow me to answer the last question first. The reason we can now finally understand Jesus teaching is because the time has come for those teachings to be realized. The resurrection that Jesus demonstrated in his physical body is now happening as a collective reality to his larger body which we are. We are those that are the first fruit of the resurrection. We will be the first in the human experience to truly overcome death and live in the immortal essence of our being. There are three main objective witnesses to this truth:

1. The great pyramid of Giza is a prophetic message in stone that has been written about Man' journey; it begins with Adam's appearance on the plane and it has a timeline that ends circa 1973 in the Kings Chamber which contains an empty, so called, sarcophagus; a symbol of resurrection.

2. Jesus, when asked concerning Herod's temple, said: *Tear this temple down and in three days I will build it again.* The reference was clearly to his bodily resurrection. Beyond that we see that a thousand years being as one day, for his greater body, resurrection happens on the morning of the third day, the dawn of this third millennium AD.

3. The tabernacle in the wilderness is a demonstration of eternal truth. The Holy place, symbolic of the Church age, has a volume of 2000 cubic cubits, illustrating a time of two thousand years, after which comes the veil. The rending of the veil signifies a release from the blindness of three dimensional consciousness.

Each of these witnesses speaks of our present time of awakening from death. To carefully peruse them in detail would make this writing far too extensive but even then it could not be the witness you and I really need. We need to hear from within the temple of our own sacred soul, the truth of the dawning of a New Day for mankind, the truth of our resurrection. It is only the voice of the spirit within that can truly confirm to you the truth of which I speak.

The second question: Why have we not been able to see what Jesus really meant? Whether a worm is crawling around aware only of its own need to eat and survive , or it is in the cocoon, trapped totally in its own awareness, it would be impossible for it to even begin to comprehend a totally different form of existence, the butterfly. So it has been for the mind of man, trapped in the thought that he is a physical being trying to become spiritual and be approved of by God. However, the time of emerging is at hand. A deep seated eternal awareness is wakening from within and the things we could neither understand nor believe are becoming our true nature.

Now, for the first question; let's get to the real issue. What was it that Jesus came to show us? It is seen in the episode with Lazarus. As you may remember, Jesus sent his disciples ahead of him to the feast

Jesus waited until the middle of the feast, and when he arrived Lazarus was already dead and buried. Remember how Jesus made such an issue that Lazarus was sleeping? After some disputing by the disciples, Jesus relented and said: *All right, have it your way, he is dead* If we can understand that Jesus walked out a pattern of experience that was itself a demonstration of truth and that Jesus was telling us that the death of Lazarus is the death of Mankind, then, in the same way as Jesus called forth Lazarus from his tomb, so is he calling mankind. Jesus mission was:

I came to call Man forth from his Grave.

However, Jesus made it plain that it was a SLEEP that man must awaken from, a sleep of many ages, the sleep of man's mortality. So we see that the grave man is awakened from *is the grave of his own mind*, his own thinking. We must understand that the physical realm is a projected reality on the screen of our consciousness created there in order to help us understand the wonderful mysteries of God, the eternal principles of existence. Until we see that, we will always be trapped and unable to hear what God has to say in us and to us.

The death that man has experienced and that we are being raised from is the death we experience as our carnality, our physical sense of being, our human nature, as we call it. However, it's not our being physical that is our death. You CAN be physical and yet be ALIVE, as Jesus said: *He that lives and believes, though he be dead* (physical), *yet shall he live* (be fully aware)" Being *alive* is *the awareness of your eternal existence;* your immortality, your God-self or, Christ as you. What is our death? It is the thought that you are physical and ONLY physical. This is the thought that separates you from the greater realities. THIS is your death.

When Did Our Sleep State Begin?

If Jesus mission is to raise us from the sleep of Ages, our death experience, then who is it that is really awakening? Clearly the one that is awakening is the one that fell asleep. This one that is awakening we call *the greater awareness of our being.* When did we lose this greater awareness? When did our sleep begin? In Hebrews the second chapter we read very clearly that Adam was LOWERED or MADE LOWER than the Angels. In the Psalms it says: *Lower than the Elohim.*

104

We say therefore that man experienced a distinct and sudden lowering of consciousness called a sleep. When did this happen? We read in Genesis that man was put asleep in order to make him man and woman, to make him two instead of one.

We conclude therefore that man's falling asleep is actually referring to his becoming Mortal or taking on a physical form.

I know that such a conclusion is drastic and sudden and takes us out of the sphere of standard Christian thinking. However, I am profoundly persuaded that all of Jesus' teaching and experience clearly demonstrate this theme. In fact, Jesus' words and his self proclaimed mission cannot be understood except in the context of this assertion.

What we are saying is that man is not a mortal being at all. In fact, he, like the Elohim, he is a God-Being that was lowered in consciousness to take on a physical body, to become human. In short we say HE INCARNATED. Carnal is a Latin word meaning *flesh* so the word *in-carnate* simply means coming into the flesh or, taking on human form.

This profound mystery has been the struggle of man's mind for long ages. Man is totally trapped, not in death or even in physical form; man has is trapped in THOUGHT, in chains around his mind. These thoughts are as grave clothes that have immobilized him like Lazarus. The awesome voice of the Son Of God is reverberating through human consciousness: *Loose Him and Let Him go.*

Since, as I say, man has been trapped in thought forms, then his release can only come by the breaking down of those thought forms or the renewing of his mind. Man must be brought to the remembrance of a greater existence, not so much in the past as in this present knowing. The mind of Christ as Paul called it. Man has always been a truly spiritual being having a death experience of his mind; almost like a powerful dream that is his human experience.

So we see then that Jesus' greater mission was to show man a picture or a true image that would enable man to see himself from the point of view of eternity. Jesus walked as a man showing all that man is capable of being. Man has power over the elements. Man has power to forgive and to heal, and he is the Son of God. Jesus, in his crucifixion, he showed that man is the Son of God, crucified on the limitations of a physical, mortal experience. The thorns in his head are the fearful pricking of his own mind. This fear is created from the lack of true understanding. The wounds on his back are the experiences of rejection and abandonment made real in the realms of physical duality. The wounds in his hands and feet are the disabling impotence of limitation, feeling trapped in the physical form. Finally, when he cried out all the accumulated frustration and pain of aloneness in a single cry: *My God, my God, why have you forsaken me?* He became the image and focal point of all of mankind's deepest fear, his fear of separation, the journey of consciousness that not only man but all sentient beings experience.

Love Is Who We Are

In that surrogate, distinct experience of one man, all men can sum up their individual pain and sense of loss and aloneness. They can look at it, embrace its seeming reality, its pain and sorrow only to step back from it and realize this awesome thought:

This entire physical realm is only a created experience. It is only how we feel. It is an image created by our mind. It is a way for us to understand a much greater truth, the truth of the eternal love of the Father; love that always forgives, that always understands, that always makes a way.

Love that has no limitations, no boundaries, that excludes none and includes all. This Love is the ultimate reality of existence. It is God, the source of all things, of all existence, all life and all being. It is the only reality that can truly define who and what we are. All else is imagery and limited by thoughts that cannot lead us to this eternal knowing. The Source, our Father, Love itself, is known in itself and of itself alone.

It is through this death of the cross, the embracing of the human experience that we come to the resurrection of conscious life in which we are now participating. Light and knowing of a new dawn are the awakening of our God-mind, the mind of Christ. Our death and separation have brought us to a great new beginning. The cross is behind us. The death shrouds of our former thinking are neatly folded in the tomb of our mind, and we step forth into the glorious awakening of all the truth that we know ourselves to be. Morning has broken. We are free.

An Invitation

We, as the newly awakening ones, children of the resurrection, are standing on the shoreline of the human experience. We are looking over the vast ocean of truth and awareness that lies before us, and are willing to loosen the ties that have bound us these long centuries of time to our former thinking. We are standing there with Jesus as he reaches his hand toward us and makes the awesome invitation from his great soul and says, as it were:

Come, my new ones of time and space. Step with me away from the shoreline of what we have known, onto the imponderable and the unknowable depths of the greater reality of who we are. Let us venture a new pathway for all mankind. Let us bring into focus the greater principle of the Father's being that have waited such a long time to find a lodging place in the human heart. Here they will find a fuller expression and bring great joy to all eternal realms.

Morning has come. Our night has passed and our long awaited freedom freely invites us to share our love and our joy without boundaries or limitations. I married you to me when I embraced all that you are in my own physical form. Now you have wakened to return my love. Let us not linger long in the shadows of yesterday, only that we might find strength and resolve for the journey that is before us. Our love awaits u. The Father's own heart invites us. Come let us go.

Rokus denHartog

NOTE TO THE READER

This ends the series of articles I selected from my previous writings. I chose the ones I did to present the theme I have referred to as *A New Theology* or *A New Theory of Reality.*

It may seem somewhat pretentious to consider the thoughts presented in this small booklet as a *New Theory of Reality,* and perhaps, so it is. However, if I am to err in my assessment I would err in an over valuation because of the import I feel deep within of the need for exactly such a theme. The planetary change of consciousness we are experiencing during these decades, I believe, will prove to be of a far greater magnitude than any of us have been able to fully appreciate.

The two email discussions, THOR 1 and THOR 2 that follow are a more detailed and organized presentation of the truth that is dawning with this present shift into the Age of Aquarius. These discussions took place in a two year period and the participation of the discussion group proved to be invaluable to me in the forming of these greater concepts.

Although I have edited the emails to make them more presentable in this book context, I have tried to preserve the original intensity we all experienced as we struggled with the synaptic grooves in our minds that always want to pull us back into old thought patterns. For this reason I have included verbatim some of the email responses of the discussion. My thanks and appreciation is hereby expressed to all that participated.

During the course of the discussions I made a summary of the thoughts presented for the purpose of discussion and review. This summary follows this note. You might wish to refer to it from time to time as you wade through the rest of the book.

If you experience even a small portion of the excitement and inspiration that we felt as we participated in the discussions, your time will be well spent and you will be greatly blessed *by NOVA ORA.*

Rokus denHartog

108

A Summary of Thoughts Concerning
A New Theory of Reality

By: Rokus denHartog
And
The THOR Discussion Group

April 2007

Dear Friends:

As time unfolds, moving us into the Age of Aquarius and as the dispensation of the purpose of the Ages is being revealed it is essential that there be A New Priesthood and a New Theology. This greater understanding is needed so we can align ourselves with the divine unfolding and have confidence to embrace the new experiences that are coming our way.

The two summaries that follow are a synopsis of the two email discussions that make up the remainder of the book. They are entitled THOR 1 and THOR 2; the title T-H-O-R, meaning **A New Theory of Reality.**

If you are like I am then you may sometimes find it difficult to wade through a lot of words to get to the meat of what different writers are saying. I hope that these summaries will enable you to quickly overview what I am saying and perhaps incite you to correspond or converse with me about it or continue to read the more extended version that follows in the email discussions. I know that we all have a deep-seated aversion to systematized theological thought. In our experience it means dead, dead, dead. However, I ask you, take time to read what I have written; you may find that you are hearing the same or very similar truth. I have no intention of locking truth into frozen language or dogma; rather, I seek continually unfolding thought content for us to communicate in this greater reality that is dawning. Words themselves are not the container, you are, but words are spirit servants into this greater reality. Please enjoy.

Rokus denHartog

THOR 1: A SUMMARY OF THOUGHTS

First: All of what we consciously experience as ourselves began with a desire in the Source, our Father. It was the desire of Love to experience itself. This desire required that **AN-OTHER** ONE begin to form to be the object of this love. This is: *IN THE BEGINNING,* the beginning of duality. I call it the journey of separation. We make this statement: **The Source itself initiated the journey of separation.**

Second: So the ONE bought forth out of itself the MANY...the Many that made up the WORD, the expression. As they were brought forth the Source blessed its own God-Seeds....blessed them unconditionally to go forth, create identity, create journey of consciousness in pure joy and freedom. This is how you and I were conceived...this is our eternal mission...to fill the desire of the Source, the Father of all.

Third: In our conceiving we became as children, innocent, without experience or knowledge only feeling the desire of the Source and its total unreserved unconditional Love. As we began to try to respond to this Love, among our first thoughts there came a thought, a question....we wondered...what if I cannot fill the desire of the Source? What if I cannot meet its expectation of me? So is it that Sin was formed, it came out of the very formation of our own consciousness...we were the creators of it, a necessary by-product of our creativity. Sin serves as goad to press us on.

Fourth: As sin was formed in our earliest formative thoughts it turned our attention inward and we learned a wholly new experience, one we have learned to excel in....we questioned our own worth of being...we created awareness of shame.

Fifth: As worlds of consciousness were created and we unfolded in this Journey of Separation into ever increasing density of form we learned the process of forming Identity. As we did we needed greater measures of organization and control. Civilizations, worlds, came and went and the questions became increasingly insistent for answers. Love and Control, seeming opposites pressed the journey on. To answer the deepest questions of our existence, sin, shame and the reasons for them, the Elohim agreed to create this physical realm and then lowered themselves into this realm in Human form.

Sixth: The creation account of Adam is our story of being lowered into physical form. Light beings lowering their frequency of vibration. As in the beginning of consciousness there were two main elements working, separation...seen in the male and female and shame, the motivating principle that drove us into this biological clothing, our humanity. The great prize for which we came was the understanding of our Journey, our eternal quest, the knowing of our Father's heart.

Seventh: As shame, our sense of un-worth, shame, the result of our thoughts of separation and sin, was translated into acts, we began to experience a whole new level of shame...Guilt. Guilt caused by acts motivated by shame. There was no way for us to understand Guilt and its mother shame, nor was there a way for us to understand that these two were based on presumptions and false images that we created in our minds about an infinitely loving and accepting Source. To make the experience of Sin, shame and Guilt real, legal and tangible...the Law was added. A people were formed, called out, formed as a nation to marry the YHWH of Israel, a covenant of Law, of performance, of conditions, requirements, and conditions. This Law gave a legal definition to sin and hence guilt. For the first time we understood how guilt is created in us through failure to perform an agreed contract and the death that results from it, separation.

Eighth: The door is now open. The lowering is complete. Sin, shame and guilt are experienced in a valid setting of Law and punishment created from agreement. The way is now open for us to begin to understand the fundamental truth of our existence. Sin and guilt and its result condemnation and death are all the result of our own mind; they were never imputed by the Source. The time of Law prevailed upon Israel until 2000 years ago when the Light of All Light appeared as Jesus the Messiah of Israel, to redeem them from the curse of the Law which they suffered for all creation. Even though the Law had come...its lessons could not be understood for the curse was still upon his people. We are ready to open the greatest chapter of the human story....the coming of the Son of Man. Jahshuah...Jesus of Nazareth. We will do so in the next series of emails, THOR 2.

THOR 2: A SUMMARY OF THOUGHTS

First: Jesus, a living picture of Mankind, identified himself in many ways. He referred to Jonah, to the Serpent in the wilderness, to Moses and used all these images to make statements if identity about himself, the Son of Man.

Second: Jesus spoke of his mission in the parables he told openly and more so in his private conversation with his disciples. He stated it was most clearly in front of Pilate when he said that he came into the world to "Bear witness of the Truth."

Third: We understand this Truth to be the unveiling of Man to himself. Man must know who he is. Jesus came to show the identity of man by taking on human form and acting out the revealing drama of his Life, Death, and Resurrection. He is us. We are him.

The picture shows this truth: **Man is the eternal Son of God, crucified on time and space in his humanity**. The death of man was his loss of eternal knowing in his incarnation. The resurrection of man is the remembrance of this Eternalness as he awakens from the death-sleep of his earthy mind. His mission is to bring the presence of eternal God into form so God can be seen, touched, and known.

Fourth: The Age of Aquarius, which we are now entering, is the Age of the Son of Man. This is the time when this awakening comes. It is the morning of the third day, the feast of tabernacles, and Jesus greater body is rising from the sleep of ages. The Dawning Light of eternal Truth has come with a whole new perception of Man. We see who he is in his connectedness to spirit, and to time and space. It is time for a New Theology...not a repeat of dogmas and teachings of yesterday... but an enlightened, continually unfolding presentation of thought. This will require the creation of new neural pathways for the thought forms of higher consciousness to come so that God may dwell among men. The tabernacle of God is with men. Let the greater drama of Spirit coming into Form unfold!

112

A NEW THEORY OF REALITY

Part 1: An Email Discussion, March 2006

Rokus denHartog And the THOR Discussion Group

THOR 1 Email #1: A New Theory of Reality...Introduction

Hello all my Friends:

Our understanding is changing continually. We are taking LARGE STRIDES. In 1986 Carolynne and I began a four year journey throughout the United States. Carolynne was given a vision. She saw veins in the ground, silver and gold. The Spirit pointed to one particular vein indicating the one that she and I came through. There were many veins, but all the veins emerged into a bowl of brilliantly white pulsating LIGHT, and the Word of the Lord was: *Now you have come into a large place. Begin to take large strides.*

Taking large strides means to STRETCH YOURSELF...and we certainly have had to do that just to keep up. All our proclamations about "Not eating of the tree of Knowledge of Good and Evil," all our determination of "not judging by appearances," are meeting the testing ground of spiritual reality...the grand here and now of our experience. We are going THROUGH the appearance of words that men say, listening for the word of truth that wants to break through the limitations of their conscious minds.

Sometimes we are hindered by our past concepts of what a scripture might mean. We may have tapped into one level of esoteric meaning of such a scripture and when someone quotes it, the mind immediately brings up that older programming which usually resists the greater truth wanting to come. So...strangely enough, one of the great treasures we have, the scriptures, **seems** to become our hindrance. Hence we say, let us come out of the shadow realm into that Brilliant White Light in which there can be no shadows. It is not the scriptures that are a problem; it is our addictive attachment to SHADOWS and the whole Shadow realm. In that grand bowl of White Light there can be no shadows because the Light is not localized, it is everywhere! Is that Awesome?

We are also being stretched to consider concepts that are larger than our perceptions. As we do so, the brain has to create new neural pathways to accommodate those concepts; enough to give one a head-ache...Pfffheww. Those of you that attended our 2005 Thanksgiving meeting may remember that Carolynne had a flash insight where she heard the word *Synapses* and saw those pathways forming in a brain.

We have known for a long time that in order for a thing to be it must first be spoken. In the beginning all things were created by the Word, the spoken word is still needed to create the new. It is my intention, with your help, to use this email discussion to speak forth those things that are newly formed in our hearts, this newness we are experiencing.

You...my friends and readers...my sounding board...my fellow travelers in the realms of LIGHT...my Friends, Lovers, Sisters and Spouses....I am asking you to go on a journey with me if you will. I need you to interact with me. I need the LIGHT awakening as YOU. I cannot speak the Awakening truth of myself, my script, my book, without you.

I need to express this Awakening Reality, to clothe it with words, with language. New concepts need a place to hatch to affect these lower realms of consciousness. I struggled for many years with the fact that I seemed to have a very limited audience...I now am VERY thankful for the limited, specifically appointed audience I have been given. A new product needs to have a market testing. Is it a saleable product? Will it stand the test of reality? The LIGHT knows ALL. It has no fear or doubt, but I...as an emissary and deliverer...DO. I will emerge through realms of doubt and fear into a more perfect expression, just like you.

My intent is to write an extended series of articles. Each one short, (shorter than this one...Ha!) and through them create a more comprehensive THEORY OF REALITY. I will clearly mark the subject line of the emails with the name THOR, standing for "Theory of Reality" simply so you can delete it if you are not interested that day or do not have the time. This will allow me to keep you on my email address list without imposing on you.

There is a great need for a clear expression of TRUTH in this hour. We need clear simple concepts to clothe our minds with so we can continue with this grand journey. There is plenty of discussion about error and deception, and this too serves a purpose. It is imperative that we take responsibility for the word that we present to the body of God. Yet it cannot escape our attention that much of this expelling of gas is caused by indigestion in the body of Christ, too much unusual food too fast; allowing the body to react should bring relief.

To me, the most healthful way for us all to proceed is in an interactive presentation and discussion forum available to all who would participate. I will do my best to serve ALL by being as true as I can be to the truth that I am hearing within. May you do the same.

What I would desire from you is gut-level response to the writings. I will then incorporate the helpful responses in the development of the thoughts presented. This will make the whole project interactive. I am looking forward to your participation.

Rokus denHartog

THOR 1 Email #2: Chick Analogy…Emerging Into Newness

Dear Readers:

Thank you for the generous response to the first email. There is definitely a need here, a need for clear language and concepts to clothe our mind with as we walk into greater realms of awareness of reality. It is true for every person that **your consciousness is your reality space.** Some of us know that truth are therefore are more open to enlarge that reality space.

Although it is true that simply by exercise of the intellect we cannot attain to greater spiritual awareness, it is also true that if we refuse to allow change in our thinking modalities, tenaciously clinging to the 'right' or 'holy' words without asking for the greater meaning of those words, we definitely trap ourselves in the rubble of yesterday's religious hurricane.

I see the situation somewhat like this. Imagine a hundred little chicks in a hatchery. As the hatching time approaches there is a continuous chatter going on among the chicks that are ready to emerge. (I seem to recall that there is evidence that this is so). They are making great and lengthy projections about truth, understanding, and future events; eschatology. Suddenly, a few chicks break out. Immediately their perspective is dramatically altered. What was all imagination and revelation, spoken as types and shadows, now is suddenly reality.

The chicks that have hatched speak about what they are looking at and experiencing in that moment. However, all the 'sleeping' chicks are hearing those words from in the context of their 'in the shell' perspective. Immediately, where there was at least some harmony before, there is now sudden discord; arguments about the use and meaning of words. The chicks that are 'out of the shell' and the chicks 'in the shell' are still conversing with the same words, but those words no longer mean the same.

I think the analogy breaks down in this way. For the chicks the change is dramatic and sudden but your mind does not allow it to be so for you, hence the change takes place relatively slowly. As an example...for several years I spoke and wrote extensively about the Cross of Christ. I showed that the Cross of Calvary is a projected hologram through the experience of Jesus of Nazareth that enables us to look at and see our Crucifixion on the cross of time and space, our humanity. As I would begin to speak, when people were free to respond, they would immediately raise the objection that I was doing away the Atoning Work. It took me a year or more to realize that the source of the discrepancy was not in different understanding of the same truth, rather the discrepancy lay in the fact the I was looking at Calvary from ABOVE,(divine intent) while the hearer was still looking at the cross from BELOW (human experience). I had hatched into a greater place and was not fully aware myself that I had re-located.

Well, I promised to keep this short each time. We have not started on THOR, (A Theory of Reality) yet but I believe we will.

Rokus

THOR 1: Email #3: Where to Begin?

Dear Friends:

In the sound of Music, Julie Andrews sings to the children: *Let's start at the very beginning, a very good place to start. When you spell you begin with ABC. When you sing you begin with Do Re Mi...*

However, it is not always that easy to find a beginning point. Especially when you realize that there are realms where there are no beginnings or endings. The book of Genesis...*A Book of Beginnings*...begins with the letter "B" The Hebrew letter "Beth." Now this letter has the meaning of "house". You might wonder why it is translated as "IN" in the King James Version:

"IN the beginning God..." Think about it. A house enables you to distinguish between the **inside** and the **outside**. The nature of physical reality is that it enables you to think in terms of opposites, good and evil, **inside and outside.**

So to begin our thoughts about a THEORY OF REALITY, I will begin with this thought:

Physical reality, Time and Space, the Earth Realm, is a created realm. It was created for a purpose with a plan in mind.

Archimedes, one of the founders of modern science, and the one who stated the principle of levers said: "Give me a fulcrum and I will move the earth." He wanted a point OUTSIDE the earth to move the earth. We also need a point of reference **beyond** this reality to begin to form an understanding **about** this reality. It is my persuasion that physical things can only be **experienced** as physical beings. They cannot be **understood** from that point of view. Their meaning can only be understood from a higher spiritual point of view.

I was in Amsterdam in 2002. I never felt so disorientated in my entire life. The canals in Amsterdam are built in semicircles and the streets radiate out from the main train terminal. How do you orientate yourself in that kind of place? Easy...get a map...get a heavenly, elevated point of view. Once I understood the layout of the streets from a higher perspective, it became easy to navigate around Amsterdam.

We need a Theory of Reality to navigate this three dimensional existence in the same way as one needs a map. When your faculties are in gear and you are engrossed in the all consuming task of LIFE, you and I need a conscious understanding about this reality to give us the confidence and power to LIVE and remain connected to our eternalness.

To those who might say that you do not need such a conceptual framework, I say to you that the thought you are presenting is rooted in a core belief you already have. It is not possible to function in this realm without a core belief, a conceptual framework. All this brings up the question: How real is this reality?

THOR 1 Email #4: The Purpose of Physical Realms

Dear Readers:

Thank you for staying in here with me. We will begin to hit some pay dirt. Pay dirt in the sense that we will hit a stump or two...Ha! We will find new awareness about this 3-D world that does not fit our conditioned programming and our traditional understanding.

One main reason for me wanting to do a series of writings and the reason for wanting your collective input is the next thought in this progressive series. What is this physical plane, this 3-D world all about? Why are we here?

Metaphysics represented by writers such as Charles Fillmore and lately Joel Goldsmith have made major contributions to our present understanding. Having said that, I must also say that very often what is being said and presented as science or spiritual knowledge is really in opposition to some truly spiritual-physical principles that the scriptures teach and more importantly that Jesus came to demonstrate to us. How do we find our way in the midst of all this?

One of the main issues of discussion and/or contention centers on the word ILLUSION. It is the idea that experiencing this plane is to be compared to one who dreams...he eats a bowl of stew and wakes up hungry. Physical experience is seen as an erroneous perception. We need a more balanced approach. This balanced approach must be accompanied by a depth of spiritual maturity and experience in the Holy Spirit.

118

We are not the only ones who desire answers. All of our ancestors and many spirituals and spiritual worlds are looking on and desiring these answers through us. I no longer have the naive idea that heaven is perfect and that distortion and error only exist in this present so called evil world. In fact, I am persuaded that the opposite is true:

Whatever you find in this world can only be here because it exists in greater worlds beyond this plane.

That brings us to focusing the thought about the purpose for this level of experience, this physical plane. We can and do use illustrations taken from this human experience to help us understand, or form a picture of things that stretch far beyond this plane. Electromagnetic waves and the electromagnetic spectrum encompass many different waves and vibrations. At one end of the scale there are X-rays that your dentist uses to examine the roots of your teeth. They have extremely short wavelengths, Millions of them in a single inch. On the other end there are radio waves, used for the transmission of information on AM and FM. Beyond these waves are even longer ones, each single wave measured in meters and yards. In the middle of all these waves is a very narrow band of frequencies called the visible spectrum. If you could see with x-rays...like Superman... then the so-called visible range would be much, much broader. For us to experience sight as we do this range needs to be limited...wow! What would happen if you could see with the whole spectrum? This narrow range of frequencies, called the visible spectrum is itself made up of the seven main bands that appear as the colors of the rainbow. Just black and white is really a limiting idea.

Why this lengthy discussion of the electromagnetic spectrum? It is a visible picture of something invisible. Reality is like that spectrum. It comes in a large range, extending well beyond the range of our five senses. The visible range, being this physical plane, is only a very small part of all that we call REALITY,

If it is small, if it seems weak and is referred to by many religious and even spiritual people as 'only' natural, it is nevertheless greatly desired by the spiritual realms. It was desirable enough for you to come and to experience it; and enough for Jesus to set aside his greater glory and take on human form, like you and me. So, the purpose of this physical reality can be stated as this:

The physical created realms are like a screen of visibility to the eternal realms where non-material principles can be clearly seen in manifestation.

Rokus

THOR 1 Email # 5: The Very Beginning Holds the Key

A brief review so far. A journey needs starting point.. This point has to be in our own consciousness, which is where we are. Our journey begins with a question: *Who am I?*

In the movie The Matrix, when Trinity meets Neo, she whispers a question in his ear. It is the question that gnaws at him, a question that begins his awakening process...*What is the Matrix?*

What was and is that question for you? Only you know what it is, and it is that question that is your great treasure. It will keep you going when all seems to fail. It is the question that eternal Spirit, the Source, whispered into your ear at the very outset of your eternal journey through realms of separation, through and to your Source, the Father of all light.

The journey you and I are on has to do with the unfolding of consciousness and the forming of IDENTITY. Who are you? Who am I? So...I began this series of articles by establishing a beginning point. Knowing WHERE we are can lead us to WHO we are. The first awareness of this realm is that this realm is a realm of duality, of opposites. Everything you experience in this grand journey is etched into your hard drive through the experience of opposites.

The first problem or opportunity at hand for all emerging chicks is to look at their FEELINGS about opposites. Generally you and I have been programmed to perceive the world as good and bad. Then we took a step further and realized that we are trapped in this world of dualistic thinking. And then we fell into the trap of thinking that 'Good' and 'Bad' thinking is BAD. We blamed the woman who blamed the serpent for this terrible deed of eating from the tree of the knowledge of opposites. Well...guess what...I think we are all beginning to appreciate the fact that we NEED the experience of opposites to develop awareness of identity; that is... to unfold consciousness.

120

So...let's go back further...before the trees in the Garden. When did the idea of opposites, duality, the idea of TWO, begin and who started it?

The answer to this question and its emotional impact on us will help us make the last break through the eggshell. The answer to this question is embodied in the Lamb that was slain from the disruption of the Worlds. It can only be found by opening your heart to eternal Love and Light. You and I need to be given a glimpse beyond this created dualistic reality to understand and receive it, yet it is the simplest and most logical answer you could imagine...here it is:

Only the ONE, the All, the Sole Existence that contains all things within Itself, the Energy that is aware of itself, the Living Light, the Abba, Father of All...could have initiated the journey of separation.

This fifth email in the series, this brief statement of truth and light, will break our minds away from all the traditional neural pathways that continually lead to experiences of destruction. You can end the present program right here and now.

THOR 1 Email #6: Separation Is the Pathway into Form

Dear Readers:

I want to share a couple of responses I received after I began the present phase of the project...the subject of Separation.

From Vic: *You are saying that the Father of All is the one who started this process of separation. What would be your take on WHY? I'm not questioning your explanation but want to know more of what you think. What is the purpose, what is the end result and so on?*

From Bill: *Sitting here in my temple, so small, so mortal, pondering this, leaves me feeling inadequate. Yet, I had a glimpse then lost it. I have wondered, could it all be found in that He created us for his own pleasure?*

Thank you, Bill and Vic, for asking. Your emotional input is so appreciated and your queries will come forth as we go. Especially the most difficult part: Why would the All Loving Source begin such a journey?

As you may well remember, the only way we can clearly speak of the invisible things is by looking **At** and **Through** the visible, much in the way that you can look at a hologram and see a three dimensional image by focusing beyond the page.

First, let me illustrate the idea of separation. There are innumerable examples of it in this reality. In fact this three dimensional plane is based on separation, on opposites. The one I love best is the idea of cell division. The physical body is formed through the process called 'mitosis.' A single cell is formed from the union of a sperm and an egg. This complete unit has all the information programmed in it to form the whole body. The program is executed by repeated division. Each division is a separation...**ONE becoming TWO. One** cell becomes two, two cells become four4 and so on until there are fifty trillion cells that make up a physical form. Then that small form has to **separate** from the womb where it was formed through the awesome almost magical process called birth. Finally, at age 35 or so, you are here, physically at least, in your body.

Now, if my contention is true, that the **visible things** show the **invisible**, then the forming of the physical body is a direct pattern to show the forming of the true body, the body of consciousness. And so we can make the following conclusion:

The journey of unfolding consciousness is accomplished through the process of Separation.

As I said earlier, the only way that **TWO** could come from **ONE** was through the expressed desire of the **ONE**. That is, it was and is the Source itself that initiated the process of separation, the journey into form.

The idea of **ONE becoming TWO** is the essential thought of separation and the journey into **FORM**. This journey completes itself in having bodies. These are bodies of consciousness, bodies of Light, bodies of emotion, and bodies of flesh. There are several scriptures that speak of a 'BEGINNING' connected with this idea of **ONE becoming TWO.**

These scriptures are found in Genesis 1:1, Proverbs 8:27 and The Gospel of John 1:1.

Thank you for being my audience...Respond if you will with comments and questions, it helps greatly. I know what I mean while I am writing, however, as you well know, any given word does not necessarily mean in your mind what it does in mine. So please ask. Your question will give me opportunity to say it clearly. Worlds of awareness are listening to us. I am feeling this awareness as we share...Rokus

THOR 1 Email #7: The Beginning...God and the Word...Duality.

Dear Reader:

As we have stated, the essence of separation is found in this concept: **ONE becoming TWO.** Clearly the ONE knows no separation; it is always everywhere the same, only the ONE. So let us look at the sacred writings.

Gospel of John 1 vs. 1:

"In the beginning was the WORD, and the WORD was GOD and the WORD was with GOD".

The idea of **TWO** appears immediately in this verse in the following ways

1. There are **TWO** main subjects here, GOD and the WORD.
2. The WORD is described in **TWO** different ways. First as **being** GOD (was God) and second as **being with** (was with) God.

Since the word Duality literally means 'Two' we see the beginning of TWO or the beginning of duality here. The phrase **was God** implies total Oneness. The WORD being **with God** implies that it is **separate** from God, standing beside or at least somehow distinguishable from God.

123

So what is it that is **BEGINNING** here? Clearly it is the idea of **TWO** making its first appearance. Duality holds the possibility of separateness. As the idea of **TWO** emerges all kinds of things begin that could never be in the ONENESS: Time and Space, all physical creation, and the idea of **An other One**.

When these ideas began to come to me, I would present them by suggesting the possibility that God, the only **ONE**, went to the dictionary because he wanted to know what the word "Other" meant. What would it would be like for there to be another ONE"?

You all know that we are the "Living word, wrapped in flesh and bone." You also know that not only did the WORD become flesh in Jesus, but it has also become flesh in you. You too are that eternal WORD made flesh. Your beginning was not when Adam incarnated or in your mother's womb or when you were 'born Again'... your beginning is in the ONE, in the Mind of God, as the **desire**, then the **thought**, and then the expression...a **WORD**. This is the beginning of consciousness as we know it. This is the beginning of the journey of separation. This is your beginning as a Form Being, as one who can share consciousness and who can create levels of identity for realms of existence. This is where you begin. This is where you hear your mission statement. This is where your purpose begins to unfold...This is your **BEGINNING**.

THOR 1 Email #8: Proverbs 8: A circle...My Beginning

Dear Reader:

It is ultimately important to connect our thinking of a New Theory of Reality to the ancient thoughts and writings. All through the Ages there have been those who were granted glimpses and insights that have served as anchors to keep us until the Dawning of the Morning, the morning that we always knew would eventually come. Peter, the Apostle, put it this way:

"We have also a more sure word of prophecy; whereunto ye do well to take heed as unto a light that shineth in a dark place until the day dawn, and the Day star arise in your hearts " That Day Star is now shining...you are the manifestation of it.

Much like the one in the gospel of John, the following scripture connects the idea of a **BEGINNING** to the idea of **TWO**. That is, the Beginning referred to is the beginning of *consciousness as we know it*. It is the beginning of the journey of separation, or if you prefer, it is the journey of wholeness.

Proverbs 8 verses: 22-27 read as follows:

I was set up from everlasting, from the beginning, or ever the earth was. When there were no depths, I was brought forth...before the mountains...I was there (*I began*), when he set a compass (*drew a circle*) on the face of the deep.

Chapter nine states that Wisdom has built **her** house. So we see that the word Wisdom has the feminine gender. Yet, in the very beginning, there is only the One. The ONE brought forth the feminine one before the physical creation. We call it **The Feminine Principle.**

The 'Face of the deep' must refer to the place where **expression** comes forth from the great deep. It is by looking at ones **face** that the expression of the mind (the deep) can be seen when you are conversing.

The 'DEEP' is referring to ALL that God is beyond the place and experience of expression. So...this act of drawing a circle in the beginning is the act of creating TWO out of ONE. Once you draw the circle there is now an **INSIDE** and an **OUTSIDE**. We now have both male and female.

All that can experience separation, consciousness as we know it, began with a **thought** in the mind of God...a thought that could be very simply stated as:

What would it be like if there was another One?

The act of drawing a circle is like the WORD, it gives an expression to a thought, it creates the possibility of TWO, as we saw earlier. The expression **was** God and the expression **was with** God. Or, as we see here, God was **IN** the circle and God was **OUTSIDE** the circle, an awesome beginning. A beginning that is so simple, so seemingly small, yet this is where I began. This is where my *being-ness* was conceived, before I had any parts or any form, before I could see or understand or even form a thought. I was conceived to unfold and become all that God can be in realms of form...Me.

THOR 1 Email # 9: Gen 1:1 ONE Becoming TWO

Dear Friends:

There is one more scripture that clearly, in an esoteric way, illustrates the connection between 'BEGINNING' and the Idea of 'TWO'. Why all this scripture? I am not really proof texting here. I don't think that you would entertain my thesis simply on the basis of these scriptures. No I want to go deeper than that. I want you to FEEL the energy that is awakening us, and then I want you to know that this energy is coming to you directly from your Father, the Source from which your being came in the beginning.

This simple direct thought, the thought that you are receiving truth from the essence of all that is, from the essence of all that you are, this knowing that you and your Father are ONE...this thought...is the most difficult for the egoic mind to allow. The strength of the separate self is the ego. It does not easily step down from its preeminent position

No matter how sublime the thought or the awareness that is wanting to come to you, unless your and my mind are in a state to receive that thought, we will simply evaluate it from old programming and set it aside as 'too simple' or 'too human' or 'too complicated.' So...here is the third and, I think, the last scripture:

In the BEGINNING God (Elohim) Created the Heavens and the Earth

The BEGINNING referred to in this scripture is not the BEGINNING we have been speaking of. Rather it is the beginning of the three dimensional realm and the spiritual realities that are anchored there. We can see that from the fact that the creators here are the Elohim, a plural word; not the ONE Source. However, even if it is not **THE** beginning of beginnings, it is **A** beginning, hence the same truth can be seen here.

126

The Torah begins with the word 'IN'. This word is taken from the Hebrew letter Beth which means 'house'. A house is made to go 'IN'; building it creates an 'inside' and an 'outside. It is also a place to create a special atmosphere of closeness called 'home.' Again, as before, we have the idea of Two from One, the process of separation.

To understand the mystery of creation, the mystery of the truth of the WORD becoming FLESH, a key was placed by a carefully chosen beginning, the letter 'Beth.'". This is the key that unlocks the mystery of incarnation, of coming into the flesh, as it is written: *A Body (house) thou hast prepared me.*

All this leads us to the thorniest of all human questions. It is asked in many different ways, depending on the place it is being asked from. If we accept the premise, and to me there is no alternative, that the Source itself initiated the thought of separation, the question remains: *What was the desire BEHIND the thought?*

DESIRE-THOUGHT-WORD-DEED...this is the sequence we experience in the creative process...we have a perfect right, even an obligation to look at the divine plan and purpose through enquiring hearts and eyes. What was that...or what IS that first, central desire? Here are a couple of responses I have received on this subject:

From Bill:

Sitting here in my temple, so small, so mortal, pondering this, leaves me feeling inadequate. Yet, I had a glimpse then lost it. I have wondered, could it all be found in that He created us for his own (fulfillment) pleasure?

From Bruce:

*OK... I'm just gonna let what I feel inside me come out. If I **KNEW** EVERYTHING and **WAS** EVERYTHING...I WOULD BE TOTALLY BORED OUT OF MY SKULL! What PLEASURE could I have if I couldn't experience the UNEXPECTED or any SURPRISES? I would have to create some experience of separation in myself.*

We will consider this thought in our next email.

THOR 1 Email #10: Why the Journey? Love and Need

Dear Reader:

Leaving the old paradigm
Creating a new dimension in Time
Let's leave the Old behind
And bring in the New

This is the first verse of a song that Carolynne wrote on one of her morning walks. What awesome words...we are indeed leaving the thinking of yesterday. Are we leaving it because it was wrong? No, not really. It is just that yesterday's thinking belongs in yesterday. As we shift into a new world, a greater world, we need greater thoughts...more sublime, more refined, simpler, and more real. These thoughts that we entertain, that come from the Spirit, are creating the new dimension in this Time-Space realm.

As I have stated before, it is the cleansing of our emotional bodies from fear and shame that is enabling us to re-connect with former and greater knowing. The shedding of blood on Calvary has made provision for you to *wash your robes white.* Your robe is your flesh body and the mind that comes with it, i.e. your incarnation. Interestingly enough, it is the nerves in the body that are truly white. So this cleansing is in reference your mental-emotional body.

It is through the emotions that we can reach back into eternal realms and experience truth in the here and now, truth that will illumine us to the origin of our own being. I want to relate an experience that illustrates what I am saying and also leads us to the thought that will answer the following question:

Why did the Source, our loving Father, begin a journey that has brought with it such deep pain and sorrow?

I was standing on a balcony in Sarnia, Ontario, observing a large maple tree. Suddenly a gust of wind came and lifted a host of maple keys from the tree. They looked like a huge swarm thrown many hundreds of feet in to the air, whirling, flying, travelers with no specific destination apparent. Some keys only went a short distance, but others flew clear out of sight.

As I stood there, I felt the tree as if it were God releasing us from His own being. I felt the depth of His love. I felt the total unconditional love that released us from Him while I could also feel that He would never, nor could He ever, leave us. Wherever we went, He would be there. Whatever we would experience, He would experience with us and as us. Along with that unconditional love, I felt the intense desire of the Source as if He was saying:

You, as my seed, go...go and create...create a journey for yourself, a journey of experience, a journey of consciousness, to make Me, your eternal Source, whole and complete.

How could the Source desire such a thing? What did it want? It wanted the only thing it could **not** have if it remained as the only One. The Love that the Source is needed an **object** to need it so that Love could become all that Love can be.

**Love needs to experience itself as Love
through a need created by separation.**

THOR 1 Email #11: Shame, the Portal of Our Incarnation

Dear Friends:

This awesome Love that all the God-Seeds experienced as they were sent out from the Source needs our close attention. Our Christian Heritage abounds with hymns and testaments to those that have experienced the Love of God. You too, without doubt, know the wonder of the realization of the acceptance of God...*while we were yet sinners Christ died for us*....as the New Testament states it.

Among the thousands of hymns of praise that have been written by saints of God from the experience of this Love...the one that stands out to me is *How Great Thou Art*. You may well know it. I quote it in part:

*The Love of God is greater far than tongue or pen could ever tell...
The guilty pair, bowed down with care God sent His Son to save.
His erring Child, He reconciled, and pardoned from all sin.*

Clearly the theme of Love is tied directly to the awareness of shame.

In fact, the greatness of this Love is revealed **because** of this awareness of shame, or, as I have been saying, the journey of separation. Shame cannot be experienced when there is no separation.

It is this experience of feeling separate from God and the feeling of shame and the un-worth that comes with it that made the way to have the awesomeness of Love revealed. Could we have known the depth of this LOVE except for the depth of Shame that we experienced because of Separation?

As we have said earlier, Genesis is not the beginning of Man; it is simply the beginning of his incarnate experience. First, the creation of man is stated:

So God (Elohim) created man (Adam) in His own image,
male and female created He them.

In the next chapter, emphasis is placed on the manner in which they became male and female...a further step in the journey of separation. They were separated out of their oneness into male and female.

And the Lord God caused a deep sleep to fall upon Adam...
And the rib (chamber) which the Lord God had taken from the Man
made He a Woman and brought her unto the Man.

Finally, in chapter two, the writer makes this notable conclusion:

And they were both naked, the man and his wife,
and they were not ashamed.

It is most remarkable that the emotion of Shame is already connected to the experience of incarnation *BEFORE* the incarnation has fully occurred. What is the point of stating that they had no shame before there was any experience that would cause them to have shame?

I say that incarnation is not fully experienced at this point because the man and the woman as yet have not been clothed with animal skins. This clothing with animal skins is the final coming into flesh form which Genesis describes.

Let me make this rather bold statement to be inferred from the above paragraphs:

The first step in the process of man's incarnation is for him to create an emotional experience of Shame.

We already understand that the physical realm is a way to see the invisible. It follows that whatever appears in this realm can only do so because it exists in higher planes. So... shame did not begin in the garden...it was given a prominent opportunity to manifest through the experiences in the garden. SHAME must be looked at so that its purpose in the journey of separation can be understood. We will go back and look at the origin of shame in our next email.

I am well aware how deeply contradictory these concepts are to our, traditional thinking...let me quote the rest of Carolynne's song to you:

> **Make no mistake**
> **This is what it will take**
> **Walk over to your cliff**
> **And Learn to Fly.**

These thoughts are revolutionary and new to us. In the higher worlds they were clearly understood by those that that initiated the program of incarnation and the plan of redemption. It is in this lower vibration of the human experience where we have never been able to understand because the time was not at hand, the morning was yet to break, the darkness still had to cover all minds to make the program effective. Only now, as the Third Day dawns and the Third Heaven is opened, can these thoughts be expressed.

Paul the Apostle had an experience in which he was caught forward into the third heaven. In this heaven he heard things that were unlawful for him to utter. I understand the first heaven to be a time period before Adam came to this planet. The second heaven lasted from Adam until now. Presently we are speaking the truths of this third heaven. It is now lawful to utter them. I am persuaded that Paul is sharing the joy that we feel as these truths are opened to us. Can you feel Paul's joy?

131

THOR 1 Email #12: Sin and Shame Did Not Begin Here

Dear Reader:

I have jumped ahead of myself in the unfolding of this Theory of Reality. We have been speaking of Shame as it appears in the events that describe us being lowered into flesh bodies in this three dimensional realm. That is the story of Genesis. True, there is reference there as well to the creation of all things, but the important subject, beginning on the second page of the text, is the beginning of Adam on this planet, our collective incarnation.

Notice the pattern as it unfolds. It shows the relative importance of the key concepts of the total journey out from the Source to its consummation when "All things are gathered back into Him." As we have said and want to repeat, this physical plane is to eternal realms what the canvass is to the painter. Out of the invisible, the artist's mind, through the creative act of the brush stroke, there appears a visible image through which the artist expresses himself, knows himself, and is known of others. This story in Genesis begins to make visible the greater, invisible pattern of the unfolding of consciousness.

Notice the important role that **Shame** has in the story. It is stated first...*They were both naked...and not ashamed*...Then, after the partaking of the tree of knowledge, innocence ends. Shame begins and...the result...they try to hide from the Presence. The story of separation repeats itself in a lower plane.

As I said above, I do not really want to get entangled in all the ramifications of this story...we may want to later. For now we need to see the intimate connection between **Shame** and **Incarnation**.

Since our incarnate experience in this plane of manifestation is like the canvass upon which things invisible are clearly seen, we must conclude that neither Sin nor the Shame that results from it began at this point...we need to look back further.

In our thoughts and conversation we often interchange **Shame** and **Guilt**. Let me briefly say at this point, they are anything but synonymous. Guilt has all the overtones of Shame but is created in the mind as a result of a mental or physical act such as disobedience, betrayal, transgression of a covenant. Guilt may also be assumed without any direct cause, such as a child assuming it **did** something wrong to cause its parents to have a divorce. However, Shame goes much deeper. It is not just the thought that I **did** something wrong, it is centered on the thought that I **am** something "wrong." It is a deep-seated sense of un-worth and in-validation of one's **Being**. The child may suffer irreparably by the thought that it, because it was **who** it was, caused all that pain of divorce.

Shame is hard to look at because it makes you want to hide from the presumed cause of your shame...yourself.

This also means that Shame itself is something you have hidden and want to hide, hence...let's not talk about it. Talking about it, looking at it, will make you feel uncomfortable and even take you back to those slimy places you were so glad to be out of. All of us, and I mean **all of us,** have layers of toxic shame embedded in our cellular structure...even our DNA. We were formed through shame. Shame was the portal of our incarnation. We assume that we learned or first experienced shame when we were molested or raped or seduced or betrayed or swindled or called names at school. There seems to be an infinite variety of ways through which we create the experience of shame in this material plane...and that is exactly the point. This canvass of three dimensional realities was created for you and by you so that:

You could have experiences of Shame and so create a visible opportunity for you to understand the invisible thoughts through which Sin and Shame first entered your consciousness.

However, before we talk about it, we will have to go back further, back before the point at which we became physical...back to the origin of consciousness itself...and ask the primary question: *Why and How did this awesome journey of separation, this journey of becoming, begin? How did Sin and its offspring Shame, begin and how were they needed in the beginning to unfold consciousness?*

We have considered the thought that it was the Source itself that initiated separation because LOVE wanted to be all that it could be. Now we consider a more difficult question...*Why is sin needed?*

133

THOR 1 Email #13: What Is Sin?

Dear Readers:

Thank you for sharing this email experience with me. It is a time of reconstituting our core thinking.

The second and perhaps the most difficult thought we need to consider is the beginning of what we call sin and its consequences...evil...in the world. The reason this is such a difficult topic is that the grooves burned into the hard drive of our conceptual thinking are really deep and will tend to continually de-rail us during this consideration. It will do us well to remind ourselves of this condition as we proceed. Remember...our purpose is to create a New Theory of Reality...one supple enough and large enough to embrace this greatly expanded experience we are now in.

To consider this very old and basic question we need to realize that the conceptual language of yesterday is not sufficient. Not because the words of truth are not there but rather that we, in the limitation of our perceptions, have tainted those words with meanings and values that are not the truth those words represent. Allow me to share an example with you. In our child-like perception of our relationship with God we saw the Cross of Calvary as payment for sin that we have committed. We taught that God could not look at sin but loved us so greatly that He took His own Son who volunteered to take our punishment.

This teaching was a projection of our own feelings onto God. It was we that could not forgive ourselves; it was we that needed atonement. This explanation was our way to relate to the great Love we felt from seeing Jesus on the Cross.

Are the hierarchies of Light disturbed about this dark shadow that we have cast upon the greatest symbol of LOVE to ever come into the human paradigm? I do not think so. I believe the LIGHT knows that darkness cannot comprehend light and so must form its own images of the truth. However, as we now stand at the dawning of a whole new day, we not only have to shed the former perceptions, we must also redeem the language that has suffered distortion in our minds from lower thought forms. The word "Sin" is an example.

I remember the awesome moments when I could receive the thought that my Guilt was atoned for. The deep seated feelings of inadequacy that I could not even formulate into conscious thought, much less understand, were losing their grip on my soul in spite of the very limited theology. I was washed in the blood of the Lamb.

**I REALLY believed I owed something to God
that I could never give him.**

That thought, the thought of inability clothed with shame, lies at the root of the experience of separation and the evolving of consciousness through worlds and ages of time.

We know from the writings of Paul that the LAW (the Torah) was given to keep us protected from harm and bring us to another realm of awareness called Christ. We can easily enlarge that thought and see that all control realms in some way serve that purpose in the unfolding of human consciousness to that intended realm of Christ, the realm Jesus clearly showed us.

The LAW, by its requirements, its expectations, created the awareness of Sin and Guilt in the worshipper. The law also provided a way of salvation. The worshipper could bring a sin-offering commensurate with the offense to the temple in order to absolve his guilt. It formalized the thought I expressed earlier:

**The thought in the worshipper that he needed to return
something to God to please Him, and so expiate his guilt, was
validated by creating the order of the Levitical Priesthood.**

I must do something in return, in response to God's love. This is the thought in human consciousness that was validated by the Levitical Priesthood under the Law. The Priesthood put something in the hand of the worshipper that he could lawfully bring to God.

Does that mean that THE THOUGHT is a correct theological thought? Is this the way that God sees man? Is this an eternal reality or is it a limited, immature perception in human consciousness? Christianity as a whole, even though we have experienced the salvation of God in Jesus Christ, has continued this perception of

135

sin and atonement by teaching Jesus as a perfected form of the animal sacrifice under the Levitical order. The root of this misperception lies in the misconstrued thought that God actually gave the Law as an absolute standard of God's requirement. In fact the LAW was given to make SIN real, not to show how you could be perfect but rather to show that man's standards of meeting God's requirements can **never** be met.

There is nothing great enough that you can give to God to deserve His Love. God's Love has always been unconditional.

Even though it brought temporary relief from the symptoms of sin, guilt, and shame, the LAW could never answer the greater question: Why do we experience them at all? In my next email I want to consider where this thought of sin originated from and give it clear definition.

THOR Email #14: The Law Reveals Sin...Let's Look

Dear Reader:

Before we actually make a clearer definition of the idea of Sin, let's look one more time at the Law. Paul said, in Romans 7 vs. 13:

...That Sin by the commandment might become exceedingly sinful...

He is expressing the thought that the Law was not so much given to heal or correct sin, the Law was given so that we sin could truly become sin and be clearly seen for what it is.

In the concordance, the word used in the Old Testament for Sin is *CHATTATH*. You will also see that the same word is sometimes translated as SIN OFFERING. Both meanings are there, the context of use determines which one is chosen.

Does that mean that the sin offering itself is or is part of the sin? Clearly this would be so if the offering REVEALS the sin. This next reference to David confirms this thought. King David, spoken of as a man after God's heart, perhaps experienced sin, regret, and shame as deeply as any man. He killed a loyal friend and servant for his own need and lost his child as if it were an offering for his sin. It is this man that said these words, they are written in Psalm 40 vs.6:

Sacrifice and Offering thou didst not desire...

How could David have this profound revelation about Sacrifice and Offering in the middle of the Age where sacrifice was instituted as the official religious order? It can only be so if the offering itself is part of the sin...because it reveals the nature and essence of sin.

What then is the essence of sin? I must relate a personal story here that finally, after much struggling on my part, gave me the key to understanding the essence of sin. Carolynne and I had just had a profound experience of realizing that our desire to do sacrifice, to say "I did it for you Lord" or "I made a sacrifice"...is simply a part of revealing sin. The Spirit spoke to us and said: No...**You** did that because **You** needed to do it." As we were sharing this thought in the Sunday Fellowship here in Oldfield, we had a visitor.

This young woman got up in the meeting and said:

"I was back in my old church, the preacher was preaching about sin...so I asked the Lord: What do you think about Sin? The Lord said to me:

...Sin is something that YOU have created"

I was totally blown away....most of all because in a thousand years it would never have occurred to me to ask Jesus what he thought about sin. I unconsciously always assumed I KNEW what he thought about it...*it is really bad stuff...I died and suffered because of all that sin you know.*

The casualness of the answer also implies that our aggravated thinking and dealing with sin is all part of the sin itself, it is sin-offering. If we ourselves are the ones that created sin and all creative effort begins in the realm of thought then Sin in its most primal form MUST BE A THOUGHT.

We are now ready to consider what Sin is, when and how it began, and to see the purpose for it.

THOR 1 Email #15: A Definition of Sin

Dear Reader:

How many men and women through the ages lived and died while still trapped in the limitation of human consciousness. Trapped in the never ending circle of questions and doubts that arise from the pain of disappointment and death? Comforted only by the promise of heaven, the so called hereafter? Paul, speaking of the heroes of Faith, concludes: *All these received not the promise...*

Why should we be so privileged to live in a flow of LIGHT and LOVE that continually awakens us to greater reality and awareness? Are we more faithful or brilliant than they? No, I do not think so. We came in the appointed time for this purpose...yet they all, with us, are inheriting realms of Light and Understanding. I am aware of Paul. I think about his great quest to bring the understanding that allowed the Age of Law to fade and bring in the age that is now passing.

I am even more aware of Jesus...I sense his ecstasy and joy as we enter into realms with him that he has waited for, realms that are a direct result of his Life and death. These were his words, spoken so long ago: *Henceforth will I not drink of the fruit of the vine until I drink it anew with you in the Kingdom.* I feel His intense Love for us, we who share his awareness...like true coitus of being...so awesome and fulfilling. *If ever I loved you my Jesus it is now!* The sweetness of that chorus...I feel it. We are drinking that wine of awareness with him now, now as I write, now as you read, as we share his joy. This is the day that has been spoken of for long ages of time. This is the time foreseen when man would awaken from the long sleep of ages, the drug induced coma of material consciousness, and begin to remember who he is, who we are. We are the embodiment of the LIGHT, the eternal Presence from whom came all things and in whom all exists.

Truth is not something we learn. Truth is the essence of us, flowing from us, bringing light and deliverance to the created realms. I came for this purpose, and for this cause was I born.

I well remember, it was about a year ago, as I stood in our living room and heard these words:

Sin is the thought or the awareness that I am not able to meet your expectation.

What is so awesome about this thought is that it is clearly a thought that must be generated by a RELATIONSHIP. It is a thought that could not come until there were two; one to have an expectation and another to feel unable to meet that expectation. This thought could be one of the very first thoughts we ever generated after we first became aware of our separation and aware of the awesomeness of the LOVE of the Source from which we were generated. Even as God-Seeds, as we took our flight on the wind of LOVE into a totally new experience of separation, of becoming a SELF...our first apprehension...gently appearing in the euphoria of totally new and first LOVE...*How can we ever return this great LOVE?....How can I ever be worthy of this awesomeness I feel all around me and in me?*

Now that we have a definition of the word "SIN" to consider, we can try to answer some questions that have been asked through all time but seemed to have no answers.

One of the very first questions could be: *If we created Sin...why did we do it or what purpose does it serve?* The very LOVE of the Source that generated us, in this beginning of duality, induced its opposite in us immediately, a thought of un-worth, a thought of inability. It is this interplay of light and darkness, of good and evil, in the created realms that propels us forward in the journey of separation; the journey of creating a SELF, the Journey of Oneness, the Journey where Love fully knows itself. That is why I describe Sin and its purpose as follows:

Sin is the evolutionary driver of consciousness

Light, physical light, is an Electro-Magnetic wave. It travels at 186,000 miles a second. It does this by alternating interlocking electric and magnetic pulses. It is a visible effect to show the invisible thing I am speaking of. That interplay of Sin and Grace, Love and Need, Masculine and Feminine, that makes this whole experience so rich and beautiful, painful, and infinitely rewarding. Thank you for being my audience...I could not do this without you.

THOR 1 Email Response #15 A: Why this preoccupation with evil?...Cheryl

Cheryl writes:

Seems to me if I think of humanity as a whole for eons on this planet, they seem to be more drawn to the negative (evil) then the light (positive). History shows that awareness. Why?

Thank you Cheryl...so does the daily news, its always "'bad". This question was clearly prompted by the emails on Sin Thank you for taking the time. Here is my response to your thought.

This physical plane, the earth realm, is a very low frequency expression of our total reality. It's like slowing down a certain play in a football game to see what really happened, perhaps to determine if the referee made the right call.

In other words, what we are experiencing here happened before in a greater realm of light. The reason we are so obsessed with cruelty, abuse, addiction and evil in general is because that is what we want to understand. We are creating these experiences to help us understand shame and guilt, the elementary drivers of the evolution of consciousness in higher spheres

What makes it so real and difficult is that our **pain** (feelings of separation) wants to keep us from **looking** at our **pain** (experiences of separation). We love our denial.

Notice how we as Christians love the thought that Jesus took all the sin of the world away when very clearly, even Bill Clinton knows, it is still around in abundance. We are in denial.

The first thing AA tells a drunk to say is: "I am an alcoholic." Only when we are able to truly look at sin and its affects can we be healed and understand; there we have the simple reason for the Cross of Jesus.

We cannot look at the issue of sin through our old perceptions. We hate it, it is really bad stuff and it should not be here...so we are in denial...we cannot look at the purpose of it, we have already turned off the screen.

If we can begin to see from the point of view of the original intent in the heart of the Source, then we can understand. Here is the reason we need a New Theory of Reality.

Thank you Cheryl for responding...Rokus

THOR 1: Email Response #15 B: Did Jesus Take Away All Sin?

Dear Readers:

I want to go to greater implications of a New Theory of Reality but we are hitting some real stumps...which I am very thankful for. I am also very thankful for the key responses I am getting from the discussion group. I am sure that many of you reading these emails have very similar gut reactions as I am quoting, as below, because it is the best way to get at the deep rooted ideas that are grooved into one's heart-mind, ideas that lock us into the old paradigm.

I pray that none of you are offended in anything that is said. If you are offended, please share it with us, or with me, so we can together come to clarity.

I wrote in email #15 A:

*Notice how we as Christians love the thought that Jesus **took all the sin of the world away** when very clearly, even Bill Clinton knows it, it is still around in abundance.*

MN responded:

Boy!!! How morbid. Forgive me, but I think this is a bunch of hogwash. And that last sentence, is denying what we are told about Jesus taking the sin. I, will admit, I just don't understand everything yet but I refuse to deny Jesus. Don't you think this has gone a little out of control to deny what we are told in the Bible, or do we just believe the parts we WANT to believe? MN

Rokus: Tank you MN for being gut-level honest with your reaction to what I wrote. Your reaction helps to illustrate what I am saying...we have a programmed idea inherited from our Christian thinking. The scriptures say, as John the Baptist baptized Jesus:

141

Behold the lamb of God that taketh away the sin of the world.

Whatever this scripture may mean...it does **not** mean what it **seems** to say. If all the Sin of the Cosmos was taken away by Jesus, there would be no consciousness of it, which is clearly not the case. When the preachers confronted Bill Clinton he came right out with it: "I have sinned."

Then what does it mean? John says "Behold." That word means: "Take a look and see." What are we to see? We are to look and see the **Lamb** that is *continually* taking away the sin of the world. This Lamb could not be clearly **seen** until Jesus appeared in time. As long as there is sin, the Lamb is always there to take it away after the sin has done its work. The "Lamb that was slain" was slain from the dawn of creation...why? It was there when our first thought of *not being able to meet the Father's expectations* appeared. How great is the Love that creates such a pathway of provision. The **Lamb** came as a Ram in a thicket when Abraham was about to offer up Isaac. The **Lamb** came in the form of the Levitical priesthood and its sacrifices. It came when Jesus appeared and became truly available, and it's here now as you, the **Lamb** slain for the Sin of the cosmos, so that sin could do its work and then be taken away.

"What we are told in the Bible"...as you say MN...needs the opening of the ear to hear...the words themselves as they appear in the King James bible or any other translation are viewed by us through the eyes of our belief system. Only as the Holy Spirit reveals its meaning can we see it.

Some of you, that know the scriptures, might say that Jesus made Atonement for Sin, ONCE and FOR ALL. That is my very point. Jesus became the point of availability for all time and eternity so we could behold the LAMB of GOD that was slain at the dawn of consciousness.

THOR 1: Email # 15-C: About expectations. Please explain.

Tony Messano writes: *Rokus, what you are saying here is a very subtle thing about expectations. I'm not saying that it is unclear but do you have any other way to define it? I heard somewhere along the way that Jesus is the final obstruction to our journey back to Oneness, in other words, our concept of Jesus is what we need to see past.*

He who believes in me, believes not in me but in Him who sent me"
John 12:44

I believe that scripture put an end to all false imaginations and idol worship from that point on. Please explain from your advantage!

Rokus responds: The strange part of it is this Tony; I do not claim to understand it myself. One of the reasons I want this discussion is that I too might be released from old programming. Believe me, it is happening to me. As I'm watching us all go through it...Ha!

First...I clearly heard Spirit say to me:

SIN is the thought or the awareness that
I cannot meet your expectation.

This happened to me after some real effort and desire in me to understand the concept of sin. I searched the scriptures, I gave it much thought. I asked: What do people commonly mean when they use the word sin?

Second: Some weeks after hearing this in the Spirit, Carolynne and I were driving home from a meeting in Knoxville, TN, and Carolynne had an experience with Jesus...She heard this song:

Don't put me in a place that I don't want to be in.
I just want to walk with you and be your constant friend.
I'm the love peace and happiness that come from deep within.
Don't put me in a place that I don't want to be in.

You put me on a pedestal, too high for you to reach.
You said I had expectations that you could not meet.
But these are just false images that you did create.
Now let me out of prison. I just want to be with you.

143

What is so remarkable is that this little chorus repeats the definition of sin the spirit gave me. I have highlighted that line for that reason. It also goes on to say that we are the creators of these false images, confirming what Jesus said to our friend when she asked him what he thought about Sin:*"Something that you created."* You might also know that Carolynne is not just swallowing something because I say so; she does respect me as I do her, but she has her own mind and is sometimes my best challenger. She hears these things for herself.

I don't know Tony if we can end all idolatry. We are ingenious in creating idols and perhaps we need them until we can let go of all denial and accept who the Father created us to be. To truly look at Jesus, not as an idol to be worshipped, but as the true image of who we are, is the road back home.

As the glorious day of our true origin and our true essence dawns we are finally empowered enough to look at the evolutionary driver that became our goad on the road of unfolding consciousness...Sin... the thought that we could not respond adequately to that great LOVE from which we came and that we essentially are. We do this even as we begin to remember our Oneness and are made whole. We are freed from pain and sorrow, our tears wiped away as we understand why the roads have been the way they had to be. We have to be cleansed from the sin-thought through our embracing of it, all in the ecstatic joy of the remembrance of the great journey and the Father's intent.

THOR 1 Email # 15 D: Response to CT. Clarifying the word *Expectation.*

Dear Friends:

The definition of the root concept of sin that was given to me has been difficult to assimilate. I did not fully realize how difficult until we actually got into this seemingly unending discussion of sin. I deeply appreciate the honest questioning done in the italicized print below in this email by CT, and I venture again to suggest that it is our emotional connectedness to the wonderful, limited concepts of yesterday that makes it difficult to rewrite our programming. Below are two quotes by CT that call for greater clarification of the prime consideration, a more basic definition of the concept of SIN. I quote:

I have reflected on your definition of SIN, and it does not ring true to me. It feels like it tends to sucks me back into a place that I once was, but no longer need to be. I am sorry old friend; your vision of SIN does not work for me. CT

And again:

I am sorry to say that the concept of SIN that you are embracing appears to be leading you away from truth. A concept of SIN that embraces the idea of "I cannot meet your expectation" appears to be based in the EGO of man. God has no expectations, HE knows. CT

The first quote brings out the realization that there are two modalities working here. First there is your and my personal perception of what the word SIN means to each of us. Even those that staunchly proclaim that they do not have any sin must have a thought in mind of what SIN means to **them**. I personally feel that many of us equate **Sin** with **condemnation**. Truly the Spirit of Christ has set us free from condemnation...if we know anything we know that. In loosening our awareness of the sin that condemned us, we readily say that we have no sin...and in that sense I totally concur. Thank you Jesus!

However when **I** speak of SIN, I am speaking of the experience of all men. The experience of Adam is clearly more than your or my personal experience yet you could never relate to the experience of **MAN** if you were not yourself a **man**. So...CT, this *Sucking back feeling* that you speak of is essential for you to experience so you can **feel** what I am talking about. It seems to me that this feeling you have actually **validates** what I am saying.

The second quote...saying that expectations are based on the EGO of man is very similar. If the Ego is *awareness of self,* then it becomes clear that there must be awareness of self to experience an expectation. So...yes CT...Ego is very much involved in the idea of Sin.

One reason we created the EGO experience is so that the feelings of *failed expectations*, created at the very beginning of the journey of separation, could be made very real and so be understood.

145

Let's also look at your contention that God does not have expectation as we experience in this ego realm. You say that God **knows.** The definition of Sin that was given to me does not say that God had expectations; it simply says that our **thought** or **awareness** of not being able to meet those real or supposed expectations is the root of Sin. Whether or not the Source actually does or does not have expectations is a very different question, an important one nevertheless.

I want to relate a very simple experience that happened today that totally helped me with the very issues that CT is raising in these two quotes.

Carolynne was sharing in meeting today how difficult it was for her to get involved in this SIN issue. She found a lot of resistance in herself to it. During this time her right ear clogged up. Perhaps she pushed some wax down inside the ear canal...perhaps it was caused by congestion. She related this *physical* ear condition to her not wanting to hear these ideas, *emotionally*. As she was sharing these thoughts and her previous experiences of sin-consciousness she said:

I just wanted my (heavenly) Father not to be disappointed in me.

This whole ear experience precipitated Carolynne making this awesome statement...one we can all relate too. What a beautiful way of acknowledging that we thought that we could not meet his expectations! If you have had children or do have children, you know how often you hide your expectations, your hopes, from them, lest you put too much on them. Instead you let them feel only those expectations that they know they **can** meet, like ...*clean your room...* or...*in bed by nine...*Why? You do it to avoid creating sin in your children towards you that they cannot understand.

How many Fathers have so wanted their sons to follow in their footsteps that they created disappointment in themselves and feelings of failure in their sons? On that basis alone we can relate to the idea of the Source having expectations of us

Expectations are the specific formations of hope. Paul said: Love hopes all things...perhaps its OK for God to have hope in you?

DEATH represents **SEPARATION**
(Visible, Physical)   (Spiritual, Invisible)

Dear Reader:

Why is it important for us to understand the concept of Sin? Here is a thought given by Mary Lou Christianson in our discussion group:

I agree that living in the Christ mind is the only solution! I believe this overindulgence in the topic of sin was birthed by the religious leaders who used it as a way to control the people by convincing them they were guilty and creating enough shame to get the people to give them their wealth to avoid going to hell (also a created image for this purpose). This was used to capture whole countries as in the case where the King of England gave his country to the Vatican as payment for his sins and those of his family, and to this day, this contract stands. This is the foundation of the bondage that exists today in the system of taxation of land and income. It is all based on a lie and is meant to enslave the people of the world to support the powers that think they be. Isn't it great that we can see what is going on so we can direct our wealth and energy elsewhere?

Thank you Mary Lou. If fear based on lies creates control dynamics at the level shown here, we can well imagine that whole worlds have been trapped in layers of shame and fear even in realms beyond the physical. Only true understanding of our journey and the nature and love of the Father can release the creation.

Paul makes a statement about sin that is worthy of note here. *The sting of death is sin.* The sting of the scorpion is the element that gives it power...power to induce fear. It is an awesome thing to watch a scorpion carry its tail above its head, ready to strike.

Death here is a symbolic word. It makes the mind think of the experience of death in this realm, pain, and sorrow. As you remember, all the images of this physical realm speak of greater, more universal truths. In this case, the greater truth is **separation.**

147

One way to test this is to ask: *What do you feel at the moment when death happens? What do you feel at a funeral?* The answer of course is SEPARATION. The body lies there, so still, but you know the person that you laughed and cried with, that you touched and held close....is gone...loneliness and sorrow are the primary emotions.

Imagine a person looking at a corpse...who is suffering the emotion of separation? Not the dead person, but the one that is still alive. Who then is suffering the experience of separation when it says: *As in Adam all died?* Clearly here the corpse represents all the children of Adam...humankind if you like...or all incarnated beings. What did they die to? Clearly they have died to the greater knowing of who they are...they think they are only mortal...they are dead to their former knowing. Then who is suffering the pain of separation? Who are those that are alive, that feel the pain? It must be those looking on and seeing us here in this physical plane. It must be those who exist in spiritual realms and experience separation there, including your greater being in realms of LIGHT. We must be here for them to understand something that they are unable to understand without us....**separation.**

Let's make Paul's statement again: *The sting of death is sin.*

Separation has power because of Sin.
or
The journey of Separation becomes real because of Sin.

Now, let's put the definition of sin in place of the word "sin." We now have the following statement:

It was the thought in us that we were unable to meet the expectations of the Source that caused us (gave us power) to create the journey of separation.

Have you ever been in a relationship where you were convinced that you were not worthy of the other? Have you ever had a sudden feeling like that sweep over you? Or, have you tried to Love someone that had such a feeling about themselves towards you?

Jacob, the grandson of Abraham, flees from his twin brother to live with his uncle Laban, his mother's brother. He is on a journey of separation from Esau, really from himself (his twin). While there he sees "Dove Eyed" Rachel, his soul mate, his love, his eternal flame. However, drunk on his wedding night, he wakes up with Leah, because she is older and culture demands it so. So, for most of his life he lives with those two women. Leah has many children, and after each child is birthed she proclaims...*Now my husband will love me!*

In the story, Rachel dies young and Leah never loses her sense of separateness, here felt as sense of not being loved, aloneness. It is the story of duality, the story of TWO, two women, TWIN brothers. It's the way the Father loves you...as Jacob loved Rachel...the first love of his heart...and the way you feel about your Father that creates the journey, like Leah....always trying , never sure, always creating more experience, more life....to find that knowing of wholeness that you know somewhere deep in you must exist. Rachel is our wholeness; Leah is our sense of separation. Leah is the productive one; her sin is the evolutionary driver.

What does the Source get out of all this? LOVE gets to **know** itself.

THOR 1 Email response #16A: Definition of Sin...Linda

Rokus, I agree that we need to know about sin, to be prepared for others who will come the way we have traveled. But, SIN is SIN. Whether it is the kind that I am thinking of, or as you said, "The SIN I am speaking of lies at a deeper level than any definition we have considered...it cannot be put away until the fulfillment of all things...or as long as consciousness is still unfolding."...OK? ". Sin is Sin. And Jesus DID take all, all means ALL, sin to the cross. Linda.

Let me summarize Linda's thinking:

1. **Sin is something that can be done away with by atonement.**
2. **The whole universe would be better off without it**

These two thoughts are deeply rooted in our Judeo Christian heritage. They are the root of all sacrifice, whether killing of an animal, doing penance, confessing to a priest, wailing at an altar, or just being penitent. All these things do is underscore the deeper meaning of sin...a feeling of inability or unbelief.

149

THOR 1 Email #17: Summary and Synopsis

Dear Reader:

I was well aware before I began this project...which by the way, I love...that I would be touching the Holy Cow of our mutual Judeo Christian heritage. That Holy Cow is the subject of Sin. Our concept of it totally permeates all our religious thought and the fabric of our culture. I have also become aware that we are like Naaman, the leper. He came to the Prophet of Israel wanting to be healed of leprosy, a type of sin. The word of his servant girl brought him there. When the prophet made no Hocus Pocus, required no money, had no difficult thing to be done only that he bathe seven times in the river Jordan, Naaman was offended. He was about to leave until his servant brought him to his senses by a simple question: *Would you have done it had the prophet required something difficult?* Perhaps our religious sensibility has such offense at the simplicity of the thought of failed expectations.

The first 15 emails I have written were all preparation so I could write email #16...**A Definition of Sin.** They can be simply summarized as follows:

5. God, the ONE, the Living Light, the Energy that is Aware of Itself, is all that exists. And God is LOVE

6. Love had a desire. Love wanted to know itself and experience ALL that it could be.

7. To do so Love needed an Object to fill a need. That need is our beginning. We are the desire of the Father's heart. He needed a Son to Love Him and to be loved by Him. The Journey of Love, the journey of Separation begins.

8. In the beginning, before any thing was created, we were created as pure consciousness. We began our journey by forming thoughts. Our very first thought was in response to the inestimable, unconditional LOVE we began to experience. It was this: *How and what can I ever give to this awesome LOVE in return for what it is giving me?* We wondered: *Am I able to meet its expectations of me?*

How strange our egos are. We require that a Theory of Reality MUST be very difficult, a very profound revelation. Surely it must take a scientist or a philosopher to understand these great mysteries, when in fact the truth of the universe, its beginning, its purpose are continually acted out in the experiences of our lives, if we will only look at them, read the opened book. So it is that some, when they hear the things I say and write, set it aside. It cannot be that human, that simple.

A thought so simple, so true in every human relationship, a thought that creates the experience of shame and guilt, surely this is too simple to be our beginning.

Carolynne and I discuss these matters a great deal, usually in the context of our lives. We were discussing this very question...*Can the beginning of all things lie in a question as simple as: Did God want an experience? Did He want to experience Himself? Did He want to know His own Love? Is that how all this got started?*...That Night she had a dream...I asked her to share it...Here it is:

*I had a dream in April of 2005. In the dream Rokus and I were in a huge auditorium filled with people. (I would estimate the auditorium held 500-1000 people.) Rokus prophesied:" Someone is going to have a remembrance of what it was like before we came here" (The earth dimension). I remember in the dream that I was very excited about hearing **what** it was like before we came and **why** we came. The next day it was me (much to my surprise) that had the remembrance during the night. I got up and said "I know why we came. We came because of LOVE" It seemed like it should be something more. However, as I said that, people began having all sorts of experiences. Some were being slain in the spirit, speaking in tongues, dancing, and singing. Holy pandemonium swept the place...*

Thank you Carolynne

As you know we do have an online discussion going. It is very exiting, many good thoughts are being expressed, and much joy is experienced. Participate if you want to. We discuss these emails I am sending all of you at length. From time to time I will share some of your responses.

THOR 1 Email #18: Post Traumatic Stress. Why Look At Sin?

Dear Readers:

Thank for taking the time to read these articles. I believe they will turn out to be extremely significant as the curtain of ignorance is drawn from our minds and we begin to see the creation and its purpose from the point of view of original intent.

Allow me to make the following observation. I have noticed from the discussion of the presented ideas on the THOR forum that the idea of **sin as we have understood it** is very deeply engrained in us. As I said before, I too am very interested in having my programming changed, to have the old grooves smoothed away and new neural pathways created in my brain. It is slowly happening to me. I am loosing my aversion to the word "SIN" as I realize that sin has to do with self-created, false expectations. The word "expectations" is already strongly associated in my mind with "sin." I am changing.

I have tried to find another word or create another word to substitute for the big "S" word and so avoid the post traumatic stress involved when we use it. However...I think...we need to walk through our discomfort, not around it.

Having said all that, I want to encourage you NOT to feel that you have to accept this new definition as the Gods-Truth. Rather do this: Help me to entertain the thought of it and see what will happen. As they say, the proof of the pudding is in the eating.

In order for the truth of our thesis to be validated, we will need to show that this more fundamental definition of the idea of sin actually harmonizes with scriptural use of that term. It must also give insight into the idea of sin that cannot be gained without it.

To those that would say that there is no Sin or think it insignificant...I might note that the idea of Sin begins with the first pair in the Garden and stays with us until the lake of fire in the last chapters of the book of revelation. Furthermore, the dominant theme of the Christian Hebrew heritage is the theme of the Cross, which certainly includes the concept of Sin. To think that we can understand the whole of our journey from Worlds immaterial and Celestial realms, through time and space to planet Earth, without addressing and understanding the subject of Sin...is... well...you put a word in there for me.

I might liken the situation to that of a little girl who was adopted at the age of five and sexually abused by her step father for almost seven years. She appeared on Oprah yesterday to tell her story, the man who was abusing her lost interest when she began to develop breasts. Carolynne and I were discussing this and wondered what may have been in the man's mind to drive him to do such extreme things. What was it he wanted? Did he want to be cleansed by her purity and innocence? If it was just sex, why quit when she becomes a woman?

Remember my thesis that everything that happens in this realm has already happened or is happening in higher planes. Is this event...this abuse...really here to be looked at so that understanding can come, not only here but in the higher planes where the deed really originated?

Man, in the process of his incarnation, and in being placed on this globe, has suffered abuse at really deep levels. We have been violated at levels we are only now being able to look at. Intelligent beings have insinuated their truth upon our being, raped our minds, while we were yet children....we had no idea what was happening to us. We have been abused. Now, as we are reaching the age of puberty, the beginning of manhood, the adoption as Sons, we need to look at what has happened to us. We need to be on Oprah, the heavenly mother...El Shadii...to tell our story so we can be free from the shame and pain and become all that we are. We need to know and say clearly that:

It Was Not Our Fault

We can remain in denial, pretending that all sin is gone and atoned for. We can desperately cling to our concepts of moral purity as spirituality and remain in "denial." Or we can discuss the subject of Sin, Shame, and Guilt, allow ourselves to see it from the point of view of the eternal plan, the Father's eyes, tell our story and be free. It's your call.

THOR 1 Email #19: Harmonizing With the Scriptures on Sin

Dear Readers:

Now that I have presented a more fundamental understanding of our experience we call Sin, it is essential that we see how this understanding harmonizes with the use of that word in the scriptures.

Please do not feel discouraged if you cannot, at this point, fully see the need or the relevance of all this discussion of sin. It is difficult to look **AT** our experience from the point of view **OF** our experience. There is not a one of us that does not intensely want this planet to be cleansed of all the filth that seems to be the cause of so much pain in so many innocent children and adults alike.

Some, whom I hold in high esteem and consider to be more gifted that I, have openly stated their disagreement with the ideas I am presenting. I am not discouraged. I realize that I need that opposition if for no other reason than to see my own resistance to greater thought. Understand that my greatest desire is not that you **accept** my ideas; no, it is rather that you **research and explore** an idea that was **given** to me from a greater realm. *It is the Glory of God to conceal a thing; but the honor of Kings to search out a matter.*

Nor would I have you think that somehow it is brain-capacity that is important here. Yes a minimal ability to entertain thoughts and consider them...but we all have that ability. It is rather your ability to hold a thought EMOTIONALLY that is important. It is the emotions that are the gateway between the worlds of Light and this present realm. Our cellular inbred resistance is emotionally based and needs to be released to let us go into the greater realms of Light.

Let us look at the understanding of SIN under the age of Law and the age of Grace, the Church age. Sin, as **Transgression of the Law** and Sin as **Missing the Mark** have something obviously in common. In both cases there is...guess what...an **expectation** to be met. Now remember...the basic idea of sin is as follows:

SIN is the **thought** or the **awareness** that I cannot meet your expectation.

154

In the case of the Law, the very clear expectation is that the worshipper is to OBEY the commandment. The failure to meet the expectation is not just a **thought**, it is real, and it is **awareness.** The Law makes sin real. Paul says: *If it were not for the Law, I would not have known (understood) sin.* Penalty and sin-offerings are provided as a measure of grace to enable the worshipper to continue, but the expectation is and remains clear to this day: Sin is the **transgression of the law.**

The expectation that is inherent in the thought of **missing the mark** is the striving for excellence. Paul the Apostle is the superb proponent of this thought. He compares the spiritual journey to a RACE and the eternal reward as a CROWN of glory. His reference is to the games that were the original Olympic competitions. The winner would receive a simple laurel wreath...crowning him. Paul also makes clear that this achieving or conquering or overcoming is not an exercise of the Ego but rather of the spiritual man...yet...and very clearly so...there is great **expectation.** Hit the mark!

It is wonderful to realize that both of these experiences of sin that have been created at different spiritual levels in the journey of evolving consciousness of Man, are needed to help us understand the more basic meaning and purpose of sin. All three compartments of the tabernacle, the outer court, the inner court and the most Holy place, each comparing to the three ages of Law, Grace and the Kingdom, have blood in them. It is written: *Without the shedding of blood there is no remission of sin.* We need to **understand** in order to go on...and as I have said before...we can leave nothing behind that is unresolved or not understood. We are looking for that "aha" moment...so we can say: *Now I understand.*

THOR 1 Email # 19 A: Sin and Mistaken Identity

Dear Friends:

The following email is a result of the discussion group on the subject of a Theory of Reality. The responses that have been so helpful are the ones that question the validity of what I am saying and I do appreciate them very much. Please feel free to comment either way...let me know if you don't want to be quoted or named...I respect your sense of personal identity even if it is somewhat mistaken. {Chuckle}

Janis Rose writes: *I just kept hearing that verse in Genesis "Sin is crouching at the door and its desire is for you and **you must master it.**" It was spoken to Cain when his countenance was fallen over something done to him that caused him to see himself differently; once again sin is shown in the context of us seeing ourselves in our mistaken identity.*

Thank you Janis...we are definitely getting somewhere. I never particularly wanted anyone to just buy into the thought that I myself wanted to assimilate...I just want you to consider it like you do here...Thank You.

May I add this as a perspective?

I do very much see the concept of mistaken identity, and I can see why one would call it sin. After all, it is "missing the mark", which was the New Testament word used for sin. Yes...we see ourselves from a lowered perspective...however the "mistaken" part also comes from a limited perspective. From the divine point of view, the lowered identity was intentional and desired, not mistaken. You and I needed this "false" identity to create the journey of separation just as much as you need the sin-thought to energize it. So yes, mistaken identity is closely connected to the idea of sin, but they are not synonymous. Allow me to enlarge.

If I may take some license here, with your permission...I would reword your sentence this way:

Instead of saying: *Seeing ourselves in our **mistaken** identity.* This *seeing* you can only do from a place of enlightenment...I would rather say: *Seeing ourselves from the point of view of our **limited** identity.* The word "limited" is without imputation of any fault. It was a purposed experience.

So...yes, *Sin* and *Mistaken Identity* appear in the same context. Let me show how I see them connected but not the same. Mistaken Identity is a thought *about* you; I do not think that the first thought that appeared in us was a thought *about* ourselves. When we look at child development, it is a long time before a child can begin to reflect on itself. Its first thoughts are spontaneous reactions to its *experience*, its feelings. Feelings are induced by environment, and only later by self reflection.

156

I consider the scenario to be like this: As our emerging state of separate self began we felt the awesomeness of our Father's unconditional love. Our first thoughts were responses to this feeling. One of our first thoughts may have been:

Oh...I do not want my Father to be disappointed in me!
OR
How can I return this awesome great love?
OR
Am I worthy of this great love?

Now you can say that these thoughts are the result of mistaken identity, but there really was no mistake about this new identity. It was just beginning to form. It was innocent as a child's. It was new and unformed. It was exactly what was desired.

Each of these thoughts **assumes** that there was an expectation on the part of the Source. Whether or not such an expectation actually existed is a different question. So...

The thought that I am unable to meet
the expectation of the Source...

precedes the idea of a fully formed identity. In fact this thought was a spring board for the formation of a separate identity, an evolutionary driver. My conclusion about the idea of mistaken identity is:

Sin is a generating force of thought that enabled us to form a sense of self, an Identity. This identity served us on the road of separation, and when we finally began to see that separation is not real, just a creation of the mind. We concluded that identity to be "mistaken."

THOR 1 Email #20: Sin Conceived Shame

Hello Dear Reader:

It seems to me, from reading the responses I get, that we are ready to proceed to the next phase. Those of you that can see my intent in defining sin as a primary thought in the development of consciousness will be as anxious as I am to explore the implications for understanding our experience. Those of you that still resist entertaining this thought about sin have heard it enough to be able to at least consider it, whether you actually see it as significant or not. Remember, whether or not our definition of sin is absolutely correct is not as important as this question:

Is this manner of looking at Sin helpful to us in understanding our journey?

Remember the analogy of the tree...the myriads of God-Seeds that were expelled? Some of them caught the high draft, going for miles and miles...others spiraled down quickly, but all of them went on a Journey, a Journey of exploration, becoming and of discovery. Remember how the Tree felt...there were no requirements, no rules or conditions...no expectations were placed on the seeds. There was only an intense longing and desire that Love might be all that it can become.

As we began in this awesome newness, in this unformed consciousness, without boundaries, without definition...we were struck by a thought that formed itself in response to this overwhelming, all encompassing love: What if we cannot return this Love? What if we cannot meet the expectations of the Source?

This totally new thought was a necessary first step in the forming of consciousness. As we began defining a separate self we experienced for the first time the most basic of all feelings...a feeling of un-worth. In the presence of such total Love we began to experience what we now know to be shame. It was not caused by anything we had done for as yet there had been no action. We created shame about our very existence...our own being...the beginning formation of the idea of a Self, the most precious gift ever given.

Sin when it was entertained conceived in us what we now know as the primary negative emotion...shame.

Nobody told us about it. Nobody forced it on us. We were not raped, seduced, or abused in any way when we created the Sin-Thought. This Sin-Thought in turn conceived in us the beginning formation of self...the program of separation kicked in. Consciousness began to form. Identity took shape, and we began the journey of the separate self.

The true understanding of this process will release us and untold generations from our deepest fear. We have fear of some force outside of ourselves that may have seduced or deceived us. A fear that always debilitates, paralyzing us, causing us to look to another and not to that of God that has always been the essence of our own being. The scriptures call it the fear of death. It is the fear separation.

The prison doors are swinging open for us and for Worlds and Realms of thought that lie beyond our awareness. They are intimately connected to us and released with us as we remember and take back the only power there is, the power freely given to us as our very essence...LOVE

THOR 1 Email 21: Sin and Grace...Descending and Ascending

Dear Friends:

> *Sin the thought of my incompleteness. Through its Shame I descend. Grace is the awareness of my wholeness. Through its Joy I ascend.*

In the same way as our vision in this natural realm is limited to a narrow band of frequencies, in the middle of the spectrum of electromagnetic waves, called visible light; so also our awareness of reality as physical beings is limited to a narrow range of perceptional frequencies called the third dimension. The scripture speak of things **in** the Earth, **above** the earth, and **below** the Earth. The Mormons speak of Terrestrial, Celestial and Tellestial Glory. Here **in** the Earth, we can create experiences that will help us **know** and **understand in other realms of light.**

We have focused on **Shame** and its cousin **Guilt** because this very low vibration of the emotional body is so important in our beginning the journey of consciousness, and finally, in our becoming incarnate. You may feel my pre-occupation with Sin and Shame to be obsessive compulsive behavior, and well it may be. However, if we take just a brief look at the society we live in, the daily fare of TV viewers, we might conclude that humanity in general has some kind of introspective compulsive interest in violence, sex, and crime. Perhaps we would like to exclude ourselves from them; however, we cannot. They are the reason we came, and our fate is tied to theirs in Love.

Let's balance the scales a little in regards to sin. We see it to exist with its polar opposite, Grace. If you can say: *I missed the mark,* then you can certainly also say: *I hit the mark!* Every child needs to experience fulfillment in a job well done and feelings of worth, the very opposites of sin. They are important feelings.

If you can ask the most elementary and painful question of your existence: *Is it okay to be me?* You can equally well affirm the awesomeness of your existence with thanksgiving and say: *I am so glad to experience all that I am and all that I am becoming!*

In fact, as is easily seen in homeopathy and in the preventive measure of inoculation, it may take a little disease to stimulate the body to health and wellness. **So the experience of Sin is essential to attain to the height and depth of Awareness of Being**. In early child development it is so important for a child, under the loving guidance of a parent, to experience the full range of its emotions through Sadness and Joy, Success and Failure. Only much later in life, if at all, it may discover that true life really exists in a much larger scope than this present realm of opposites.

Most important in considering all this is the fact that the emotional body is the doorway to ascension. It was used to lower you to the nakedness of mortality through shame. You may use it now, through joy, to ascend, clothed in the Glory of your greater knowing.

To truly experience the fullness of Joy needed for ascension you and I will have to totally embrace, with thanksgiving and with understanding, our experience of sin and shame.

It is important for us to UNDERSTAND Sin and Shame so that our emotional bodies can be cleansed. Our fine twined linen garment needs to be washed in the Blood of the Lamb. The deep seated toxic Shame is so removed from the cells of our bodies. Our chakras can be opened, unsealing the book of our incarnate experience. We are as the Lamb that has been slain. We are receiving the book from the One who sits upon the throne of our being.

It is in the reading of this book of our incarnate experience that we finally understand. We know. We remember. We ascend, clothed with the Glory that we had with Him before the worlds were.

THOR 1 Email 22: How Deep Is Toxic Shame? Will You Look?

Dear Friends:

In the movie "The Matrix," Morpheus has the challenge of explaining to Neo that what he sees to be real is in fact not real at all. It is only real to his mind. He must explain to Neo that the Matrix is a computer generated reality program that Neo is experiencing only in his mind and in reality his body is in a factory with thousands of others being used as batteries to produce energy for the machines that have taken over the planet. At one point Neo is given a choice, a blue pill or a red pill. The blue pill will let Neo go back to where he was; remove all remembrance of recent events. The red pill will take him into the unknown, the unexplored greater reality which Morpheus compares to the Rabbit Hole in "Alice in Wonderland." Of course, Neo takes the red pill...just like you did.

What am I saying? That which Spirit is talking to us about, **reality**, the **old paradigm**, and awakening from the **dream state**, is very much a parallel to that Movie. The shift happening in our awareness and our thinking about who we are, who God is, and what reality is for us, is as earth shattering to us as it is for Neo in the movie.

This shift in us cannot happen simply by entertaining new ideas. Our minds, programmed in their thinking and perceptions of what we believe, will not change those ideas simply by a process of thought; simply by considering ideas that are truer than others. It requires the Holy Spirit creating situations in our lives and illuminating our heart-minds. It takes places of impossibility where we either plunge off the cliff or draw back to the security of old thought patterns. It requires a time when the still small voice of God in you whispers a thought that takes you in a direction that you did not desire; a direction that seems impossible and that causes you to loose everything you have but an impulse that you cannot refuse. To not receive that thought, and not go where it bids you to go, is as impossible for you as it was for Neo...it is your destiny.

We are of those that will make a change for all men that have been on this planet and all men that shall yet be born here. It is a change of perception. It is an opening of the understanding, and it is a shift in awareness. You know it if you are part of this change and

161

you cannot resist its demands on your life. You would rather give up your life here than disobey this call, this apprehension to purpose. You are Neo, the new One...the ONE that is to come.

To become fully aware of this change in your perception of the world of reality, you must be willing to review the beginning, the journey, and the end of all that Man is. You must let yourself feel and reconsider what Sin is and how it has served man's evolution. You cannot walk past the drunk on your path or the abused child in another...you must look and consider...you came for this reason.

You must let yourself experience shame, feel its awesome downward pull, its very low vibratory frequency...feel it, know it, see how it is the child born from Sin that was conceived in the mind. You must see its awesome devastating yet purposeful effect on the evolution of consciousness. Embrace both...then release all the pain that was used, in ages of struggle, to birth and bring forth a wholly new concept of Man on the planet. This stage of cosmic evolution...this eternal drama on the screen of Human consciousness...this book...as yet unopened...sealed with seven seals...is in the hand of Him who sits upon the throne.

We came here into this physical reality, this place where all can be seen and where all is manifest. We came to see what we could not fully understand, SIN and SHAME. They are the root reasons behind our journey, our evolutionary drivers. So why would you refuse to look?

THOR 1 Email 23: Rachel and Leah, Shame serves our journey

Dear Friends.

As I have stated before, this experience of incarnation, being in the flesh, is like a book that needs to be read. It is a book, or a drama on a stage, purposed to make clear and visible the invisible things such a Love, Joy, Shame, and Sin.

As I have said, the reason it is so difficult to look at shame is because it causes you hide, hide from yourself. That is what denial is all about. We need to understand it.

162

Shame is what was used to propel us into this physical 3-D experience...almost as if we were betrayed. Jesus had to be betrayed to experience his Cross. All of us have experiences of shame and betrayal, experiences that eventually push us into God.

The bible also is a storybook of many incarnations used to display our journey. Almost every event recorded there has multiple layers of esoteric meaning that Spirit can unveil to you to help you understand your path. The story of Jacob, Leah, and Rachel is like that.

It is a beautiful and painful story of Love and Betrayal. Jacob is fleeing from his other half...his twin brother. Already a context is created for the duality we experience in this realm. He meets Rachel at the well, and Leah when he arrives at his uncle's place. The story says: *Leah was tender eyed but Rachel was beautiful and well favored.* In other words, Rachel was a knock-out. Well, you know the story...read it in Genesis chapter 29. Jacob serves seven years for Rachel. Laban makes a great feast...Jacob wakes up the next morning...not with Rachel as he supposed but with Leah....surprise, surprise...Laban, you betrayed me! Well, Laban said....fulfill her week and I will give you Rachel also...custom demands Leah be married first.

How would you like to be Leah? The older one, unattractive, undesired, passed off by guile, now married to a man who clearly prefers the younger sister in every way. Her pathway is paved with shame.

What happens in Leah because of this shame? She becomes fruitful. The scriptures say: *And when the Lord saw that Leah was hated, he opened her womb.*

The story goes on to record how Leah bears four sons. She names each son from the experience of her heart and her desire. The first born, Reuben, means **"Look**, a Son"** and she says: *The Lord hath looked upon my affliction, now therefore my husband will love me.* Her next son, Simeon, means **hearing. S**he says: *Because the Lord heard I was hated therefore hath he given me this son.* The scriptures record: *And she conceived again and bare a son; and said: now this time will my husband be joined unto me because I have born him three sons, therefore his name was called Levi.* Levi means **joined** or **attached**.

163

Notice how deep the sin thought is in Leah's heart "I am not able to meet my husband's expectations." Her desire to please him drives her on. Feel the shame in her life. She compares herself to an image, her sister. She has feelings of being afflicted, abandoned, and hated, and through them, she conceived her sons. Conceiving her sons typifies the creating of her experience and her awareness of self. The motivation of her life comes from her shame, always believing for God to hear and see her predicament.

Finally she bears again. This time she lays it all down. She realizes some deep inner truth and says: *Now will I **praise** the Lord* and calls her next son Judah which of course means **Praise.**

Notice that this time she does not name her son from something she requires of the Lord or something she desires from Him...she has come home...She says: *I will praise the Lord.*

The story of Leah and Rachel is the soul's journey in material worlds through shame to fulfillment and realization of inner worth and wholeness. The two sisters are in continual conflict over their mutual husband, material consciousness...the deep intense desire, their seeming way to attain worth, is to please the husband...someone outside, apart from themselves. The story is full of conflict, competition, love, achievement, and fulfillment. It is the story of our Ego journey in physical form. It is the story that displays the root thoughts of our beginnings in consciousness...the desire to please rooted in the sin thought of not meeting an expectation. The thought that we are NOT pleasing, creates the desire TO please.

The thought that we are NOT worthy, shame, is the driving motive to prove ourselves, to create and procreate unto our perceived husband.

The story ends with Jacob reconciling to his twin. He purchases a plot of land and raises a sacred altar unto the Lord calling it "El-ELOHE-ISRAEL," The Mighty God of Israel. He uses his given name on this altar. Jacob, by using his new name Israel, is saying:

I have overcome the realm of limitation, the Ego realm. I have come to my greater knowing. I know who I am and I worship only the One true Father of all, the source of my being.

THOR 1 Email 24: Owning Our Experience as Beings of Light

Dear Reader:

We have completed a step and need to evaluate our progress in our journey of creating a New Theory of Reality. Much has been said about Sin. Many evaluating names have been ascribed to it: unbelief, missing the mark, transgression of the law, fraud, wrong doing, and so on. These are names of awareness created from our experience, the scriptures, and our awareness of truth.

Some of these have to do with acts, acts of commission and acts of omission. *"To him who knows to do good, and does it not it is sin."* Such acts cause guilt, and guilt needs atonement.

Sin in the sense of Mistaken Identity or Sin as another personality in you that is making you do what you do not desire to do, lies at a deeper level of awareness of self. Paul knew of this reality when he said: *...if I do what I would not then it is no longer I but Sin that dwells in me....* Such awareness of Sin is rooted in Shame, Shame that causes one to hide from true self and create an alternate personality. Paul also understood Sin as a principle. We see that when he wrote: *...the Law of Sin that dwells in my members...* It is time for a change!

The most important reason for discussing and searching for a true understanding of Sin is that it is ultimately important for us to begin to own our journey.

The time has come for man to stand upright and to shake off the victimization that is rooted in blaming anything separate from himself for his place in consciousness. Man must own his experience and his journey of evolving consciousness.

How can he do this? How can you do this? You need to understand this: *That which has been the seeming cause of all your pain and sorrow was actually of your own creation.* You were the one who first created Sin and Sin consciousness. How did you do that? You did that by a thought, a thought that you created in your infancy of consciousness. It is the thought that you are not able to meet the expectations of the all loving Source of your being, expectations that you imagined yourself.

165

As long as you and I think that there is an external agency that causes you to sin, you will forever be imprisoned by that thought. Even if you were cleansed of all blame towards such an entity or impersonal cause, still, in your memory, you would have a sense of debilitation or powerlessness that would cause you to deny yourself that ultimate emergence of power and glory of being that the Source of all Light and Life gave you as the spark of who you are.

Many of us have thought that our troubles began in the Garden of Eden: the innocence, the lie, the betrayal, the blame and shame, and our subsequent 'fall' into material form and Serpent mentality. However, as I will show more clearly as we go on, that point of our incarnation into material form was actually a sort of final step in our descent from the highest realms of Light and a major turning point in our journey of realizing consciousness and identity.

As I will show, one of the major remedial purposes for this physical experience was to accomplish this very ownership of the journey that we are now considering in this email. As you, in your present experience, free yourself from all entrapment and victimization, then you also free your consciousness of those same feelings in greater realms where they were first created. The whole story created in material form, the Garden, the call of Abraham, the giving of the Law, the Cross of Jesus, his resurrection, and now this emerging of a body of consciousness in a people of Light, was planned and intended from the beginning when Elohim said: *Let us make man in our image and likeness.* In other words....*Let us, by our incarnation, create a video of images for all to see who we are and what the purpose of the Father is.*

THOR 1 Email #24 A: Mary Lou, Subjection to Vanity

Mary Lou writes:
"For the creature was made subject to vanity, not willingly, but by reason of him who hath subjected the same in hope," Romans 8:20.
Vanity, being self consciousness which also encompasses sin consciousness, was imposed by whom? Though your theory about this may sound good, it really isn't the whole picture Rokus, unless you see yourself as the one who did the subjecting of creation to this vanity to bring your theory to this realm. This was clearly done by one to another and not by anyone to himself.

Dear Mary Lou. Thank you for the input, and yes, at first sight it does seem to imply that we are unwilling participants in this so called creature venture, perhaps there are many in flesh that do come in such a way. Paul does not specifically say that to the church in Rome. Reading the scripture more carefully reveals two subjects in this chapter, the creature and the Sons of God. Verse 19: *For the earnest expectation of the* **creature** *waits for the manifestation of the* **sons of God***.* Paul is speaking to the sons of God about the creature when he says:..*made subject to vanity...not willingly..in hope...*

Why is Paul raising the subject of willingness here? Clearly he means that God is responsible. How? Is he saying that God is directly responsible for sin, death and disease, that we have no choice? I do not see that. In Romans Chapter 8 Paul is in the middle of releasing the Roman Christians from the bondage of Law. I hear Paul saying:

Look at the creation; do not put blame on them. Do not lay on them the Law that I am taking from you. If you must hold somebody accountable then blame God. He was the initiator of the journey of separation in hope and you are the fulfillment of that hope. You will deliver the groaning creation

THOR 1 Email #25: Are You Frustrated At Our Progress?

Dear Readers:

We are slowly progressing through worlds of thought that have been on this planet for many ages. It is difficult to clearly think about beginning things because our experience has already taken us beyond them. We are already breathing fresh air. It seems we are taking steps backwards in talking about Sin and the Law.

Yet we need to understand the old paradigms and our limited, perception of them in order to clear ourselves for take-off. We are going into the stratosphere and space beyond where greater reality awaits us. This greater reality, that is so intensely inviting, requires us to leave the past behind; all its joy, its lessons, its ecstasy and sorrow. Yet we cannot do so until true understanding comes. We need the understanding of beginning and purpose that enables us to look at the whole of the experience of humanity. We can then agree with the Light, and say: *It is Good.*

Some of you, my dear readers, take my writings very personally and try to fit the whole of it into your experience. I am aware that you need your personal experience to be able to relate to the truth we are considering, but you and I are only a part, not the whole.

Let me quote from an email written to me from our very excellent discussion group that is formed around these writings. If the person who wrote these lines reads this email I hope he can accept the thought that his response greatly serves my purpose for these writings, and I am truly thankful for it. Whatever frustrations any of us have are all miniatures of the total and deep frustration in the human experience itself. We want to understand who we are and why we are here.

Dear Rokus: Please do not send me anymore of these writings. I do not need someone to try and rewrite the Bible. Sin, shame, guilt and Lord knows what else. Jesus Christ Rokus! You are not bringing in any new revelations, all I hear is you trying to re-write what already has been done. Sin, shame, guilt, evil...no evil, we are God, we are not, we are... if we could only remember who we are? What if we can not? My God, guys and girls, what are we trying to do here?

Again, to the writer of those lines...thank you for expressing yourself with such punctuation. You clearly show the frustration that we all have.

You that are reading these lines have already dealt with sin, guilt, and shame in your lives. If you had not, you would not be able to read any of this. It would be meaningless to you. We are like a spaceship in orbit around a planet. The gravitational pull against our take-off has exhausted most of the fuel that we took on for that very purpose, and we must now cast off the burners and empty tanks that will only be a hindrance to our journey through space. It is essential that we do look at those things we no longer need, recognize the purpose they served, know that we need them no longer. We can then rid ourselves of such excess baggage and point our ship for the stars...go into hyper-drive!!!! Yahooooo!! Here we come!

I am writing you again, as I have done before, to let you know how much I need you to write these emails...including particularly the one who wrote the quote above. As you read, whether you reply in writing or not, you are responding. Your response stimulates me and thoughts come in me that I did not know I had. I have a general sense of the truth. It becomes clear in me as you agree with it or resist it. Thank you all again for reading and reacting; stay with me.

THOR 1 Email #26: Your Physical Experience, A Living Dream

Dear Reader:

To understand this experience of being physical from the point of view of our greater being, our existence in heaven, we need to look **AT** our experience. It holds the key. **The physical realm helps us to create visual and tangible experiences for the purpose of understanding.** We gain understanding in the here and now, but even more so in the greater realms where we eternally exist.

In most dreams the elements and events are symbolic while the feelings you experience are real. Up until the time my daughter Eva was three years old, she often dreamt of literal events, events that would happen the next day. One day she came down the stairs...*Mommy, Mommy, I am going to have chocolate cake today.* Mommy of course knew that there was no chocolate cake in the house...but Eva was not to be persuaded...*I dreamt it Mommy!* Sure enough, about noon she was invited to a birthday party, chocolate cake and all.

However, after she became a little older, it seemed that she made a shift. As she was more integrated into her physical experience her dreams ceased being literal and became as we all experience dream life. Our dreams are the connectedness between the realms.

In the same way that you dream symbolically about your earth experience, your earth experience can be seen as a symbolic dream about your eternal existence. I like to call specific physical events "Living Dreams." Such "Living Dreams" need interpretation in the same way we interpret the dreams we experience normally.

We are all aware that this present experience of ourselves is happening in what we describe as a lower frequency. Events in this life are specific, concrete, clearly defined, and create opportunity for judgments, decisions, and choices to be made. We can look at the experiences of this life, the physical ones, as if they are a dream. Each element in the dream represents something or someone in a different plane of existence. Sometimes scenarios that we collectively experienced are slowed down and repeated on the stage of an individual's life. There is a powerful story of Love and Betrayal told in the scriptures in the Book of Hosea. The story starts out like this:

And YHWH said to Hosea: Go take unto thee a wife of whoredoms: for the Land has committed great whoredom, departing from YHWH.

Have you ever read the story? He marries a harlot, has children by her, and is told what to name each child prophetically foretelling what will happen to the nation of Israel in history. She then leaves Hosea for another man...ends up on an auction block where Hosea is told to go buy her back, even told how much to pay for her. In the end, she lives with him in faithfulness.

Hello...are you hearing me? If Hosea's life was contracted to display greater purpose do you think it is possible that your life too is contracted from before you came here? Moreover, can we conceive the thought that Adam came to display a certain scenario on this planet, a Living Dream, in which each element has a specific and significant meaning so that all on-lookers from cosmic realms might **see** and **understand?**

I want to share with you a specific living dream that was acted out in my house, that will help us understand the purpose for the creation of material worlds. If YHWH could use a man's life to portray His relationship and dealing with the children of Jacob throughout their generations in time, is it too much to assume that The Light can use my house and the people in it to create a scenario to confirm to me what I am hearing about our journey in Time and our descent into Matter?

Here is the story: A young woman was visiting in our home. She was depressed about her self loathing. Someone had told her to take a mirror, look at herself and say: *You are beautiful...I love you.* One morning, as I went down early to check the woodstove, she was lying on the couch, looking at herself, and saying those words. She was somewhat embarrassed and explained what she was doing. I talked

170

with her for a minute and as I went back up the stairs I commented: *Maybe something happened in your childhood that caused you to have this deep seated shame...this self-loathing.*

At the top of the stairs, I took a peek into Eva's bedroom. She was sleeping there along with a niece and her sister Cornelia. As I opened the door, I noticed an unusual, pungent, odor but strangely enough, I just closed the door, wondering at the odor but not interfering.

I had been in bed for perhaps 15 minutes when there was a sudden commotion in the house, like herd of elephants. Cornelia had awakened the rest, the room was full of smoke, and blankets were smoldering and being pushed into the shower. Eva was running down the stairs with sooth on her face.

Apparently a hot curling iron had been left under the pillow. It burned a hole one foot in diameter and an inch deep, into the mattress before the smoke became pungent enough to awaken, not Eva but Cornelia who was sleeping on a mattress on the floor. The curling iron itself was a twisted melted mass of plastic and metal.

The young woman on the couch awoke with a start. The first thing she saw was a young girl, Eva, running down the stairs with sooth on her face. That visual event triggered a memory. When this woman was just a small girl she had an easy-bake oven and had used the light bulb from it to read by in bed. Apparently she fell asleep with the hot light on the bed sheets. The bed caught on fire. It burned the house down in the middle of winter.

As she saw Eva coming down the stairs, the memory of that event flooded back in her mind. The house had burned down with all the Christmas gifts for the whole family. She remembered standing in the snow, watching everything going up in flames, and hearing her mother say to her: *Look what you have done!*

Here was the source of shame and feelings of unwarranted guilt that had locked her into self loathing for thirty years of her life. The cause had been repressed in an attempt to live with the shame...but the shame, deep seated as it was, persisted, waiting for a time when she could take responsibility for her journey and see the event for what it really was...not her fault.

That is the Living Dream...what of the interpretation? We too in our infant humanity contracted a false sense of Guilt and Shame about ourselves that has locked us into self loathing these many long ages. The young woman is all of us, Elohim kind, our greater being that desired incarnation. We are looking into the mirror created by our physical experience to help us understand what happened to us to cause us to have shame and self loathing. You and I are doing this as we read this email. Reading with the easy bake oven light represents experience with limited understanding, earthly wisdom, what you and I have called carnality. It is the knowledge of the flesh, the tree of knowledge of good and evil. The bed is the place where you choose to sleep. The sleep is our incarnation. Burning the house down and loosing all our gifts is the loss of our house from heaven, our greater knowing, the glory of true understanding and eternal relationship. Loosing the giftedness is our feelings of disempowerment. The mother that accused the child as being the original cause of all evil is the lie we were told by Mother Religion about ourselves in the Garden. Eva represents our child-like experience of humanity, our lowered knowing of self. The sooth on her face is the repeated experiences in this realm that remind us of what happened in what we call the Fall, our descent, the staircase she is coming down. The steps down are the continually repeated lies, deceit, blame, and shame...all the feelings and attitudes described and experienced by Eve in the garden. I suppose I am the Angels that watch over but are not allowed to interfere...the drama must unfold as planned.

To sum it up we could say that in our childish perceptions of reality, the Garden experience, we took on a self loathing because we accepted a lie, we could not understand. *Look what you have done.* That explains WHAT happened to us

After the whole experience was over and I let myself think what could have happened...what if...what if.....Why did I not install a smoke alarm? I do think we should take responsibility for our journey! We need to tell our children what drugs, alcohol and sex can do. We can put safeguards in place....however...in our lives, those of us who have come to redeem this planet and restore true knowledge to creation, our lives our not our own, nor are our children's lives, we belong to the eternal purpose for which we were sent and the Angels will protect and keep us for that purpose.

What are we learning? The shame that we have is rooted in lies, lies we have been told, lies we have created ourselves, lies that blame us as the cause of evil because of disobedience to our Father. The truth is that we came here in obedience to the Father to create an experience, a living dream.

Our Real Shame is an image we created as a result of sin. Sin is a thought we created that acts as an evolutionary driver of consciousness. This shame needed to be re-enacted in the flesh worlds in order for understanding to come to our higher being. The events in the Garden, like the scenario in my house, are a created reality to help us get at the real cause of our shame and sin...so here is my concluding statement:

Material reality was created by the Elohim for a Living Dream that would help all worlds understand the Journey of separation and know the Love of the Father.

The truth about you is that you are a being of Light, a being of great power and Love, a being that totally loves the Father of Light. You have come into material form to do His will...You are exquisitely beautiful!

THOR 1 Email 27: WHY Elohim Incarnated As Man

Hello Dear Reader.

I have said it repeatedly and will say it again...thank you for reading these articles. I mail quite a few of them, in my scale of things, but even if only a few of you read them it is incentive for me to write again. I have an expectation that drives me; a bit humbling to think that way, after defining Sin as the thought of a failed expectation.

I am experiencing the unfolding of these thoughts as I write. If you can find a minute to respond to something that inspired you or that raised a question...you can experience that unfolding with me.

For some years I have known that our **view** of what we call the 'Fall', the story related in Genesis, was wrong. I knew we were viewing awesome events there but the glasses of shame that filtered the light of our understanding caused us to experience more sin-consciousness and we always turned away condemned. The key to unlock this dilemma is first to realize that the **Garden** Story is indeed **NOT** the same as the **Creation** story in the first chapter. Eden, is NOT the beginning, it is only the beginning of the incarnate, lowered sate of man. The book of Hebrews describes it: ...*made him a little lower*...I prefer to read it: ...lowered Elohim into his Adamic form

To give a different context to the word: *The Lord God planted a garden*, perhaps a comparison to what we call real life might illustrate. Hitler was looking for the allies to invade Europe, to create a beach head. He consulted with psychics and apparently to the last minute was convinced they were coming across the English Channel. There was a great deal of disinformation being propagated by radio and other means to help him think that way. To keep the landing spot and method of arrival a secret was very important. The enormity of the operation was awesome, we were successful, we managed to land our soldiers on European soil with loss yes, but the mission was a success. Many gave their lives for the cause of freedom.

So it is with the lowering of Adam into this hostile environment of the three dimensional plane. Deceit, confusing thoughts and erroneous ideas have shrouded the truth of our beginning for many ages. We could not see or understand. Jesus purposefully told his truth in parables, by his own admission, so that the ruling element of his day might deceive themselves into thinking they knew what he was a saying when in fact they knew little or nothing of what He said. Jesus himself had to take the disciples apart and show them the sacred meaning of his words.

To this day, certain religious elements are totally misled by the first few chapters in Genesis. Some scientists use it to scoff at the scriptures simply because the King James mistranslation uses the word "day" for a period of time. Priests have used it to condemn women for all time. Religion in general has built a prison called original sin, to enslave the minds of men.

What do I say? I say that Sin did not begin in Eden. When Paul says: *By one man sin entered the world,* it means what it says. The experience of sin, which existed from the beginning, took on a whole new color. Sin became more easily recognized when man took on a physical form. Sin became an act of disobedience. Shame also, in this lowering, became more real and intense; it was felt as NAKEDNESS, the loss of eternal awareness and glory. A new dynamic, guilt, the consequence of wrong doing, became our experience.

Why did all this happen? Why was it necessary to make sin and shame made more real? For one reason and one reason only, so they could be clearly **seen** and **identified** in order to be **understood.** This plane of manifestation is not the realm where things originate; it is the place where the invisible things of eternal awareness are made visible.

Let's consider the prevailing religious concept about the creation of man. Imagine a scientist who by genetic engineering and cloning creates a new species. He sets up a scenario to test his new creation to check out its moral qualities. When this creature fails the first test, he is disobedient; will he lock the creature away forever? I do not think so. A wise man would not do so, much less a wise God.

Not only the HOW of the incarnation of MAN but the WHY must be answered. Let me make this tentative statement for consideration:

The creation of Man on this planet is a progressive step in the eternal plan of evolving consciousness to satisfy the original intent. Man is a Glorious, Powerful, Beautiful being of Light who descended with intent and purpose to be here at the cutting edge of unfolding consciousness.

THOR 1 Email 28: The Cosmic Story Book Is Opened, We Have A Vantage Point.

Dear Reader: The March 2006 issue of National Geographic, the current issue as I write this email, bears this title on its cover:

The Greatest Story Ever Told
The Journey of Man,
The Trail of Our DNA

Perhaps they anticipated me saying the following:

The incarnation of Adam, his journey on this planet, is a Cosmic Story Book. It is a primer to help non-physical realms understand the journey of Separation.

The above statement above creates a point of view from which to look at the whole journey of Man. It is difficult to understand the words of the Angels who exulted at Jesus birth saying: *Peace on Earth and goodwill towards men;* as we see that same region of the globe filled with turmoil and hatred and ready to explode into a nuclear holocaust. We need a greater vantage point to understand those seemingly irrelevant words. Some would say that Jesus has come and gone. Men have made a religion in his name that has filled the earth through bloodshed and we now have more war and hatred than when he was here. Yes, we need a greater point of view.

One of my readers expressed his frustration this way:

Please do not send me anymore of these writings. I do not need someone to try and rewrite the Bible. Sin, shame, guilt and Lord knows what else. Jesus Christ Rokus! BT

BT is a dear friend. He was honest enough to express the frustration of a lot of people, not necessarily my readers, who find it hard to make the adjustments necessary to accommodate to this new perspective. To Bill it seems that I am rewriting the scriptures, and in a sense, I am doing just that. However, it would be more properly said this way.

The Bible will seem like new book to you and me once we learn to look at it, from above instead of from below.

The first two chapters of this record of Man shows him being lowered into this three dimensional world of opposites through the agency of shame and blame. The effect is dramatic, pain in childbirth for the woman; sweat of the brow, thorns and thistles, and futility, for the man. The serpent gets a from-the-belly point of view, and a diet of dust. These are the opening lines of this awesome story. Yet we through our religions have based all our self loathing and rejection of self on a concept called original sin. We have, compounding the first

176

few lines into many chapters on the same subject, shame and sin. This inability to understand ourselves and our journey is the underlying cause of all our wars.

Peace and goodwill toward man, the dawning of true understanding of *Who you are* and *Why you came*, is now available, because of a man who came and demonstrated the truth of man and his journey. He opened the Cosmic Primer, the Story book. We are reading it. The angels were right after all.

The LAW and obedience to it lies at the core of the three major religions. Some aboriginal people don't even have a word in their language for GUILT; it seems that it is a specialty for us. The next chapter in our Story Book will deal with the nature of LAW and the role it plays in unfolding consciousness. Paul, the teacher of the last Age, called the Law a Schoolmaster, referring really to the Slave that accompanied the child to school to ensure his arrival there. Today we might call him the Bus Driver.

That single statement by Paul, who was the master student and teacher of the Law, will be a springboard to help us understand why a people had to be separated and sanctified and be a Holy nation, a royal priesthood for the cosmic story to unfold. It will be the subject of our next email.

THOR 1 Email 29: Descending and Ascending, the Journey Through Form

Dear Reader:

Jesus, the way-shower, made this statement:

No one ascends to heaven but he who first descends from heaven even the Son of man who is in heaven.

It follows that the key to understanding **ascending** lies in looking at **descending** or lowering. No one who is still mortally engaged in the place of being lowered has much interest in looking **at** it, their only desire is to be here. To those who are free and wish to ascend, to you this writing will be significant.

We have seen the beginning of the journey into separation, Sin and Shame. We have seen how incarnation or being lowered further into FORM gave the picture of the 'Eve' taken from the 'Adam' even as our being came from the Source. It is a replay, on the stage of materiality, of our greater beginnings in consciousness. Shame became the portal for our incarnation and Guilt immediately colored our first acts, yet we still could not understand this pain, this awesome remorse that drove us to try to please, to perform, our sin. All we found was pain in child birth, the birthing our being in form, and thorns and thistles, the resistance and opposition to our progress.

It is the Law, given to a people on Mt. Sinai, that was to accomplish this last degree of lowering to help us to understand Guilt, Shame, and Sin. These are spiritual qualities that are our companions through the valley of the Shadow of Death, the journey of Separation, along with Goodness and Mercy. They must be expressed in the realm of form to be clearly seen and understood.

It is the Law that gives a legal definition of Sin and makes Guilt real and understandable.

The strange thing about the Law is that it shows the truth by showing us what the truth is not. I will return to that thought later.

The book of Genesis does mention creation in the first chapter. The lowering of Man takes two or three more chapters. However, the unfolding story really slows down when it tells about Abraham, Isaac, Jacob, their descendants and their journey into Egypt. Again we see a re-enactment. Even as Adam and his children were lowered into the realm of materiality, so the children of Israel went down into Egypt. There they came under the rule and bondage of the Pharaoh. Egypt and its Pharaoh represent for us Material Consciousness and the rule of the Ego. Remember our thoughts about a living dream.

Much could be said and has been said about the Story of Abraham, the Father of the Faith walkers, and the journey of Israel through the ages of time. All this is beyond the scope of these few emails. We wish to concentrate on that particular aspect that will give us understanding of our lowered estate so we can be fully released to ascend. Every stain of darkness must be washed from our soul so that we can take flight into the realms of Glory and Light that are our inheritance while we are still in these matter bodies of limitation. The law that was given to the descendents of Abraham is the critical element we need to look at:

The Law of Moses is and was a legally binding contract between two parties, a contract to perform and a stipulation of penalty for non- performance. It was a MORT-GAGE.

There is no other covenant or contract ever made with man like this one. Our next email will examine this contract and its significance for all Time and Ages.

THOR 1 Email 30: Law, the Legal Definition of Sin, Review

Dear Reader:

Thank you for persisting with me through these simple yet disturbing and uprooting thoughts. The reason the process seems laborious is simply because new neural pathways need to be created in our brain as we learn to process the greater thoughts of reality that are awaking within. These thoughts are rising up from the 'deep' as it were; they are thoughts of remembrance.

Recall our original thought defining the idea of SIN:

Sin is the *thought* or the *awareness* that I am unable to meet your expectation.

Only yesterday I received a call from a dear friend who has been reading these progressive emails and asked me the question: *How can God have expectations? How can it be sin to have expectations?* I was a little taken back! Have I been so unclear in my presentation of the most cardinal thought of all these emails? Have I left the impression that sin is having expectations? Surely not! However...just to make amply sure that I do NOT leave that impression, note carefully:

SIN is the **THOUGHT**
Or the
AWARENESS

What is that thought or awareness?

"I am unable to meet your expectation"

Notice that this leaves the question whether or not **God** has expectations, completely open. Neither does it decide whether these expectations are real or imaginary.

Let me say how I see this. To me this is clear. The Source has a purpose, this purpose is an expectation. However, especially in our immaturity we cannot perceive that expectation; so **we** create an imagination, false images of that expectation. Then we decide that we cannot meet those self-imagined expectations. Can you see how difficult this must be to resolve? Ever raise children? Can you see why an elaborate plan of redemption has been put in place from the beginning? The awesome wonderful perfect Law of God that David the Psalmist so eloquently emulates was given to Israel for the whole world, for all the cosmos, to see the enactment of this Sin Principle.

When Paul says that the Law came and sin revived, it means that the Law came to make the **thought** of sin into **awareness,** an experimental reality. Notice the word **awareness.** The Law brings **awareness of sin** by imputing guilt. It is called a ministry of condemnation.

When the Law makes a requirement and you make an agreement to keep the law then you KNOW when you have failed to meet its expectation, you are CONDEMNED. The Judge says: Will the jury foreman please read the verdict: "*Your Honor, we find the defendant guilty as charged.*"

The wonderful thing about the Law and Guilt created by that Law is that the guilty one can repent. Atonement can be made, restitution can be given, and punishment can be measured out and served. Let me say it again:

The law was given to make sin a real, tangible experience so that guilt could be felt and understood as to its real cause.

THOR 1 Email 31: The Law Is a Contract between Two Parties; A Mort-(En)Gage

Dear Reader:

Have you ever felt victimized by the Law? We all have. Perhaps you were half asleep and you ran a red traffic light at three AM. There was no traffic in sight, no one was hurt or even endangered. There was no one around except you and the police in a car, a half mile away, who just happened to see that your brake lights did not come on. Criminal law requires proof that intent to harm or actual be committed for conviction, not so for traffic offenses. And well traffic law should be that way, if for no other reason than to enforce safe driving habits. Yet, you cannot help but feel that somebody took advantage of you when you pay that $100 fine and get points on your driver's license without any harm intended or done.

What is the principle here? In a free society like ours the ideal is that those that govern do so only by the consent of the governed and that only laws passed in harmony with the public will are truly valid. The opposite is Dictatorship or simple Authoritarianism, *it says: I have the right to rule over you because I am more powerful than you.*

Here is the most important aspect of the Law that needs to be considered. The Law that YHWH, gave to Israel was activated as a **contract of agreement** between YHWH and the Nation of Israel. A Mortgage is not legal or enforceable unless it is signed by both parties of Contract, the Lender and the Property owner, so is it with the Law of YHWH.

I want to very carefully show, from the scriptures, the nature of the Law and its power to impose its punitive conditions. The whole reason and purpose for the Law is based on this principle: The Law was not an imposed requirement; it was an agreement to perform

In chapters 20 to 23 in the book of Exodus the laws governing the social and moral requirements are stated. They are worth a close scrutiny, far beyond what we intend to do here. In chapter 24 is the critical verse I want to show you. This verse holds the key that shows the giving of the Law to be a legal contract between Israel and YHWH, it reads:

And Moses came and told the people all the words of YHWH and all the judgments: and all the people answered with one voice and said:

All the words that YHWH hath said we will do.

There is the "I Do" of the marriage contract. In chapter 27 and 28 of the book of Deuteronomy Moses gives instructions for a ceremony to be exercised upon crossing the Jordan River into the Promised Land. The significance is shown in Chap. 27 vs. 9 where we read:

Take heed and hearken, O Israel; this day thou art become the people of YHWH Elohim.

It reads like a benediction after a wedding vow. The ceremony consists of some tribes standing on one mountain reading the curses resulting from failure to meet the expectations of the Law, while other tribes are standing on another mountain reading the blessings that result from the keeping of that same law. After each curse is read this instruction is given: *And all the people shall say; Amen! Amen...* meaning..."So be it".

In Chapter 19 of Exodus Moses instructs the people to bathe and to sanctify themselves. They are to refrain from conjugal relations and to present themselves to YHWH as in a wedding ceremony. The promise is given this way:

Now therefore if ye will obey my voice indeed and keep my covenant, then ye shall be a peculiar treasure unto me above all people: for all the earth is mine. And ye shall be unto me a Kingdom of Priests, a Holy nation.

And again...in verse 8 we read this critical statement:

And all the people answered together and said; All that YHWH hath spoken we will do.

The evidence here is abundant. This is a legal contract, duly executed and signed by both parties. The expectations are clearly spelled out as are the penalties for nonperformance

Sin is no longer just a thought, a thought perhaps based on an imagined expectation. Sin is now legally defined by this contract:.

Sin is the transgression of the Law.

Not only is Sin now clearly defined and understandable, so also is guilt, the result of sin. The Law condemns the transgressor by his own agreement to perform and his failure to do so. A man stands condemned by the very Law he agrees to keep.

A modern equivalent to this Law is the execution of a Mortgage. The lender and the title holder make covenant. The borrower agrees to meet certain conditions, a mortgage payment, usually once a month, for a specified amount, interest and duration. Failure to meet those conditions causes the *DEATH* of the owner, that is, he is no longer the owner. Ownership passes to the Lender, hence the word *MORT.* Mort is French for *DEATH*, as it is written, *the soul that sins it shall die,* The transgressor forfeits his rights, and looses his identity..

The giving of the Law and the Priesthood was a national experience that held force for fifteen hundred years. We might ask why such an elaborate experience was created for several million people, nomads, shepherds, the children of one family. It is a plan that spans centuries of time, many generations, awesome prophecies, great pain, and deportation of whole populations for hundreds of miles by foreign potentates, all told by many inspired writers and prophets. A plan that today still holds the answers to the earth's crises now unfolding in the Middle East as we live under the shadow of the fear of destruction.

I say it was all done so that we, standing now on the Cusp of Ages might understand the basic principles of the journey of unfolding consciousness. It was done so that a people, today, might inherit, not a physical inheritance of land, such as Canaan or the USA or Palestine, but the promised land of the unlimited potential of Adam. This is the great cosmic prize of the Ages, The Glory of Man as the Tabernacle of God; Oneness; the answer to Jesus prayer.

In our next email we will try to sum up the significance of the Law.

THOR 1 Email 32: Why the Law? Source Does Not Condemn.

Dear Reader;

We come now to the heart of the question. Why was the Law given at all? History shows that the nation of Israel never did keep the law. Over and over the prophets came and rebuked them. Over and over their dire predictions came to pass. The nation was torn apart. The tribes were scattered, separated from the temple worship in Jerusalem for long ages. What a powerful story. The writer laments and cries out: *Did God fail? Did God cast off his people whom he fore-knew?* Paul answers these great questions clearly and carefully in the book of Romans. It will suffice for us simply to ask the following question: In light of all this suffering and pain experienced by those to whom the Law was given, we ask:

Why was the Law given?

We notice that the covenant of the Law was ratified by the sprinkling of blood. That blood was shed before the Law was even broken, before transgression came. Yet the purpose of shed blood is the remission of sin. We understand that the Spiritual realms that gave the Law also knew that the law was given so that SIN would become real. Sin would be revealed. The law was given so that the people would break it and so they did. Hence they were called a Nation of Priests; they all gave their lives to show the reality of Sin and Guilt. The fact that the Law was given with Priesthood, to make atonement for the worshipper as a measure of grace, verifies this thought.

Law had to be given to show what is true when there is **NO** law. It came so that the following can be said:

Where there is no covenant of Law, no sin can be imputed, no curse can be exercised, and no death penalty can be imposed. There can be no condemnation administered if there is no Law.

Do we understand what condemnation is? Yes we do. Many Ages have unfolded, many saints have given their lives, and yes we know what condemnation and guilt feel like. The Law came, we agreed to its terms, sin became real, and we suffered the consequences. Now we know and understand. Why is this so important?

We needed to know what guilt and condemnation are so that we might know this simple truth:

The Source, Our Father, Does Not Condemn Us. We Do It To Ourselves.

THOR 1 Email 33: The Grand Father Clause, Our Beginning, Abba, Father

Dear Reader:

There is a legal principle called the Grand Father clause. It works like this. In 1964 I bought 5 acres of land from a farmer friend in Ontario Canada. I bought it for $2000 and began to build a cedar log cabin. I cut, skinned and carried the trees to build my 30 by 40 cabin in the woods.

Chris, the land owner, did not want to give me legal title at the time of purchase because the mortgage holder would have required the money to be paid against the outstanding mortgage.

Three years later a law was passed preventing strip development along county roads. It was a law that prevented farmers from selling lots along the roads of rural Ontario. When I tried to sell the property in 1970, the real estate told me I could not sell. I had no title and could not get title because of the law that had been passed recently.

How did I sell? The real estate sold the property for me to the new owner and then the new owner took me to court, to get a title. In court I was able to establish that I in fact owned the property before the law preventing its sale was passed and hence had an inherent right to sell the property even if the present law forbade me from doing so. I could show ownership by dated photographs that showed the building of the cottage and the canceled checks showing the monies I paid for the land. I sold the property for $16,000. It was the Grand Father clause that protected me:

A Law Passed Later Could Not Cancel Out
A Legal Transaction Made Earlier.

Paul the Apostle uses this principle to explain how the Law which came later could not cancel out a covenant made with Abraham made five hundred years earlier. The covenant made with Abraham had no conditions and no requirement to perform. There was only one party making covenant. God, *having no greater to swear by swore by Himself saying, In blessing I will bless thee.* The law of curses that came later could not cancel out the covenant of blessing made earlier.

What am I saying? I am telling you that Guilt, Shame and Sin which are made real by the Law were never imputed from the beginning of consciousness when the Source blessed every seed that came from him to go on the long journey. It was a beginning without conditions or requirement or any agreement. Sin was not imputed in the beginning of our incarnation either. Again, there was no contract required, no agreement made, no signatures put down, and hence no sin imputed.

The accusations, the Shame and Blame that have petrified us all these long ages, have never been imposed from the Source. It has all been of our own doing. We did it with the help of darkened intelligence, and our own sense of self loathing created from imagined failure to meet the expectations that were never spelled out or required. We ourselves have condemned ourselves. We have been unlawfully been our own judge and jury.

The Lamb that was slain from the foundation of the world, and the blood shed in every age, all testify to the great unconditional love of the Source that cannot leave or forsake its own, ever, in all worlds and all ages. His love is unconditional and unending in power and grace.

No law, no power, no intelligence that speaks or utters any law or curse can ever cancel out the original LOVE and INTENT of the Source when it gave of its own self and covenanted with itself to begin the great journey of Love, the great journey of becoming, our beginning in consciousness. Abba...Father.

THOR 1: Email 34: The Law Is Like A School Bus Driver

Dear Reader:

I remember riding the school bus when I attended High School in Ontario Canada in the fifties. If you were the first to be picked up in the morning you were also the first to be dropped off at night, the school bus thing was not an experience you looked forward to. It was mostly a way to get somewhere else, to School. One older student, he came on the bus about halfway, was always smoking as he stood waiting for the bus. If you have ever smelled a smoker who smokes on an empty stomach then you have some idea of the odor that permeated that school bus as he first stepped in the door. Yes, the school bus experience is the experience of what is not your true being. It is a trip to show you what you are not, so that you can choose who you are.

Now we understand that the law was given to create a legitimate context to experience Sin, Guilt, Condemnation and Death and that the people who bore that curse of the Law were really a nation of priests who carried it as a cosmic object lesson for all men and angels, we can understand why Paul called the Law a Schoolmaster (slave) to lead us to Christ.

The word Christ literally means "Anointed", so the statement really becomes:

The Law ministered condemnation to us so we could see and understand that it is really we ourselves that condemn ourselves and so bring us to the empowered life.

It is written: *There is therefore no condemnation in Christ, to those who live not after the flesh but after the Spirit.*

Our child like interpretation of reality formed the first thoughts of sin. These sin thoughts in turn conceived the thought is us that there was something innately faulty about us that disabled us from pleasing our Father-Source and so shame was born. We carried this shame with us as we were lowered in consciousness into this plane of manifestation. We needed to understand Shame that is now lodged deep in our cellular structure. This shame then drove us to become better and, caused us to create an atmosphere of Law. Law that says: *I will do better tomorrow. I will please God. I will do all his commandments and fill all his expectations and so please him.* That spirit of Law has worked in our members from the beginning. It is self effort to improve what needs no improving, just unfolding. The Law given on Mt Sinai made this Spirit real and tangible. That spirit of Law, so important in everyone's experience, is the pathway to Christ, the anointed, the empowered life. In Christ we know that we are pleasing to the Source because we are its seed, its offspring, its own essence and life. That acknowledgement is what Jesus showed to all creation and is therefore named after him when we say:

There is therefore no condemnation in Christ Jesus.

THOR 1 Email 35: A Personal Note from Rokus

Dear Readers:

Thank you again...those that are still reading. I have finished what I believe is the most difficult part of THOR. A summary of the first thirty five emails follows. Our next series of emails should be very exciting; a whole new awareness of who Jesus is and why he came to a small planet on the periphery of a small Galaxy, the Milky way. Again, any reaction to my writings is greatly appreciated...Rokus

THOR 1 Synopsis: The Source Never Condemned Us...We Did

Dear Friends:

It is time for a synopsis, an overview to check our progress in developing a new Theory of Reality. I am very satisfied, from the responses and discussions prompted by these writings, that our old programming is being scrambled. The debris is definitely floating to the surface, ideas and perceptions that just do not help us understand who we are and why we have come.

Chronologically we began with observations and conclusions about this physical realm. We saw it to be a place where invisible eternal, things manifest to be seen and understood. We then used that principle to begin investigating those eternal things. Here follows a sequential series of thoughts concerning a new theory of reality:

First: All we consciously experience of ourselves began with a desire in the Source. That desire, reflected in all creation, is the desire to produce after ones kind. This desire in the Source to experience its own Love, and so know itself in a way that could not be in the Oneness alone, required that an OTHER ONE begin to form. This is the beginning of duality. We call it the journey of separation. We say that the Source itself initiated the journey of separation.

Second: So the ONE bought forth out of itself the MANY; the Many that made up the WORD, the expression. As they were brought forth the Source blessed its own God-Seeds unconditionally to go forth, create identity, and create the journey of consciousness in pure joy and freedom. This is how you and I were conceived. This is our eternal mission, to fill the desire of the Source, the Father of all.

Third: In our conceiving we became as children, innocent, without experience or knowledge only feeling the desire of the Source and its total unreserved unconditional Love. As we began to respond to this Love, among our first thoughts there came a thought, a question, we wondered: What if I cannot meet the desire of the source? What if I cannot meet its expectation of me? So is it that Sin was formed. Sin came out of the very formation of our own consciousness. We were the creators of it. It was a necessary by-product of our creativity, a goad to press us on.

Fourth: As sin was formed in our earliest formative thoughts it turned our attention inward and we learned a new experience, one we have learned to excel in, we questioned our own worth of being. We created awareness of shame.

Fifth: As worlds of consciousness were created and we unfolded in this Journey of Separation into ever increasing density of form we learned the process of forming Identity. As we did we needed greater measures of organization and control. Civilizations, worlds, came and went and the questions became increasingly insistent for answers. Love and Control seeming opposites pressed the journey on. To answer the deepest questions of our existence, sin, shame and the reasons for them, the Elohim agreed to create this physical realm and then descended into this realm in Human form.

189

Sixth: The creation account of Adam is our story of being lowered into physical form. Light beings lowering their vibrational frequency. As in the beginning of consciousness there were two main elements working, separation, seen in the male and female, and shame, the motivating principle that drove us into this biological clothing, our humanity. The great prize for which we came was the knowing and the understanding of our Journey, the revealing to us of the Father's heart.

Seventh: As shame, our sense of un-worth and the result of our thoughts of separation and sin, was translated into acts we began to experience Guilt. Guilt comes from acts motivated by Shame. There was no way for us to understand Guilt and its mother Shame, nor was there a way for us to understand that these two were based on presumptions and false images that we created in our minds about an infinitely loving and accepting Source.

A people were formed and called out as a nation to marry the YHWH of Israel. This marriage was a legal contract, a covenant of law that gave a legal definition to Sin and hence Guilt. For the first time we understood how Guilt is created in us through failure to perform an agreed contract. We understood the death that results from it, separation.

Eighth; The door is now open. The lowering is complete. Sin, Shame and Guilt are experienced in a valid setting of Law and punishment created by agreement. The way is now open for us to begin to understand the fundamental truth of our existence: *Sin and guilt and its result, condemnation and death are all the creation of our own mind; they were never imputed by the Source.*

The time of Law lasted for fifteen hundred years when the Light of All Light appeared as Jesus the Messiah of Israel. He came to redeem them from the curse of the Law which they suffered for all creation.

Even though the Law had come its lessons could not be understood for the curse was still upon his people. We are ready to open the greatest chapter of the human story, the coming of the Son of Man, Jahshuah, Jesus of Nazareth. We will do so in the next series of emails.

Rokus denHartog

190

A NEW THEORY OF REALITY

PART 2

An Email Discussion
by
Rokus denHartog
and
The THOR Discussion Group

THOR 2 Email # 1: Introduction, Who is Jesus?

Hello all my Readers:

Thank you for responding to my invitation to participate in the second part of our ongoing email discussion: *A New Theory of Reality Part 2*. I wish to continue our exploration of greater thought forms by which man will experience the next phase of the eternal purpose for this planet.

The central awareness around which these ideas are evolving is the thought of our eternal existence in all worlds. We ARE so much more than flesh and blood, yet it is this very flesh and blood in which we experience the greatest of transformations thanks be to the eternal plan of our Father-Source.

My simple analogy of being disorientated in Amsterdam still holds great truth. We need an eternal perception of this drama we call the Earth Experience in order to really find the power to "walk it out." We MUST be able to see ourselves from a larger and higher perspective to find empowerment, the divine energy to be human.

Much has been written and said to inspire us toward God-Hood, and I am thankful for all of it. However, the greater challenge is that we, for the first time in the human journey, might truly become human; truly incarnate. To do so we must gain awareness of our Deity, our Divine origin and essence. Only from the divine perception's higher perspective can we embrace our humanity. That in us that is human, and believes in human-ness apart and separate from deity, can never fully embrace the human experience. We have too much guilt and shame locked into the cells of our bodies.

How are we to gain that heavenly perception? This is where Act 2 of *A New Theory of Reality* opens. Enter the most controversial figure ever to walk the shores of human consciousness, Jesus of Nazareth.

Where to begin speaking of him? Should we address all the religious images created around his person? Should we try to scrub away centuries of thought, of caked layers of penance and sorrow experienced along the painful journey of our tortuous past? Shall we release him from the prison we have created mentally for him, locking him away from ourselves by religious images and thoughts? I say yes, he must be released. Can we do so? I think we must.

In this first email we address the thought of WHO Jesus really is. We might remind ourselves of the fact that he referred to himself repeatedly as the **Son of Adam.** We might say that he made the claim: **I am Human**.

I am, and I show you all that you are and all that you can be. I am not separate from you; in fact, I am truly you. I am more you than you have been able to think or perceive yourself to be. I have come to release you from the prison of your own limiting thoughts about yourself. Soar with me into worlds you did not even dream existed. Come up so high with me and descend so low with me that you will grasp the whole of all that is me, as you.

THOR 2 Email #2: The Great Journey and Jesus Mission

Dear Readers:

This is the second email of Part 2 of THOR. I have significantly reduced my mailing list. Thank you for staying on. I am starting Part 2 by questioning the main thesis: *Is man truly an eternally begotten being of Light having an experience as man?* If this be so, then the image that Jesus brought should bear this out. We will look for it in the words he said about himself as well as those of his disciples. Let's examine this issue carefully. Your input will be appreciated.

The Great Journey of separation, as we have called it, is the journey of creating **AWARENESS** ...awareness of being...the unfolding of consciousness. This awareness and unfolding can only come through the formation of **IDENTITY**, the ability to say 'I AM". This awareness of our identity as separate entities that **come from** the source, **exist in** the source, and **return to** the source is what we call the journey. It is the journey of separation. We could equally well call it the journey of wholeness; it depends on which leg of the journey you are experiencing.

It is a journey that goes nowhere. It is always truly in the **now** and is always where you are, **here**. It is the **now-here** journey. The past and the future, real enough to the mind, exist primarily in the mind and give context to the experience which is always created in the now. The great prize of this journey is **awareness of being**, something that still lays somewhat undiscovered before us.

How do we experience this awareness of being? It comes in the realization of worth, the expression of devotion and worship. We experience it most of all in Love and in the sharing of Being. This love and sharing of being is the heart desire of the Father from the dawn of time.

Jesus told his life mission in a parable. He said that the Kingdom of Heaven, the Divine Intent, is likened unto a man. This man discovered a treasure hidden in a field. For the joy of this treasure, he sold all that he had and purchased the field in which the treasure was hidden.

If AWARENES of BEING is the prize we speak of then the treasure spoken of in this field must be the people that can carry the promise of this awareness, a people in the Earth.

A people were sent for this very purpose. The field represents the world, three dimensional reality. The treasure is the experience of Man. Man is the carrier of this quality of Identity that is able to focus awareness of being. The great mission of Jesus is to unearth this treasure and make it his own. He is to gather this people and bring them to an awakening of who they are and why they have come. They are called his children because they are begotten of the truth he came to bring.

193

Apparently a price had to be paid to gain legal ownership of the treasure. The whole field had to be purchased. Another element had taken possession by default. The cost to him was the giving up of his greater knowing. He had to leave the realms of his greater existence and participate in the human drama, calling himself the "Son of Adam" or the "Son of Man."

The scriptures confirm this thought in Hebrews 2 vs. 13-16:

13. Behold, I and the children which God hath given me.
14. Forasmuch then as the children are partakers of flesh and blood, he also himself likewise took part of the same.
15.And deliver them who through fear of death were all their lifetime subject to bondage.

The death which is spoken of here is the loss of our greater awareness in the realms of LIGHT and the taking on of our mortality. The children here, for our purpose, are those that carry the hope. The ones who came for the purpose expressed above. The ones who need to awaken and remember their journey. The ones who came, not only to learn lessons in repeated life times, but who came consumed with the desire to understand, to help to deliver, to bring release, and to allow the love of the Father to be experienced by all.

According to verse 15, it is the fear of death that keeps these 'children' of Jesus unable to become all they came to express and to be. This fear of death is the fear of their own mortality, the fear of embracing this physical reality, the fear of being in a body. This fear keeps them in bondage to perceived limitation.

In verse 14, we see the point I want to focus on and to add emphasis to, the reason stated for Jesus' coming:

His mission was to incarnate in the same manner as the children.

Why is this so important? Why did he have to become human like us? The reason is plain. Our fear of incarnation, rooted in false shame and sin, holds us bound, unable to fulfill our mission. This one, who came directly from the Father, came specifically in human form so that we in our humanity can **identify** with him. In seeing who we are, we can release our fear.

The Consummate Realization Is This Simple Thought:

It's OK to be Human

THOR 2 Email #3: Jesus, His Mission, Defining the Argument

Dear Reader:

Jesus is and was, without doubt, the most controversial figure to ever walk the experience of man. Jesus again is in the news because of Mel Gibson and his movie. It is a movie that Hollywood would not finance, a movie that became an all time box office success, where millions of people flocked to experience Jesus in the twenty-first century. News week magazine, on its April 2006 cover, carries a picture of Jesus crowned with thorns, wearing a red robe with the title:

<u>CHRIST'S MISSION</u>

New Debate About The Role Jesus In The World

The controversial book about Jesus, the "daVinci Code" hit the best seller list in 2005 and its movie version, after a court challenge, is about to make another awesome success story. It's all about the humanity of Jesus and his relationship with Mary Magdalene. In short, yes, Jesus is in the news.

The grand questions: *Who is Jesus? What truly is his mission?* demand answers. The unfolding of light and awareness in this dawning age requires not only a truer look at this most controversial figure but more so at the message he brought. This message is about the Love of the Father, true. It is about forgiveness. It is about the passive resistance that changed India through Gandhi. It is about all the issues the church has used and abused for two thousand years. But the heart of his message, the true and essential reason for his incarnation, has remained illusive. His message is about to take on great clarity as mankind graduates into the age of maturity and responsibility. His message in truth and reality was **to** Man **about** Man. It answers the deepest and most important questions of man's existence: *Who am I? Where did I come from? Why am I here?*

I wish to make a simple irrefutable argument to state both the identity and the mission of Jesus. I wish to make this argument from his own clear statements about himself as recorded in the gospels; not from Newsweek or Mel Gibson's movie; not from anything written about him by Paul, the Church Fathers or novelists; not even from things he has spoken to me personally or from my experiences with him. The Gospels are the best records available about him.

This may get a little tedious but I want to be simple and clear in the argument that will connect the age of his disciples to the Age that is now dawning. The church age is passing, and the age of his Kingdom is at hand. I will take time later to establish, again by his own words, that he considers this present Age, the Age of Aquarius, as His true coming. This is the day of the Son of Man.

First we establish that Jesus spoke of himself as the Son of Man and the Son of God. His closest associates believed him to be the Messiah, the Son of the living God. The reason given by his enemies for crucifying him was that he stated himself to be the Son of God, thereby, supposedly, making himself equal with God. This was considered blasphemy, a sin worthy of death.

Secondly, by his own words, we will establish his mission. From his mouth we will extract his mission statement. We will then make a conclusion concerning the most awesome and most profound question of man's existence, the Who, Where, and Why as stated above. This statement is the deep unconscious knowing that lies un-awakened in the subconscious mind of man. It is a deep, almost forgotten awareness, a memory that needs to come forth so that man can rise as in a resurrection to take his place in the great drama unfolding on this planet.

Email #4: Jesus the Son of Man and Jesus the Son of God

Dear Reader:

We begin the statement of our argument by pointing out that the phrase "The Son of Man" occurs eighty eight times in the New Testament. Eighty one of these are Jesus personally calling himself **The Son of Man**. We recognize that the Gospels repeat the same events. Thirty two of these references occur in Mathew's Gospel.

So the fact is that of all the recorded words in the New Testament, Jesus refers to himself as the Son of Man at least thirty two times. There are four references **about** him as the Son of Man; thirty six references in all.

This is remarkable if only for the fact that the phrase **Son of God** only occurs twenty eight times in the Gospels, including repeats, and only five of those references are quoting Jesus referring to himself as the Son of God. All of these five references are found only in the Gospel of John. There are also two places where Jesus is called the Son of God by Peter or the High Priest. In either case, Jesus does not deny the reference.

Interestingly enough I could find no direct references to Jesus as the **Son of Man** in all of the letters of the various apostles to the Churches or the theological treatises by Paul. This is so remarkable because Jesus clearly preferred to call himself the Son of Man instead of the Son of God, thirty two times as opposed to five. The writer of the book of Hebrews uses the phrase **The Son of Man**, quoting from the Psalms, but does not directly associate that phrase with Jesus. The book of the Revelations uses the phrase twice about Jesus in a glorified state and the book of Acts once as Stephen has a vision of Jesus at the right hand of the Father.

The simple conclusion we draw from these facts is that the revelation of Jesus as the Son of Man was not given to the Apostles who taught the early church nor was it necessarily understood by them. Jesus, as the Son of God, brought the Holy Spirit to mankind on the day of Pentecost. That visitation is still the core of the church age.

The age that is passing experienced Jesus primarily as the Son of God. It remains for this Dawning Age, as Man begins to understand who Man is, to see Jesus as the Son of man.

However, for the sake of our argument, we conclude that Jesus clearly understood himself to be both the **Son of Man** and **the Son God**. Jesus referred to himself as the Son of Man because he knew himself to be Representative Man. This powerful, key awareness will become more clear as we look at Jesus own perception of his mission.

THOR 2 Email #5: The Mission of Jesus in the Passing Ages

Dear Reader:

We look first at Jesus Mission as it pertains to the ages that have passed. The simple reality is that Jesus was crucified at the celebration of the ancient tradition of Passover. I do not know how anyone could possibly give appropriate credit to the revelation of Jesus mission as the Passover Lamb. Paul was used, with his fine legal training and his expert knowledge of the traditions of the Hebrew people, to bring this revelation to the world. We cannot begin to measure the impact this truth has had. It has transformed the experience of humanity, even if this truth has not been truly fully seen to this very day. In fact, the greater truth of Jesus as the Lamb of God still lies hidden in the shadows of our limited perceptions. Much has been said and written of this awesome truth, in whatever depth we have understood it. Uncountable numbers of individuals in history for over 2000 years have testified to the saving grace of God they experienced in Jesus Christ and have shown it in the transformation of their lives.

This revelation of Jesus as the Passover Lamb, a theme deeply imbedded in Judaism and the History and traditions of the Children of Israel, brought to an end the dispensation of the Law given on Mount Sinai. In Jesus own words we learn that he came to fulfill the Law, not to destroy it. We see that every aspect of the Lamb of God, shown in the type and shadow of these rituals, can clearly be seen in the Life, Death, Resurrection and Ascension of Jesus. Looking at the contract of the Torah then helps us see more clearly the mission of Jesus to the whole cosmos. He came as the Eternal Lamb of God to release the creation from limitation and bondage.

It seems a total injustice to the awesome scope of these eternal truths to dismiss them in a couple of paragraphs. It must be remembered that Paul's writings will remain forever as the standard and great interpretation of the Law as it pertains to the atoning work of Jesus.

We have no wish to repeat any of this great teaching, only to acknowledge it, that we might step forward into a greater revealing. As we leave the age of Pisces and enter the Dawning of the Age of Aquarius, Jesus the Son of Man is appearing.

The first time Jesus came it was to those born under the Law, the nation of Israel. He paid the penalty of death incurred through the covenant of the Law on Mt Sinai, fifteen hundred years earlier. He was the spotless Lamb needed to satisfy the demands of the Law.

The understanding of Jesus' Mission as it was seen during the Church age is best summed up by the statement made by Jesus favorite disciple, John. It is the most famous Evangelical scripture of all time, John 3:16:

For God so loved the World that He gave His only begotten Son that whosoever believes on him should not perish but have everlasting Life.

Even though this scripture has been understood only from the very narrow perspective of our fundamentalist Christian thinking about heaven and hell, the peace it has brought to millions of fearful hearts and minds is awesome. There are not sufficient superlatives to describe what I feel about it. Is there any way to imagine what civilization on planet earth would be like had it not been for this outpouring of grace that came because of Calvary? It is so awesomely amazing to see the Love of God given freely to man in spite of man's continued resistance and inability to accept heavenly truth and understanding. We can see clearly that John saw Jesus not as representative man but as representing and revealing the heart and the Love of the Father; hence the phrase: "His only Begotten Son" or **The Son of God.** This is the mission of Jesus as seen by John and as it has been interpreted by the apostles and church history. During these two thousand years, in a limited way, we have been able to grasp the thought: **God so Loved that He gave**. John's gospel expresses the core of this truth. It is the one that defines Jesus five times as the Son of God.

Jesus himself referred to his own mission and Identity many times. We will list just some of these now for comparison:

1. *I came that ye might have life and have it more abundantly.*
2. *When you've seen me, you have seen the Father.*
3. *He whom the Son sets free is free in deed.*
4. *No one cometh unto the Father but by me.*
5. *I have come to seek and to save that which was lost.*

These statements are all wonderful and rich and will require attention. Most of them have not been understood in the light of the limited theology of this passing age. We will review them and others in this new and greater perspective of Jesus' mission and the truth of the Cross. However, to state the simple argument we wish to make, we need only have a quotation from Jesus himself about himself. He made this statement when asked a direct question by his enemies and in conversation with his disciples. We will reserve this powerful awareness for a separate email.

THOR 2 Email #6: Jesus Mission and Identity...the Disciples

Dear Reader:

I am slowly outlining the argument that I am presenting in these first few emails about Jesus' identity and mission. I am headed for a clear statement concerning his mission, particularly as it pertains to us; we that are awakening from the ages of fear-induced sleep that has so severely limited our awareness of self and so our expression. As the Age of Light and Joy dawns on the creation it is truly incumbent upon Man to take his pre-ordained place in this greater reality. After all, that is why we came. It is my contention that this awakening, this ascension in awareness, cannot come to man except through a greater appreciation of the death and resurrection of Jesus Christ. In short, we need to understand his mission.

I know, in his age of tolerance and expansion of thought, it may seem to some that I am advocating a step backward. It seems I am inviting more loyalty and reverence for a person who is already worshipped beyond his own will and desire. However, if you will stay with the argument and let me truly make it, I think you will see that in fact I am doing the opposite. Even as God has from the beginning, I am opening the door to greater awareness for Man about Man so that you may become all that you are and all you are intended to be. I am inviting you to accept responsibility for your own being.

We wish to take a look at the exact recorded words of those closest to Jesus. His own disciples, the ones he entrusted his mission too, and also his enemies, the ones he so greatly needed to accomplish his journey, the ones who falsely accused him and put him to death.

200

Let's look at the disciples first. Notice that Jesus opens the following conversation to discuss his identity, they hesitatingly respond. He then confronts them directly and makes them verbalize the impossible dream, that he in fact is the long awaited Messiah, the Redeemer of Israel. Matthew 16: 13-16:

When Jesus came into the coasts of Caesarea Philippi, he asked his disciples, saying: **Who do men say that I the Son of Man am?** And they said: Some say that thou art John the Baptist, some, Elias; and others, Jeremias, or one of the prophets. He saith unto them, but whom say ye that I am? And Simon Peter answered and said: Thou art the Christ, the Son of the living God.

Here it is in unmistakably clear language. Jesus, identifying himself as the Son of Man, elicits this awesome response from his disciples. Peter acknowledges the heart longing of every true Israelite for at least seven hundred years since the destruction of the nation of Israel if not for fifteen hundred years, from the cry of deliverance from Egypt and the 40 years of wandering when Moses exclaimed: *One like unto me will YHWH raise up from among you, Him will you hear!* Can you hear the cry of desperation in the words of Moses, one of the world's greatest leaders, the exasperation of people unable to hear truth?

Here in this most famous, most debated scripture of all time, we have a clear, if indirect assertion that the Son of Man, Jesus of Nazareth, is in fact, in the context of divine history, the Son of God, the promised Messiah.

Note Jesus' response here: *Blessed art thou Simon bar Jonas, for flesh and blood have not revealed this unto thee but my Father which is in heaven.*

Jesus, who clearly claimed to have been sent from the Father above, knew his origin to be in greater parallel realities. Here he also places Peter in that same reality by stating him to be the recipient of divine revelation. It seems as if the stakes in this conversation are really high. Clearly all the great claims of Jesus concerning his purpose and origin would have little effect on the world or humanity if it did not meet with a corresponding response from within their own being.

The Father himself must testify on behalf of the Son or the Son's testimony cannot be established. He did so in Peter.

The great issue of the Ages, the great quest for Identity and acknowledgement of it, is stated here as if in open court. It's almost as if Goliath has issued the challenge and David has taken the field with only a slingshot of words, words of Age abiding truth and reality, words of power and empowerment, words of identity and Mission. The court drama has had its opening statement, it is this:

The one you see as the Son of Man
Is in fact
The eternal Son of God

We reserve Pilate and the high Priest for the next email.

THOR 2 Email #7: Jesus' Mission and Identity...His Enemies

Dear Reader:

There was and still is an ancient custom in Britain that requires the next heir to the throne to establish the legitimacy of his claim to it. This is accomplished at the coronation by the reading of his genealogical descent back to antiquity. When a police officer stops you in traffic, on a public highway, he has legal right to require you to identify yourself. In more gentle times this requirement simply meant that you had to answer him when he asked you: Who are you? Today it requires you to show an ID card or a driver permit. Times have changed. When Jesus is confronted by the High Priest and the kangaroo court of the Sanhedrin, with Jesus' friends in High Places conveniently ignored or absent, the issue of his Identity, after other futile accusations, is made the central theme of his accusers. Listen to the words:

Matt 26:63-66: *And the high priest answered and said unto him, I adjure thee by the living God, that thou tell us whether thou be the Christ, the Son of God. Jesus saith unto him, Thou hast said, nevertheless I say unto you, hereafter shall ye see the Son of Man sitting on the right hand of power, and coming in the clouds of heaven. Then the high priest rent his clothes, saying, He hath spoken blasphemy; what further need have we of witnesses? Behold, now ye have heard his blasphemy.*

Again, amazingly, Jesus does not gainsay the charge but still refers to himself as the Son of Man. It is the powers of these present orders, those that seemingly control the consciousness of man; they are making identity the issue. They set the stage. They ask the question. Jesus uses the power of his words, as David used stones to slay Goliath. Words like stones to penetrate the mind of man with a thought; this thought being that the Son of man is truly the Son of God. My friend and mentor used to say concerning Goliath: "Nothing like that ever penetrated his mind before." So it is with Man.

It is very clear to me that the real reason the religious leaders of that day wanted Jesus crucified had nothing much to do with his teachings or his so called blasphemy. Their primary concern was the influence he had with the people. It was said of him that the common people heard him gladly, the envy of every politician and religious leader. This is the one who was practically worshipped as a King on what is now called Palm Sunday, when he rode into Jerusalem on a donkey and all the people hailed Him as the Son of David. They remembered what was written in their sacred writings: *Fear not, daughter of Zion, behold, thy King cometh, sitting on an ass's colt.* They feared that this one would not only unseat their place of authority but even cause another Jewish uprising against the Romans. The real issues were not spiritual or even philosophical, they were territorial. Nevertheless, the stage was set for Jesus to proclaim the truth of the Son of Man.

Almost as significant as the words Jesus spoke before the High priest are the words that he did not speak. He made no attempt to instruct or educate. He showed not the slightest desire to illustrate spiritual principles or defend or promote a cause. He made no mention of payment for sin, made no defense: *As a lamb is silent before its shearers so opened he not his mouth.* He was dumb.

In our next writing we will see Jesus in the judgment hall of Pilate, the power of Rome; the most powerful of world empires. What does Jesus have to say in the Arena of the power of Man? What words will he choose? Where will his focus be?

203

THOR 2 Email #8: Jesus and Pilate...the Mission Stated

Dear Reader:

If we can see that the unfolding path of consciousness is purposed for Love, that Love may fully know itself as Love, and if we can see that Love for its expression needs an object, then we can also see that the great quest of this eternal Journey of Wholeness, this journey of Separation, is the formation of identity, the forming of the separate self. What a price has been paid for this treasure. What a depth of love for the Eternal Father to totally give of Himself, His only begotten Son, to pay the price for this journey, this unfolding. As great as our love of the Savior has been, seen through the eyes of our great need and our self depreciation, so much greater will this Love appear when we see it from thanksgiving and the treasuring of awareness of being.

In the judgment hall of Pilate he stands, the King of Love, confronted by the powers of control and manipulation. The great question has to be raised. It must be raised, not by Love, for Love has no contention. It must be raised by the powers of control. *Who are you? Why are you here?* It's not just Pilate, concerned about Caesar and his political career. It's not just the High Priest and his manipulation. No. It's every man that has become trapped in the tremendous struggle on the Journey of consciousness. It's every man that died by the wayside, feeling lost, feeling empty and not understanding why. It's every woman that wanted a child and could not have one; every man that wanted to create order and only found chaos and defeat. The whole of the created orders cry out for the understanding that will bring release. This one, the King of Love, came, not in power, but in weakness to state the answer, the key that sets us free, the loosening of the seals that will enable us to read our book. Here are the recorded words:

Pilate therefore said unto him: *Art thou a king then?* Jesus answered:

*Thou sayest that I am a king. To this end was I born, and for this cause came I into the world, **that I should bear witness unto the truth.** Every one that is of the truth hears my voice.*

In this place of ultimate human authority, before the representative of Caesar, the final statement is made by Jesus himself, the statement that answers the question of his identity and his Mission. It confirms what we have seen already. The proclamation at the river Jordan...*This is my beloved Son*...the witness of Peter, the affirmation of Jesus' silence, Jesus' own reference to himself as the Son of Man...But here....Jesus goes beyond answering a question. He makes a definitive statement. Allow me to reword the above statement:

I am sent from the Father of Light to be a witness to the truth of Man's identity and purpose. What you see me to be is the true identity and purpose of Man; therefore I have called myself the Son of Man. In every respect the demonstration of my Life, my Death and my Resurrection is a projected reality, a perfect parallel, to show the truth of Man. As I was sent of my Father, so were you. As I am the Son of God, so are you. As I was born in a stable, so your consciousness was formed in the bestiality of your human nature. As I have power to forgive sin, walk on the lower elements, transfigure, heal and make whole, so do you. As your eternal being became incarnate, took on physical form, was crucified on the limitations of human consciousness, so I was crucified on a wooden stake, stripped of all of my glory, naked and despised, so I could be like you, so you might know you are truly me. I have faced all your fears, felt all your doubt, and tasted the salt of blood and tears. I have cried, been weary, felt forsaken and lost. I have loved and lived and celebrated and exulted. I know who you are. I am you and you are me. We are forever one. We have overcome.

It is so ultimately important that the truth of man MUST be stated and witnessed because this third dimensional reality is a PERCEPTION. Every definition of man presented to him over the ages as to his origin and purpose is a perception. They all have an element of truth. All are presented by someone with intent to persuade, to direct for some design and intent some loving and noble, some self serving and deceitful. For that reason they are all false. Jesus said: *All that have come before me are thieves and robbers*, because they seek to gain from man by directing his flow of consciousness. Jesus claims to have no intent of his own. He claims to be sent from the Source itself, from the Father. Only you can know if he came for you. Can you feel his truth? Then you are part of him.

205

THOR 2 Email #9: The Argument Completed

Dear Reader:

At the beginning of this series of articles, I made the statement that I wanted to make an irrefutable argument. Here is a synopsis of that argument. Perhaps we can decide whether it is refutable or not.

If Jesus is representative man as I contend, then the war that has raged about him for these two thousand years is really the war in Man's own heart about the question of his own identity. Jesus and his experience as Man becomes what we have called a "living dream" showing the greater truth about collective Man.

Are we, as science claims, the accidental by product of evolution? Did we come from a chemical reaction in some primal ooze as a single cell to somehow, accidentally, in a world of infinite possibilities, finally be here in these 50 trillion cells of community called man? Are we, as Zechariah Sitchin and others claim, the offspring of the Gods, the Annunaki? Are we then the product of genetic engineering and crossbreeding, with resident pre-human species, by extraterrestrials? What are we to understand from the Genesis record? Are we truly a perfect immortal species, created in innocence, fallen from grace, and doomed to death and hell as some preachers would have us believe? The questions can be and have been stated much more eloquently than I can do in a few sentences. Volumes have been written. Poets and songwriters and philosophers have asked this question in so many ways it cannot all be told. Every one that ever allowed himself to feel his journey has in his or her way asked this wonderful, terrible, question in the context of his own life. Who am I? Why am I here? Many have in despair settled for the thought that there really is no answer or have turned to any number of addictions to drown out the quiet questions that will not go away. Science has determined that the observer and the observed are really one and cannot be separated. So how can we hope for an answer?

This one who came among us, as one of us, gave no philosophy, no doctrine to believe. He just offered himself as the answer to our deepest need and questions. Was he sent for me? My up welling emotion, my joy of knowing, they are my answer but can that serve you? Can my argument here, in just a few emails, clear away the fog of doubt and unbelief of ages? Yes, I believe it can because it is time. It is time to answer the question asked for so long. It is time to know reality. It is time to rise up. Resurrection time is here.

The simple argument is this. Jesus, attested by the Spirit and by Word, claimed to be divine, the Son of God. He demonstrated power and glory. He was able to truly manifest his acknowledged divinity, yet he called himself repeatedly the Son of Man. He identified himself with mortal man. He showed himself to be truly human in every respect, sharing the fears, the rejection, and the abandonment in his personal crucifixion on a Roman cross. This same one, when confronted with religious and political authority that speaks for man, clearly and unequivocally **stated himself to be the witness of the truth!** What Truth? He was the truth about MAN; Man whom he claimed to be and so represent and truly did represent in his life, death, and resurrection. There is an eternal truth waiting to be born in every human heart, longing for manifestation, longing to be seen and understood. This truth is found in this simple yet profound acknowledgement of existence. I will state it as it might have come from his mouth or your own:

You are, as I am, incarnate deity. You have been sent from the Father, born into limitation, crucified on time and space in your human form. You are the eternal, pre-existent Son of God, now ready to rise in the resurrection of this awakened consciousness. I am the witness to your truth.

If this be so, then may this be our prayer:

I return to thee Oh Father of Light, to my greater awareness as an eternal being of Light and Glory. I am ready now to fully accept this human form into which I have been sent for the divine intent and purpose that all the creation and all creatures in all realms might know thee Oh Holy Father and remember the joy of your great immeasurable Love.

THOR 2 Email #10: The Meaning of Death and Hell

Dear Reader:

We are standing at the Dawn of a New Age, the Age of Light and understanding, the Age of the Son of Man. Yet the Light that is breaking in our being is like the light of a bright room coming through the crack of a partially opened door. We are yet to enter its greater reality.

It is essential, as we leave the imprisonment to the limited reality of material consciousness, that we understand the symbolic nature of the imaging we have thought to be so real and substantial. The best way for me to illustrate what I mean is to speak of one particular part of that imaging: Death and the Grave.

Death and the Grave belong together. Death is an experience and the Grave is where you locate that experience. In the classic movie, The Matrix, Neo, whose name means "New" or "New One," at his introduction to a greater reality is instructed by Morpheus to "Free your mind." So we must do. So also Jesus exhorted and enabled his disciples to do when he confronted them with the greater truth about himself on the road to Emmaus. They were in deep conversation concerning the events so recently transpired, the crucifixion, the death of the Master. They had believed him to be the Messiah. How could the Messiah die? They had believed that he was the ONE.

Jesus helped them to free their minds to receive a greater perception of all those events they had just witnessed. He used words they had heard since their childhood, words from Moses, Isaiah and all the prophets. Those words became reality as they listened and, as they described it, words that made their hearts burn within them.

Here too we stand. We do not fully understand but we know that we are the recipients of a greater reality, a reality dawning in us as a new day. Religion as we have known it has fulfilled its purpose. Its structured dogmatic strength is broken, no longer needed in a world that is evolving into a new paradigm; God in Man, God as Man. Our hearts are young and open to this reality as were the disciples. How our hearts burn in us as we hear this greater perception of the truth of Man.

We will easily understand the greater significance of the Easter story, told more often in this last age than the story of the Exodus was in the age before it. Strangely enough the two stories are truly the same story, each signifying the collective release of man from the bondage to material consciousness.

Let's look more specifically at these two symbol words and their value in interpreting reality, the words Death and the Grave. They are used throughout the scriptures. I will mention just four. Hosea said these words: *I will ransom them from the power of the grave; I will redeem them from death: O death, I will be thy plagues; O grave, I will be thy destruction: repentance shall be hid from mine eyes.* David in the Psalms left us one of the most often quoted graveside scriptures in all history: *yeah though I walk through the valley of the shadow of death, I shall fear no evil.* Paul quotes Isaiah when he exclaims *Oh death where is thy sting? Oh grave where is thy victory?* John in the Apocalypse heard Jesus say these words: *I am alive forevermore, Amen! And have the keys of hell and death.* All of these are awesome statements of truth concerning the experience of man as we will see if we can only loose our minds from seeing only their immediate physical meaning.

The first thing to note is the use of the word **hell**. The meaning of the Greek word used here is actually Hades, meaning the abode of the dead. The old English word is really a good translation; it also means a pit or a hole in the ground hence a grave. It was used to describe covering something with earth as in "helling" potatoes. Its modern meaning of a burning place of torment is really incorrect. We will use the word Grave as a better translation.

My main thesis is as follows. The words Grave and Death are symbol words that describe our experience of becoming human, our incarnation, our coming into the earth realm.

If **Death** is in reference to the **experience** of man living in a human body... dead to his greater spiritual being...

Then the **Grave** must refer to the **human body**, the location of the experience.

209

Interesting indeed that modern usage of the word hell has been erroneously substituted for the grave or the place where we experience humanity. So in truth all the horrors we have assigned to this place called hell, the eternal torment, the unending regret, and the gnashing of teeth is really our perception of our own human experience. It shows the depth of our pain, the feelings of abandonment and rejection that we have localized in these human bodies. No wonder we have such staggering health problems. We are a nation addicted to prescription drugs, plagued by heart disease, diabetes and Alzheimer, all names we have created to describe our dysfunction and pain.

If **Grave** means the body and **death** is the experience in the grave then it follows that the word Death has a symbol value representing a primary experience that we have in these physical bodies. What is that primary experience? What is the most important feeling we experience here? Listen to the words of David:

"Yeah though I walk through the valley of the shadow of death", we translate here as follows: *Yeah even though I am in the human experience.* Whatever follows here must be the negation of the normal human experience, here it is: *I shall fear no evil for thou art with me.* What is the evil I fear? I cannot experience it, for thou art with me:

It clearly follows that the fear that we experience here in our humanity is the fear of separation, our aloneness.

We say this: The primary purpose of our embodiment, our human experience, is the experience of separation. Death then has the symbol value of **SEPARATION**. Now separation is a mental and emotional experience hence is referring to the **MIND**. You must **believe** that you are apart, away, separated from, in order to feel aloneness. Physical death, a human body lying still and cold, a graveside experience, is the three dimensional equivalent of what all the greater realms experience as **SEPARATION**. Separation is simply the belief that we are apart from the Source, from God.

Paul understood this concept of death. *"To be carnally minded is death"* is a clear definition of this thought. It can be said this way:

To have your mind focused on the experience of being in the flesh is the death experience of your spirit being.

Death = Mind (experiencing separation)
Grave = Body (where it happens)

We are often left to wonder, in the midst of painful irresolvable situations, what is the purpose for all this that we call the human experience? I too, as many of you, scoffed at the suggestion that we are the creators of our own experience. I thought that if I did, I must have been out of my mind! If we understand that it was separation itself that was desired by the Source so that Love could become all that it is, then we can see why an experience of separation created in this level of density we call physical would be such a great asset for evolving through states of consciousness. Understanding separation emotionally in a physical body is an inestimable benefit to create attitudes of acceptance, forgiveness, reconciliation, and hope. These are primary qualities needed in the great journey toward wholeness.

The powerful emotion experienced at a graveside, at the passing of a loved one, is the feeling of aloneness. Our minds try to grasp the thought of never again being able to touch, to look into the eyes, to share a feeling. This is the most powerful and impacting experience in the entire human journey, the feeling of separateness. These feelings that we create in the material realm are meant to bring understanding about separation. They allow us to emotionally focus it. Our understanding must become so deep and real that eventually we can say NO to the whole of the experience of separation and KNOW beyond all uncertainty that separation is not real. It is through this very process that we will finally come to realize that we have never been separated from our Source, from God.

Paul utters this thought in an exclamation: *Oh death where is thy sting?* We might say: *Oh separation where is your pain?* Paul here acknowledges that sin, the evolutionary driver of consciousness, only has power because of our belief in the experience of separation.

Paul continues: *Oh grave where is thy victory?* In his ecstatic joy of Calvary Paul foresees a day when man will no longer be trapped in lower degrees of awareness of this physical plane, no longer bound to material consciousness, no longer held by the pangs of death, the pain of separation.

It is the body that is either a place where you glorify the Father when you say: *A body thou hast prepared me, I come to do thy will oh God,* or it's a place of imprisonment and failure when you say: *Oh wretched man that I am who shall deliver me from this bondage to corruption!* What is it that man needs at this juncture in time? Does he need an immortal body that cannot die or suffer? I say NO, a thousand times, No! Yes, physical immortality is on the agenda, but what is it we need now?

We need to understand and be in a place where we see this present physical form as awesome, beautiful, and perfect in every way to accomplish the purpose for which it was created. It was created gloriously and beautifully by those who designed it for the eternal purpose of the evolving journey of consciousness. We need to know that it is only our fear of being in this body that locks us into the limitations of the body. The body itself is beautiful and perfect.

This is the message of the DEATH on the Cross and the Resurrection from the GRAVE that Jesus proclaims through John when he says: *I am alive forever more Amen! And I have the keys of hell and of death.* What are these keys that he has and desires to share? These keys are understandings about the Mind-Body connection or the Death-Grave connection. Death represents the mind of separation that lives throughout the body. The mind that can be bound to carnality, to physical-ness, and the body holds and manifests the mind, locking limiting perceptions of self into our very cellular structure. This is the grave we are buried in. We are released from its imprisoning power by the eternal truth we receive as we behold the True Man, the Son of Man, crucified and raised. We were buried in our carnality, our limitedness, trapped in physical consciousness. We are now awakened by His love as we realize the truth of our being. We are the eternal Son of God, crucified on time and space in our humanity now rising in the power of the resurrection to a new eternal day.

Jesus left the grave clothes neatly folded in the tomb. It is the sign of your reverence for the physical experience with which you are clothed in your human journey. Those grave clothes are your thoughts of separation, your rejection of it, and your pain. It was a needed path. To be truly and fully released from it, you must hold it in great reverence indeed. You could not have gained the eternal value of your earth experience without those grave clothes.

212

Three days and three nights Jesus spent in the earth. It is the picture of your embodiment in Earth Consciousness. His rising from the grave is the guarantee and assurance that you too can rise up into the eternal awareness of who you have always been and why you came to this plane.

Jesus' resurrection prophesied the collectively awakening of his greater body on the morning of the third day. From the time he seeded his consciousness into human awareness to this hour is two thousand years, two prophetic days. A thousand years is but as one day to the Lord. This dawning age, this new millennium, is the morning of the third day. It is resurrection time. Our resurrection is at hand. Our mind is being freed. We are ready to fold up the limited awareness of being and take flight on the wings of this new morning into an eternal day of gladness and joy. It is our time to live. For the first time in all of human history we are truly here, realizing our divine Sonship with God as The Son of Man.

THOR 2 Email #11: Lazarus, a Living Dream

Dear Friends:

Spiritual evolution is all about perception. It's not so much **what you look at.** Its all about **what you see,** or what you do not see. In order to SEE or PERCEIVE, we are given or we are continually creating what I call *"Living Dreams."* These experiences help us to awaken from the centuries of sleep or death, the entrapment in material consciousness. Jesus experienced such Living Dreams, and in fact, for us, He was a living dream. He was a projected reality into our realm of awareness. These Living Dreams are simply *orchestrated physical experiences*

When he heard the news that his friend Lazarus had died, Jesus became immediately aware that this experience was significant for him and had to do with the opening of his awareness about his mission and purpose. This is evidenced by the fact that he referred to Lazarus as *being asleep* when speaking to his disciples. The disciples strenuously objected to his terminology, *if he sleeps, he does well!*

Not only did Jesus refer to Lazarus death as a sleep, he remained yet three more days, arriving late for the funeral to the dismay of

213

Lazarus' beloved sisters, Mary and Martha. The conversation at the graveside is illuminating and reaches to the core of Jesus' Mission and Purpose. Here is his response to Martha when she complains about his tardiness and her exclamation that Lazarus would rise again in the last day:

John 11:25-27:

I am the resurrection and the life: he that believeth in me, though he be dead, yet shall he live: And whosoever liveth and believeth in me shall never die. Believest thou this?

Jesus immediately has a major reaction to the thought of the **Last Day** mentioned by Martha. He breaks the bondage in our minds to linear time and claims himself to be the key or the portal through which we can be released from looking at reality through the perceptional window of Time and Space. He is saying that reality is not physical and time based, it is SPIRITUAL. It is always here and now. It lies in your own embodiment, it is the Kingdom, it is attainable. He says all this in a simple comprehensive phrase:

I Am the Resurrection

The phrase, *though he be dead,* is referring to Lazarus, but it is really referring to all those that are in physical bodies, the living dead. All that are incarnate and dead to the greater awareness of who they are. *Yet shall he live,* meaning that even though you are physical, **yet** through me you can become aware again. You can awaken to the greater reality of your being while still in the body.

When Jesus goes on to proclaim...*and he that liveth and believeth, shall never die*...I hear him say:

And when this awesome awareness that I bring begins to awaken you, you will lose all fear of death. Death will no more have power over you in this realm or in the invisible realms. The pain of separation will pass from your spiritual being and you will be alive, with me, forevermore. You will be truly free.

He that *lives and believes* is he that is *awake and sees.*

214

Jesus knew that some major event, like raising Lazarus from the dead, would validate his Mission. It would bring into human consciousness the truth that he is and came to be, the ONE to awaken every Man. When he groaned, wept, and called Lazarus forth, Jesus experienced in one intense emotional moment the depth of his purpose and calling. He identified with the vibration of the Father's Love when he prayed: *Thou hearest me always.*

The report by John goes on to say that the time of the Passover was close. The Jews conspired to take him and Caiaphas made his now famous statement. John 11:49-50:

And one of them, named Caiaphas, being the high priest that same year, said unto them, Ye know nothing at all, nor consider that it is expedient for us, that one man should die for the people, and that the whole nation perish not.

Jesus knew all this when he heard the report of Lazarus death. Jesus, was aware and awake. He could hear and see.

THOR 2 Email #12: Review of Jesus' Mission and Identity

Dear Friends:

Jesus, named Jahshuah by the Angel Gabriel, and his mission are the subject of this writing. This is perhaps the most controversial subject of all time.

There have been many great teachers that have come into the world. As we lose our fear of being deceived, realizing that much of what we have understood has been at least incomplete and at worst a deception in its own right, we venture out and listen to such teachings and understandings from other religions. Jesus is and was honored as a prophet, a master, and certainly a teacher by many other than his followers. Deepak Chopra has just written about the Third Jesus and liberally quotes the historical Jesus in that writing. All this intensifies the mystery. Who is that one that was called the Son of God yet claimed no more than to be the Son of Man?

215

Jesus did not seek to be worshipped. He said: *They that worship the Father must worship Him in spirit and in truth.* He was truly magnanimous when it came to his followers. When the disciples found some who did cures in Jesus' name, yet were not walking with him, Jesus made this remark: *They that are not against me are for me.* If all the followers of Jesus through the centuries had been as magnanimous as he was, the world would be a better place today.

Considering all these things I must conclude that the understanding of Jesus' person and mission as seen in the writings of the letters to the new testament Churches and in the Church doctrines of the passing age are only sufficient for that age and are incomplete and wanting for the Age that is dawning.

If, as I state in previous mailings, the greater mission of Jesus is only now coming to Light, at this dawning of the Age of Aquarius, then we must also acknowledge that we truly have not known who he is and our passionate desire might be, as Paul the Apostle wrote: *That I might know him in his resurrection.*

And it is in RESURRECTION that we DO know him...not so much in Jesus' resurrection but in our own, unless you can see that the resurrection of Jesus from a physical tomb is in fact your resurrection. It is the guarantee to you of your resurrection from the tomb of human consciousness. That resurrection, our rising up from the lower planes of imprisonment to human perceptions, is now in full swing.

If you will listen, in the recesses of your own mind, you can hear him saying to you:

Fear not the death you have experienced in your mortal mind. It was only for a brief moment. It was the precursor to an eternal resurrection, a remembering that you were with me in the worlds that once were. You can walk with me now and I with you in planes of Light and together we will know the purpose and plan of the ages as we see our Father's will done in Earth as it is in Heaven.

To fully see the purpose of Jesus' death and resurrection, we must examine more particularly the events immediately before and after his death on Calvary. That will be the subject of the next few emails.

THOR 2 Email #13: The Greater Meaning of the Cross

Dear Friends:

Most of us have lived long enough and died enough in our living to realize that our human identity is not so much an experience of physical fact as it is a PERCEPTION of those facts. The best illustration of this thought is the idea that there are always two sides to any story; at least two, or as many as there are participants in the story.

A small boy, raped by an uncle, may grow physically into manhood but a part of the personality, because it is a perception, will most likely stay as a little boy, afraid to trust, afraid to reach out. This entrapment, caused by shame, can only be broken after there is a sufficient amount of life experience gained by the victim to enable him to understand that as a little boy there was no fault attached to anything that happened to him. He was truly a victim. However, even if the mind gains enough understanding and life experience, the adult victim can still be taken back emotionally to the event of the rape and there bring realization of the truth to that little boy's mind, the mind now trapped in an adult body.

This process of taking us back in our emotional awareness to the traumatizing event was accomplished for us collectively by Jesus dying on the cross. It is only effective for you if you BELIEVE. That is, if you allow the Holy Spirit to emotionally take you back to the event of the cross, realizing that it is really you that was crucified, that it was you that experienced the wounds of fear, separation, abandonment and disempowerment.

Jesus thus becomes your savior when he, by taking your sin upon himself, (your belief in your failure to meet eternal requirements, and your feelings of shame and guilt), shows it to you. As you watch in wonder and amazement, identifying with all the pain and agony, you can hear him sweetly say to you:

All these feelings you have experienced, all this pain, are the results of a lie that you have believed; a lie that was whispered in your mind that you made real; a lie that said that you could not meet the expectations of your Father-Creator; a lie that made you believe that

His love for you is conditional and imperfect; a lie that caused you to create a separated identity, lost and alone.

The truth is that you, like me, were crucified, not on a stake, but on the cross of time and space in your human form. I am only the image of your truth. Your cross is not made of wood. Your cross is material consciousness. You are trapped in the thought that you are only human, the thought that your perceptions of self are the whole truth and nothing but the truth. In reality, you are the Son of God even as I am, and you are doing the will of your Father who sent you.

Amazingly enough, the power of the cross, the atonement provided there, is effective even when there is little understanding of the greater truth it represents.

The greater truth is the fact that you as an eternal spiritual being took on a human form of limitation and imperfection and in that process became trapped in material consciousness. Trapped, in a human body, by your limited perceptions, you died.

Most of us have experienced that redeeming power, the cleansing of the blood of Calvary, the wonder of forgiveness, and being born again. However as we walked on into greater light, we began to realize that even if we were "born again", forgiven, heaven bound, we still had pain and fear, and we still created lives filled with disappointment. Hypocrisy was never far from our soul. Even though we experienced the power of the cross, we had no truth or understanding to appreciate its full and greater message.

Today we stand at the crossroads of humanity. In order for man to inherit the eternal Kingdom of Light breaking on this planet, he MUST remember the greater journey. He MUST go back past layers of shame and guilt and remember that he is the Eternal Son of God. We must remember that in obedience to the Father's will, man was lowered into the human condition to prepare the way for the Dawning Light of God to come into the creation through materialization of divine consciousness in man, Christ.

Only the message of Jesus, the greater message of the cross, can break the power of shame that keeps us from the realization of our ONENESS. Suddenly some of the words of Jesus become plain:

I am the way, the truth and the life, no one cometh unto the Father but by me. The way is the way of remembrance. The truth is the truth of who you are. The life is the eternal consciousness that you had before you died in your humanity.

We will continue this line of thought in later emails, but first let's take another look at our humanity.

Email #13A: Shedding and Embracing our Humanity

Dear Friends:

This present email writing is a response I received from Tony Salmon to email #13: **The Greater Meaning of the Cross.** I want you to hear from Tony how the trauma of life became the pressure point that took him inward to God and finally drove him to embrace the dark moments and the pain in order to know all that God is. Tony refers to our incarnation as an incarceration or an imprisonment. We will spend some time to compare these two valid perspectives of the human experience. One is from the pain of our experience based on a feeling of limitation; the other is from the desire of the eternal realms that seek this plane of manifestation as an opportunity.

Tony Salmon writes:

When I read these words I am reminded of how we, in our true essence, have been incarcerated in age-lasting chains under ignorance until the judgment. We incarnate into this time/space continuum by inheritance, borrowed genetics. We identify with coded information in the genes, the double helix becoming the parenthesis, the earthen boundaries, and our identity becomes based in all of the information contained within it. The genetic links or chains become the bars of death and our true essence becomes the prisoner of this cell until the time appointed of the Father. We have somehow lost our way, lost our identity. The unthinkable happened; we were brought into the sphere of limitation. We were made subject to death

I am learning to embrace my humanity. Oh, it's been a long time coming. When I began to hear the trumpet, when I began to awaken and remember my true estate, I was all too happy to quickly abandon the human experience with all of its pain and tears.

Why wouldn't I want to escape? I was held captive for so many years with a horrible fear of rejection and fear of abandonment, fear of being left alone. I remember the times when I would drive to a place where no one could hear me scream... and cry very loud to release a groan from a gaping wound that was cut so deep. I remember being doubled over in physical discomfort because the emotional pain was so intense. I could not understand this human drama, it made no sense to me. I could not understand why a loving God would not instantly pick me up in His arms and make all the pain go away. After all He is my Father, right? I ran to my daughter every time I heard her cry, hoping and praying that her injuries from falling off the bike were not serious and that I would find her safe from harm. Oh, every parent knows the horror of wondering what we will see when we run to our crying child, and every parent knows the relief of realizing that our child is safe and not seriously injured. At that precise moment we know that everything is perfect, a little ointment and a band-aid and our child is as good as new, but the child doesn't know that. The child is experiencing trauma and so we pick the child up in our arms and provide the love and comfort that the child is reaching for. My God, are we better than our Father?

Yet He came to me so many times. He always had a way of showing up when suicide became the most comforting of thoughts. He came to me at the times when I did not feel safe from my own hands, fearing that they might indeed have more power to squeeze the trigger than another part of me had to stop them. At these times the heavens would open and I would be lifted into very high realms.

And yes, He came at other times as well, showing that I am never really alone. The very gift of preaching that the Father gave me also proved that within me is the power to break the chains that kept me in torment. In many of my lowest and darkest moments I would stand in the pulpit and literally lift myself into the celestial City where there is no night, no sorrow or crying. After being in such a meeting I was amazed to discover that I could remember all of the things that were troubling me before, but there was absolutely no pain attached to those thoughts. I was able to be objective and look at the circumstances from the bird's-eye view. There were times when a thought would come that the pain I was experiencing was not my own, but I was feeling the groan of creation.

Oh, the words of Job, *"I know that my redeemer lives and IN MY FLESH I will see God!* AH! He lives and will manifest in my FLESH! Now there is light; now there is understanding. The void and the deficit is the very place where He must manifest. The death, the decaying organic matter, and manure provide the perfect place for the seed to grow! Thank you, Father, for the void, the dark place! You have made the pavilion of darkness your home! In the very darkest place of my heart is the place where you must manifest! AH! The glorious Light of His kingdom shining in the darkest recesses of my soul! Thank you, Father; thank you Yeshua!

Love and mercy to all from Tony.

THOR 2 Email #14: The Human Body...Temple or Prison

Dear Friends:

Hope you enjoyed the response from Tony Salmon. You notice that his use of the idea of the human cell as a prison reflects the victimization humanity has suffered under so many long ages. It is this very feeling of victimization, the power of sin, that Jesus came to destroy by the brightness of his appearing, his Truth. There is a legitimate use of the idea of imprisonment in the incarnate state as a corrective measure as referred to by Tony. It was imposed on the Angels that transgressed as described in the book of Jude and the book of Enoch.

This same contrast, Temple or Prison, is seen clearly in the following references to incarnation, one from the Psalms: *A body thou hast prepared me, I come to do thy will oh God!* Here the physical body is seen as a Temple. When Paul refers to this same experience of incarnation he cried out: *Oh wretched man that I am, who shall deliver me from the body of this death?* Here the physical body is seen as a cell of imprisonment.

The following are some comments from the group, first Esther:

Whoo-hoo, bring it on :) I love the whole concept of Jesus' death on Calvary being a representation of something greater to us. His death on Calvary as a representation of our own experience with humanity is in keeping with his use of parables. Just like he didn't mean those stories literally, it would seem natural that his death has greater meaning too... Love Esther

Here is Archy Hafichuch, relating a vision concerning Jesus:

Just picture a rough hewn table top, but smooth on the surface. At one end is the hand of our Lord, resting on the table, yet, not resting but leaning on it and yet not leaning but using the table to convey His strength and compassion. His hand is rough from carpentry, yet warm and firm. I saw that I was in His arm and yet also part of the hand. It was so real, like being right there, part of Him, in Him, and yet I felt the power and strength in his hand like I was the hand. I can still feel and see His hand. Words are so inadequate.

What a powerful experience to relate to us Jesus passion for identification with our human experience. Wood is traditionally humanity; carpenters use wood to create habitation.

THOR 2 Email #15: Humanity: Our Experience not Our Identity

Dear Friends:

I would like to make a few more remarks about the perspective of our humanity that may help us in receiving the Light that is coming from higher realms about our incarnate state.

I love Tony's remarks about the cell, the basic building block of our human bodies, being as a prison cell. Jude makes reference to those Angels that fell and were bound with *chains of darkness*. What an apt description of the double helix that makes up our DNA. It contains the primary programming and information code of the physical body. The strands of the double helix can certainly be seen as BARS that limit human consciousness. To break free from the imprisoning and the limiting effect of the two strand-DNA on our consciousness we must break the THOUGHT that we in fact are only human. We must shed our blood as Jesus so clearly showed us, let go of identity.

It is our belief that we are human and only human that incarcerates us. No one could imprison you if you did not believe in the imprisonment. You were the one that believed the lie.

The awesome truth of that wooden Cross is that you are the **Son of God** crucified on it, wood symbolizing **humanity**. You are NOT that cross. You are not humanity. You are simply crucified ON it. Humanity for you is not your IDENTITY, it is simply your EXPERIENCE. You are an eternal being of Light having a human experience.

The power of the Cross and blood of Jesus is the enablement it brings to you to change your **perception** of self. Since only your mind can lock you in debilitating imprisonment to the human condition, it is only through the mind that you can be freed from that same condition. Right perspective is the key. Truth is the key. You shall know the TRUTH, (the truth of your eternal Son-ship), and the knowledge of that truth at a deep emotional level as you behold the crucified Son sets you FREE; free from the lie that has imprisoned you in your human identity. The Cross and the blood shed there are absolutely necessary to reach down into the subconscious layers of debilitation, through shame, and free you from a self-imposed thought that keeps you bound; the thought that you are human and only human. Only through the blood of Jesus, the blood that speaks the eternal truth of who you are, can we be saved from the lies that have entrapped our consciousness in bars of limitation.

It was never your body, your cells, your DNA, that imprisoned you. It was the belief in your mind that bound you. It bound you through your false identification with the body. The Light breaks and you are reconnected with your greater knowing, your greater identity, your Light body.

From the point of view of this greater knowing, you can now look at your incarnation and instead of seeing a limiting prison cell, you can now see the most Glorious opportunity for a Light being, the opportunity to be lowered into form and bring the Glory of the Creator-Source, the Father of Spirits, into material consciousness. You are no longer asleep under the alluvial deposits of centuries of human consciousness, but awakened as Christ to show the Glory of the Father in manifest form to all created realms. Not only Christ formed in you or you forming in Christ, but you **as** Christ bringing the Father of Light in form. This is the intention of the redemptive program in Adam-kind.

Without the shedding of blood, there is no release from the imprisoning effects of sin, the thoughts of inability to meet divine appointment. Without the **shedding of human consciousness as the identity of your eternal self,** there can be no true awareness of your eternalness to re-connect you to your greater Glory. Without the death of Calvary, there can be no resurrection of your greater self. Without the greater awareness of your divine being, there can never be an embracing of your humanity.

Human thought and human ability alone can NEVER embrace humanity. It will always be imprisoned by it. It is only in your greater awareness as the eternal Son of God that you can embrace being human as a Glory and an appointment. It is only **God** that can embrace being **human.** Only the Son can say: *I have come to do thy will, a body thou hast prepared me.*

THOR 2 Email #16: Breaking the Hold of Old Imprints

Dear Friends:

I have shown that the Age of Aquarius is the Age of the Son of Man, that is, the Age that will see the fulfillment of Jesus' mission as the Son of man. We continue to pursue our search into that mystery. Jesus himself, when confronted by the Pharisees, counseled with his disciples that he did not really want the Pharisees to hear what he had to say. He wanted them to hear the words of his parables, draw their own conclusions, but not to hear the truth he was bringing to this planet. He purposely intended for them NOT to hear his truth. His explanation to his disciples went like this: *Unto you it is given to know the mysteries of the Kingdom.* The Mysteries, or the *Musterion* in Greek, are the sacred secrets shared only with initiates of the order. It is little wonder then that the religious world to this day understands little of the divine purpose of the Ages.

The full purpose of Jesus as a gift to this Planet from the realms of divine purpose has not been revealed until this time, this time of awakening of the Body of Christ. In fact it has been purposely kept from the consciousness of men until now. Now is the time of the revealing of this sacred mystery he spoke of to his disciples. It is now, especially, that we as his body must know these sacred and holy thoughts to comfort us and enable us to walk away from every paradigm of truth and reality this world has known into a brilliance of truth and remembrance of being that comes from being re-connected to our Light Bodies.

In that Jesus rose from the dead, we are to know that we can and will also rise from the deadened consciousness of physical mortality into the remembrance of our own eternalness while yet we remain in these physical mortal bodies. This is what Jesus meant when it is written: *I have the keys of* **death and hell.** Meaning this: *I have the understanding that you need in order for you to live in the* **mind-body connection** *of the human condition. I have truly made the way for you to fully incarnate in this physical plane and so bring the glory of eternal awareness and light into every realm of darkness.*

Tony with such excellence told us of Samson, representative of the Son of Man. He related how Samson grasped the two pillars **upon which rested the whole house**, and in his blindness and seeming failure completed his mission when he tore it all down. My heart lept for joy at such beautiful words. It is you and I that so shatter the forces that have controlled the minds of men through the imprint in the DNA, the two strand pillars upon which the whole house of lies has rested these long ages. No longer will man be held from the greater truth of his being by the imprinted consciousness programming of his DNA. Man will bypass all the layers where he sought residency and now receive the greater knowing of his own being from a true remembering of the imprint in his own Light Body. The DNA of his physical form will now serve only the intended purpose, **a body thou hast prepared me, I come to do thy will oh God**. All the nobility of the Philistines died that day. All the powerful thoughts that have ruled the minds of men are broken and made powerless. Rulership is being taken from the Angels and given to the Son. Our words are Spirit and they are Truth; they break the strongholds of dysfunction from the minds of men. The force of Evil cannot abide in this Light.

225

I am persuaded that Mel Gibson was commissioned from the Spirit to do his re-enactment of the crucifixion of Jesus Christ. At the beginning of this, the Age of the Son of Man, there must be a review of the mission of Jesus. We cannot bring the full intent of the incarnation of our eternal beings into conscious awareness without the empowerment of the Holy Spirit through the imprinted image of Jesus on the Cross. This is what I believe Jesus meant when he said: *No One cometh unto the Father but by me.* We might say it this way:

> ***No one can come to the full realization of the purpose
> and intent of their incarnation experience
> without the truth I am bringing.***

Or to say it in a positive way:

> ***I am the one that was sent of the Father to bear witness to the
> truth of your being so that you can overcome and fully
> manifest God in this plane and so be one with
> the Father and His purpose.***

It seems difficult for me to get away from restating the mission and purpose of Jesus. Perhaps this is so because we cannot really see this purpose in his actual experience until we have a more clearly defined perception of his over-all mission. The "grooves" in our mind concerning past concepts about Jesus and his purpose are deep and well worn. It is almost impossible for our minds not to slip into that old groove.

What is that old thought pattern? Simply stated it is this: **something went wrong, we screwed up, and God has come to fix it.** As I have said before, I am not entirely opposed to this remedial approach to the divine intent. I myself have been full of regret and blame at times and have needed true forgiveness and a cleansing of my soul from sin and sin consciousness. It is this very fact of our need for forgiveness that makes the old ruts so attractive to our minds. If it had no validity at all, it would be easy to discard. The very fact that there is great validity to forgiveness, salvation, and redemption makes the road into a greater awareness, a new paradigm, difficult if not almost impossible. Except for the enabling power of the Holy Spirit, we would be like those children of Israel that could not let go of the slave mentality of Egypt and so did not enter into the greater promises. They all died in the wilderness except for two, Caleb and Joshua, two as a witness that it IS possible to overcome.

It is that very addiction to a perspective of victimization deep in our cellular structure that we must leave behind; hence so great a need for the Holy Son of God to whisper into your ear:

Psst...It's OK to be human. Relax and listen to your heart.

THOR 2 Email #16A: Inheriting the Promised Land

Dear Readers:

One of the great themes of scripture is the idea of a *Promised Land.* It is first seen in the promise to Abraham, a promise that his descendants would inherit real estate. They did.

Come to find out that the real estate they inherited was just a piece of desert. Had the Promised Land moved? Paul makes the comment that Abraham was looking for a City whose builder and maker is God. Perhaps it was more than a piece of real estate after all.

Well, I am persuaded it is all true. It **is** real estate. It is Palestine. It is the USA. It is the planet if you like, but it's much more than that.

Jesus left us with these words to ponder when we moved to this little piece of real estate in Missouri:

> *So won't you come on in with me?*
> *Into this Place of Ours,*
> *Together we'll walk, hand in hand*
> *And inherit the Promised Land.*

I love what Gary Sigler has to say in the following response to email #16:

Hi Rokus,
I have seen for some time now that our purpose is to fully incarnate

227

into this physical realm. In the book of Hebrews Chapter 11 we are told that all the men of faith died not having received the promise. We have thought in the past that the promise was a natural land or a land up in a heaven somewhere, but we are beginning to see that the land that we are to inherit is our body. Heb 11:15 says: "And truly, if they had been mindful of that country from whence they came out, they might have had opportunity to have returned."

Thank You Gary!

THOR 2 Email #17: The Wounds of Your Crucifixion

Dear Reader:

We are finally seeing Light at the end of the tunnel, so to speak. The long dark pathway, stage one of our journey, incarnation, is coming to the Light of Day, the day of true awareness. Jesus said: *He that hears my words shall not walk in darkness.* It is my persuasion that we are among the first who are beginning to hear the true import of his words.

Not only the import of his spoken words but more importantly the reading of the pages of his book of incarnate truth, the word that became flesh and dwelt among us. That word of truth, enacted on the stage of human consciousness, is the word I am speaking of. It is primarily the truth revealed in his Crucifixion.

We well know that the religious interpretations of the event of the Crucifixion are inadequate, although they are not without beautiful significance. The simple fact that David proclaimed a thousand years earlier: *Sacrifices and burnt offerings thou hast not desired, thou hast opened mine ear to thy word,* is enough to put to rest the thought that Jesus' death was payment and retribution for sin to appease the justice of God. More clearly understood, we see that it was the LAW that required restitution for Sin. It was the Law, the Covenant Israel entered into, that had to be satisfied. It was a covenant that mankind needed in order to create the experience of legal guilt, atonement, restitution, and forgiveness. These are awesome truths and sacred understanding, but they do not add up to the full significance of the truth and purpose revealed in Calvary..

The Prophet Isaiah writes these awesome, beautiful words:

He was wounded for our transgression, He was bruised for our iniquity, the chastisement of our peace was upon Him, and by His stripes we are healed.

The connection here is between the **wounds, bruises, chastisements and stripes** that Jesus received and our experience of **transgression, iniquity, conflict, and disease**, in short, the dark side of the human experience.

These qualities of experience called iniquity, transgression, conflict, and disease were experienced by him and displayed by him as WOUNDS in his body.

We recognize that Jesus on the cross is enacting the woundedness of Mankind. He is creating an image through the medium of his own physical body, a reflection as it were of our inner woundedness. This woundedness has manifested in our lives as transgression, iniquity, conflict and disease; woundedness we purposed in the eternal realm to carry to this plane and manifest. As he puts himself on display, he is saying to us:

Look at me and see the thing you are hiding from yourself. See the way that you feel about yourself deep within. Let go of the pretense and denial that keep you in a religious frame of mind and allow yourself to feel. Feel your feelings of loss, abandonment, and pain. Recognize that like me you have carried these in your body for a greater purpose.

Clearly then the purpose of the Cross and the shed blood of Jesus are to create a pathway of emotional release for all that are trapped in distortions of self awareness; hence Jesus' claim of being the Way, the Truth, and the Life. The Cross of Christ is not so much about FIXING as it is about ACCEPTING. We see this clearly in the words of Isaiah when he writes: *As a Lamb was dumb before its shearers so opened he not his mouth.*

What are the wounds that are displayed for us to see in his crucifixion and what is the emotional significance of each of these inner wounds? The first woundedness Jesus experienced happened in the garden of Gethsemane. As he travailed in his soul over the impending agony he was facing it states that he sweat drops of blood. Under extreme stress the peripheral capillaries in the forehead can burst and mix with the perspiration, the result being drops of blood on the forehead.

Let go of the thought that because you experience stress you are not truly spiritual. Release yourself from the unjust demand of perfection that says that a spiritual person should not have pain. Know that stress is part of the driving force that presses you on in your quest for awareness and understanding.

The wounds he experienced in his body are as follows:

1.   The pricking of thorns in his head...*Fears of the mind.*
2.   The stripes on his back...*Rejection and Abandonment.*
3.   The wounds in his hands...*Powerlessness, inability to perform.*
4.   The wounds in his feet: *Feelings of imprisonment, locked in.*
5.   The wound in his side...*Disappointment and Betrayal.*
6.   The drops of blood on his forehead...*Stress.*

These emotions are the debilitation of the human experience. Mostly they are debilitating because we have perceived them as evidence of lack of worth and lack of spirituality. We have said to ourselves that because we experience these emotional states we are therefore not qualified for God-Hood. We discredit ourselves from the divine awareness within and without. We have used these feelings to justify our feelings of shame and un-worth, imprisoning ourselves in the lowered consciousness of the human experience.

The very fact that the one we esteemed to be without fault or blemish, the one who called himself the Son of Man, the one who was crucified because they said he claimed to be the Son of God, supposedly making himself equal with God, that one...experienced every emotion for which you disqualify yourself.

'As a Lamb led to the slaughter so opened he not his mouth,' are the words recorded about him describing the way he embraced the cross. In so doing, so he showed clearly that you, as the Son of God, crucified on the limitation of your human incarnation, are perfectly acceptable and truly honored in the courts of heaven. He showed you

that your seeming weakness, fears, and disappointments, instead of disqualifying you, are actually the divinely appointed pathway of your becoming. They are your pathway of ascension and resurrection into divine awareness and enthronement.

The shedding of blood at the cross of Jesus symbolizes for us the letting go of attachment to our humanity as a sense of identity. It is not the fact that we are human that limits us, it's our identification with our humanity that imprisons us. We think that being human is the whole of what we are. Being human is the experience of our higher being, it is not who we are. It is the ATTITUDE toward our own humanity that is so critical. Jesus came to show us the higher way, it is the attitude of ACCEPTANCE and EMBRACING.

.

Your human experience, as your Cross, instead of being seen as a place of defeat and shame is in fact the place of your qualifying. It is the place where you clothe yourself with the divine attitudes and divine awareness you so intensely desired in your disembodied pre-incarnate state.

You, your higher being, desired to participate in redemption. You are part of a collective Lamb that came to take upon itself the sin of the cosmos. You are a redeemer. This is why you became human, to do the will of your heavenly Father.

THOR 2 Email #18: Shedding Our Blood...Some Responses

Here is a response from John McGill in Hawaii:

Hey Rokus,

I just re read # 17 and it gets better and better as the words sink in deeper. You have found the gold that everyone, without knowing it, have been looking for but never thought they would find. Jesus is now back in vogue. He is no longer an appendage or some side trip. He really is us and we are Him. Hurrah! Love: John

Again, may I remind my readers, I appreciate your comments and responses. They stir me to write and encourage me, and you don't even have to agree with me, {chuckle}. If you do NOT want me to include your name and or address in the quote, let me know. I like to connect people when I can.

Because of the response above, and to clarify the importance of the awareness of our higher being, I will write this particular email about the shedding of blood referred to repeatedly in these emails and in scripture in general.

The holographic image created by Jesus' life and particularly his death on the cross is given to us to LOOK AT. The writer of Hebrews, when raising the question: *"Who is Man?"* raises the question of identity. He then proceeds to describe Adam Man as a glorious, overcoming, creature of Light to whom God put all things under subjection. When the writer acknowledges that we are unable to see the truth of this greater identity, he cries out in despair: *But we do not (yet) see all things put under him (Man).* Notice the *yet,* it is not in the original text; hence I have placed it in parenthesis. Then the writer makes this awesome statement:

But We See Jesus.

What I am emphasizing here is the main thesis of all these present emails, the imaging of our eternal truth and identity in the cross of Christ. It is by looking at that image that we CAN see that all things are subject to us.

Let us look at the main theme of the cross, the shedding of blood. It was literal blood that drained from his wounds and soaked into the ground, and that blood HAD TO BE PHYSICAL to be significant. However, it is the metaphysical truth of the blood we want to see.

Any person present at the cross could see the physical blood draining. It takes an illuminated eye to SEE the TRUTH that the blood represents. We want to see by the eyes of the spirit as we have been enjoined to do all during this past age.

Since *The Blood* has been used almost as an incantation without a great deal of understanding when we sing: *There is power in the blood,* many have turned away from the truth represented here. Many have exclusively associated the blood with punishment and retribution, hence the aversion. We can no longer conceive of God that way. We need to take another look to see the awesome power of the blood and the cross for *it certainly will never suffer loss,* as the hymn writer declared.

When we look at Jesus on the cross, the first question that arises is: *Who is this man?* The answer is two-fold.

The Roman centurion strikes his chest and says: *Surely this was **the Son of God.*** Jesus says: *Who do you say that I, **the Son of Man,** am?*

So, the answer is simple. When you look at the one on the Cross, you are looking at yourself. You are seeing, not your humanity that you thought you were, but your eternal self having the human experience: The Son of God dying as the Son of man.

If this be so...then who is shedding blood? Clearly it is your eternal being, your greater self that is shedding its blood. I say *it's* in a non-gender way, meaning your Christ or eternal being. But your eternal cannot shed blood, it has no blood; here in lies the wonderful mystery.

The blood shed on the cross that flows into the earth is representative of the experience of your incarnation.

You and I died in Adam when our consciousness, represented by blood, entered the earth and we embraced and were limited to an earthly identity. This identity is defined by genetics. We have struggled with it, have cursed it and have tried to release ourselves from it ever since because we did not understand why we were here.

When the awesome truth comes to your spirit man and you see that as Jesus blood was shed on the cross so you too poured out your life as an eternal being and took on the consciousness of man, then you can no longer see as you have seen yourself for thousands of years, your perspective has changed forever.

Let us make this conclusion. It is not your nature that needs changing or fixing, nor is it your participation in the genetics of Adam that is your problem, neither is it your cellular structure that imprisoned you. Rather it was through your PERCEPTION of those things that you were LOWERED into the earth realm for a divine intent and purpose. You died to your eternal awareness on the Cross of limited human consciousness to do the will of your Father.

THOR 2 Email #19: Without the Shedding Of Blood
There Is No Remission of Sin

Dear Reader:

Now that we have clearly stated the case, we can see some very obvious conclusions that will help to shift a paradigm of perception that we have struggled with for a long time. The question is:

Why is the shedding of blood necessary for the remission of sin?

Blood is the single most important element in spiritual ritual in the Old Testament. Animals were ritually slaughtered and their blood applied to persons and holy objects to ritually cleanse them. The Children of Israel were instructed to apply the blood of a Lamb to the doorposts and lintels of their doorways to prevent the Death Angel from entering their homes. The High Priest could only enter the Holy Place with blood. Paul the Apostle continues the significance of blood but elevates the ritual to a spiritual level. He states that the rituals of the law were ineffective to cleanse the worshipper shown by the fact that they had to be repeated over and over. These sacrifices, because they were simply images of the truth, not the truth itself, all pointed to another day, another time, and another realm. The benefits of the sacrificial offerings came not from the offerings themselves that the worshipper sacrificed but from his OBEDIENCE; as it is written: *Sacrifice and burnt offerings thou hast not desired, thou hast opened my ear to thy word.* And again: *Obedience is better than sacrifice.*

Since the blood shed on Calvary is symbolic of something that happened in the eternal realm, the lowering of your consciousness, then clearly the blood was not shed primarily for any sins of omission or commission in that earth realm. We were just not there yet. The sacrifice of Calvary took care of sin consciousness in the human plane simply by removing the curse of the Law. It was effective, once and for all. The Law of just deserts, of retribution and karma, no longer ruled human consciousness. So...when you hear another person testify that he found forgiveness of sin at the Cross, be happy with him and for him because he was taken out from under the law and found grace, for it is the law that creates sin-consciousness. The experience at the Cross is greater than our theology about it.

How then does he shedding of blood remit Sin? We understand the symbolic meaning of **shedding blood** to be the *letting go* of eternal consciousness, *giving up* of your greater reality: *your incarnation.*

We restate the question as: *How does the experience of INCARNATION release you from the imprisonment to sin?* We understand that SIN itself is not the problem; sin is needed in the evolving of consciousness. It is the evolutionary driver that takes us on the journey of separation. It is the **imprisonment** to the **power** of sin, enacted by **Shame,** that debilitates you and keeps you from progressing into greater realms and experience. It is not Sin that caused you to hide from the Light, it is Shame, and again, like Sin, shame is needed to enact the divine intent of this awesome journey of consciousness. When shame became so toxic that it debilitated you to the point of locking you in a fetal position, then you needed a release, a remission of your sin.

Sin is that awesome thought you generated at the beginning of your eternal journey, something that began in your thinking when you first received the power to form your own thoughts. You need this thought formation process in order to begin the journey of developing your own creative ability. You began to discover the 'secret,' the fact that you draw experiences to yourself by fixing your desire and intent. Sin was that first thought conceived in you questioning whether or not you would be able to meet the expectations of the loving Father-Source that created you; the Father that gave you the seed of self awareness, consciousness of being.

Our incarnation releases us from the power of sin by making real what has no essential reality of its own, that is, our shame. Shame that came as the result of sin, is the imagination in you that you are not pleasing to the Source because of some perceived limitation or imperfection.

Shame has no reality of its own. It had to be given an artificial reality in the flesh in order to be emotionally understood.

In other words, only in the body of flesh could you create the experiences needed to help you understand the true nature of shame. Shame that in this physical plane is made real so that ultimately, after the experience, you can see that shame experienced by your greater being, is not real. Shame is only a creation of the mind. We came here collectively to unlock the mystery of sin and shame and so set the creation free to progress on its eternal quest for unfolding of consciousness.

THOR 2 Email #20: Oh God, Why Do I Feel So Alone?

Dear Reader:

We continue the theme of the Cross. The Cross represents a three dimensional image, a hologram, of the truth about you and me. As we see the truth, not flinching, not pulling our eyes away, we can allow ourselves to feel the pain of our own existence, pain that we have been in denial of, pain we pretended not to have.

Jesus, referring to himself and his purpose, made this remark: *As the Serpent was lifted up in the wilderness, so must the Son of Man be lifted up.* He took this metaphor from a time when the children of Israel were journeying through the wilderness and had been bitten by fiery serpents. Instructed by God, Moses raised a brass image of a Serpent on a pole. If anyone would exit their tent and LOOK at the image they would be healed from Serpent bites which were causing them to die. In other words:

They were LOOKING at the thing that bit them
and
The mere act of LOOKING brought healing.

We understand the principle: *In order for something to be healed it must be revealed.* In SEEING Jesus on that cross we are SEEING ourselves. We are looking at the thing that bit us. We see what we **perceive** our human condition to be. The things that have bitten us, our feelings of rejection, of disempowerment, and most of all our intense loneliness, have left us on the beach of our incarnation, disconnected from all greater reality, blind and dumb.

As we look at him and allow our emotional body to receive the imprint of our own suffering, his love for us enables us to **feel.** We can feel again, releasing our deepest pain and fear, the fear that God has abandoned us. We feel this fear in the agony of his soul as he cries:

236

Eloi, Eloi, Lama Sabachthani?

My God, my God, why have you forsaken me?

As we begin to realize that we are the creators of our own experience and we ask ourselves: *Why would we create and endure such pain? Why would we even want to be here at all?* We are pressed to the greater truth hidden behind the surface of our experience. It is the realization that it is not truly the human that suffers at all; it is the Son of God that is crucified on human flesh. It is our greater being in eternal realms that reaches to understand its journey of separation. Our higher being intensely desires an emotional experience to help it focus its feelings of abandonment and rejection in order that it might ultimately understand, not so much the feelings created by your own mind, but the counter-positive. It desires to know the deep undemanding, unending Love and unconditional acceptance of the Source itself. Finally, we will understand, or will know, that we are really one with the Source itself. God is having the experience as us. Then the saying will come to pass: *We know as we are known.* Truly, in reality, we have never been, nor could we ever be, separate from all that we are. We are whole and complete.

THOR 2 Email #21: Jesus Has Come To Your House!

Dear Reader:

Our quest is to bring understanding to the most elementary questions of human existence. *Who are we? Where are we?* and, *Why are we here?* Jesus has appeared in time, sent from the Father, as you have been, to bring real tangible answers these awesome questions.

Science has a significant input. The book of the DNA has been opened. Religion tries to maintain the status quo. New Age teachers are doing their best to help. Psychics and mediums through different sources are encouraging mankind to take a step forward. Much effort has been given for many centuries to meet the human need which is now a crisis of major proportions.

Can we bring a positive note? Can our word, our being, bring Light and Salvation? If we look at the lowered vibration of man, we have little hope. But when we tune our ear to Spirit, wonderful music is playing, awesome encouragement is heard, unlimited possibilities are in view, and a powerful word of Light and Truth is bursting forth from within. We are the precipitation of Divine Light and consciousness that has waited many ages to come. Now we are here. We are the long expected one. Christ has come.

Several significant words are in vogue today describing who Man is and what is happening to him. Some of these words are: Spirit, Soul, Soul groups, the subconscious, the over-self or greater self, true identity, identity in Christ, and so on. Whatever our words may be, there is a common theme to all of this. This theme is well illustrated by a little chorus Carolynne received a few years ago:

You're more than you know,
You're more than what you see,
You're bigger than this flesh you're in,
And all that's in between.
You're great and you're wonderful,
All things under feet.
Now walk in this knowing,
And never claim defeat!

This great and wonderful being, your greater unconscious self, needs to become your conscious self. You and I need to awaken. That inner awareness in you we call Christ is the awakening of your being. He is you and you are him. He has always been you, you have always been him. Now is the time for sleeping beauty to awaken at the kiss of her lover. Your higher being has never slept; only relative to your lack of awareness is the idea of sleep meaningful. You need to have greater synaptic pathways created in your brain to accommodate this new and awesome awareness that is flooding your conscious mind. Are you ready, willing, and able?

The truth and awareness that Jesus brought and manifested in this plane is the seed crystal for this universal awakening. Perhaps we are the eyelids of mankind, fluttering open at the first tremors of greater consciousness flooding through our collective self. However it may be, the joy is irrepressible, it is contagious, and it is wonderful. *Then were our mouths filled with laughter, when the Lord brought again the captivity of Zion.*

238

When your inner eye looks at Jesus, crucified on the cross, it is your inner, un-awakened self that responds to what you see. Your mind may not grasp what the inner eye beholds, but your inner Spirit man responds to the Light. It awakens, and for the first time is able to let go of a long held belief in shame and un-worth. Your core belief in separation is shaken. Life and consciousness for you will never be the same. Jesus has come to your house.

THOR 2: Conclusion

Dear Friends:

This concludes Part 2 of THOR, *A New Theory of Reality*. Since the primary subject of this part is the mission of Jesus, we would be amiss not to include some reference to the resurrection since the resurrection of Jesus so powerfully prophesies of the destiny of mankind.

Jesus clearly stated that he had *power to lay down his life and to take it again.* We see the evidence of that in his dying on the cross and his subsequent arising from the tomb.

If Jesus' death on Calvary is a picture of us being lowered into the earth realm from realms of glory and light, then we realize that we too had power to lay down eternal life and to take on the human experience. Jesus went on to say:

This commandment have I received from the Father.

We too came by our Father's command to do His will. No one forced us. There was no mistake. We did not stray from the Father's purpose and even the deception involved in our lowering was by divine arrangement.

Even as we see Jesus take his life again in the resurrection so we, the first fruit of his resurrection, can and will rise again! Rise, not so much from a physical rock-hewn tomb, as the master did, but arise from the dusty layers of Adamic consciousness that have trapped us in the realms of earth. Now we, like so many seeds can germinate and rise into the greater expression we are beginning to experience.

239

We can know and fully waken into our eternalness even while we still remain in this mortal flesh. That is the great promise of Jesus in the resurrection.

Soldiers are trained to routinely kill so that in the moment of conflict, when the choice is kill or be killed, there will not be a fatal hesitation caused by moral reprehension. In like manner, we have been trained to master the doubt created by self induced shame

It is in viewing the evidence presented by the Master, the first begotten from the dead, that we attain to the resolve necessary to cut those last strands of attachment that tie us to the lower earth consciousness that has been our death. Honor and praise well up within us as we see the wonderful dawning of this first fruit of humanity. This is the greater beginning that Jesus came for. Our awakening and rising is the hope that was set before him, the hope for which he endured the shame and the agony of the cross.

I am glad and delighted to walk with you and with Jesus in newness of life as this new creation man. Here is his song to us via Carolynne. He sang it to her…through her… when we first came to Missouri.

There's resurrection power, in my very being
There's resurrection Glory in this hour
It's a whole new way of living
A whole new way of walking
And it's just beyond the open door

So won't you come on in with me
Into this Place of Ours
Together we'll walk, hand in hand
And inherit the Promised Land

Rokus denHartog

ABBREVIATED SUMMARY OF THOUGHTS

Dear Friends:

Here is an abbreviated set of thoughts summarizing the whole of A New Theory of Reality, the core of this writing. I hope that it will help you to quickly review the main thoughts of its thesis as you ponder the implications.

THOR 1

First: The Source itself initiated the journey of separation.

Second: The ONE bought forth out of itself the MANY.

Third: Sin is the first thought or awareness: *I cannot please you.*

Fourth: Sin thoughts create SHAME, sin and shame serve as evolutionary drivers of consciousness.

Fifth: To answer the deepest questions of our existence, sin, shame and the reasons for them, the Elohim agreed to create this physical realm and then lowered themselves into human form.

Sixth: The great prize for which we came was the knowing and the understanding of our Journey...the revealing to us of the Father's heart.

Seventh: The Law was added to make the experience of sin, shame, guilt, and condemnation, legal and tangible. All of them are all the result of our own mind. They were never imputed by the Source.

Eighth: Jesus came to show, in his own body, the truth of Man and Man's experience, and to reveal the Father and His great love.

THOR 2.

First: Jesus called himself "The Son of Man."

Second: His Mission was: "I came to bear witness to the truth."

Third: The truth Jesus came to bear witness to is: Man is the Son of God crucified on Time and Space in his humanity.

Fourth: The Age of Aquarius is the awakening of mankind, the resurrection of Jesus' greater body. Spirit is taking on Form. This is our grand hour.

May the great love of the Father, who has begotten us in the beginning, make these words a reality in your heart.

Rokus denHartog graduated in 1963 from the University of Western Ontario with an Honors degree in Mathematics and Physics.

For fifteen years he taught Mathematics and Science in Canadian High Schools before becoming a free-lance minister and an explorer of spiritual thought.

Today he and his wife Carolynne travel and minister throughout the USA and abroad.

They live on ten acres in rural Missouri where they pastor a Christian Fellowship.

Rokus denHartog

Made in the USA
Middletown, DE
28 December 2021